1958   1970   1975   1980   1985

1962

LOST HOT RODS II

Pat Ganahl

| 1990 | 1995 | 2000 | 2005 | 2010 | Current |

More Remarkable Stories of How They Were Found

CarTech®

CarTech®, Inc.
838 Lake Street South
Forest Lake, MN 55025
Phone: 651-277-1200 or 800-551-4754
Fax: 651-277-1203
www.cartechbooks.com

© 2012 by Pat Ganahl

All rights reserved. No part of this publication may be reproduced or utilized in any form or by any means, electronic or mechanical, including photocopying, recording, or by any information storage and retrieval system, without prior permission from the Publisher. All text, photographs, and artwork are the property of the Author unless otherwise noted or credited.

The information in this work is true and complete to the best of our knowledge. However, all information is presented without any guarantee on the part of the Author or Publisher, who also disclaim any liability incurred in connection with the use of the information and any implied warranties of merchantability or fitness for a particular purpose. Readers are responsible for taking suitable and appropriate safety measures when performing any of the operations or activities described in this work.

All trademarks, trade names, model names and numbers, and other product designations referred to herein are the property of their respective owners and are used solely for identification purposes. This work is a publication of CarTech, Inc., and has not been licensed, approved, sponsored, or endorsed by any other person or entity. The publisher is not associated with any product, service, or vendor mentioned in this book, and does not endorse the products or services of any vendor mentioned in this book.

Edit by Scott Parkhurst
Layout by Monica Seiberlich

ISBN 978-1-61325-542-1
Item No. CT506P

Library of Congress Cataloging-in-Publication Data

Ganahl, Pat.
 Lost hot rods II : more remarkable stories of how they were found / by Pat Ganahl.
    pages cm
 ISBN 978-1-934709-93-1
 1. Hot rods--History. I. Title. II. Title: Lost hot rods 2.

TL236.3.G3625 2012
629.228'6--dc23

2012018501

Printed in the U.S.A.
10 9 8 7 6 5 4 3 2

All photos are by Pat Ganahl or from the Pat Ganahl Collection, except on these pages: 20 (both): Steffon Hoppel; 24–29 (all): Trent Sherrill; 30 (right): Ken Roble; 33 (bottom left and right): Frank Fernandez; 34 (right), 35 (both), 36 (all): Mark A. Oltjenbruns; 38 (both): Mike Besoyan; 44–45 (all): Fred Steele; 46, 47 (all), 48 (top): Jim Griepsma Collection; 49–51 (all): Dwain Rogers; 52 (both), 53 (top and middle): Mike Hilborn; 76 (both): Vince Weatherby Collection; 79 (both), 80 (bottom): Bruce Heather Collection; 91 (top left, middle, bottom), 92 (all), 93 (both): Andy Bekech Collection; 96–98 (all): Johnny Bedell; 99 (right), 100 (both): Andy Cohen Collection; 102, 103 (top left and right): Lupe Serrato; 106 (top left and bottom): Bruce Heather Collection; 108–109, 113, 114 (top and middle left): Darrell Mayabb; 114 (middle right, bottom left and right): Ed Koski; 121, 122 (top left): Nick Osborne Collection; 129–131 (all): Gary Weckesser Collection; 133 (right): Bill Bartlett Collection; 138–139: Conrad Garcia; 143 (top): Ron Rothstein Collection; 150 (bottom): Butch Gardner Collection; 154–155 (all): John Boyle & Boyle Collection; 156–158 (all): Burly Burlile & Burlile Collection; 159: John Harvey Collection; 175 (top): Greg Sharp Collection; 175 (bottom), 176 (all): Bill Andresen; 178 (top): Sidney Allen.

Front Flap: *The Himsl Brothers (see pages 59–61)*

Frontispiece: *The Al King Chevy Caper (see pages 11–12)*

Title Page: *The Cunningham Forty (see pages 79–81)*

Back Cover Photos

Top Left and Top Right: *The Blue 1932 (see page 27)*

Afterword: *1933 in the Basement (see pages 116–117)*

DISTRIBUTION BY:

Europe
PGUK
63 Hatton Garden
London EC1N 8LE, England
Phone: 020 7061 1980 • Fax: 020 7242 3725
www.pguk.co.uk

Australia
Renniks Publications Ltd.
3/37-39 Green Street
Banksmeadow, NSW 2109, Australia
Phone: 2 9695 7055 • Fax: 2 9695 7355
www.renniks.com

Canada
Login Canada
300 Saulteaux Crescent
Winnipeg, MB, R3J 3T2 Canada
Phone: 800 665 1148 • Fax: 800 665 0103
www.lb.ca

Contents

Introduction 6

Chapter One: Search and Find 8
The Al King Chevy Caper 13
Joe Bailon's *Candy Bird* 15
Harry Luzader's Deuce Coupe 16
The *American Graffiti* Merc 17
Eddie Dye's 1929 Model A 18
The *Charlie's Business Coupe* 19
The *Modern Grecian* 20
Steffon Hoppel's 1939 Ford Coupe 21
Sy Gregorich's *The Victorian* 22
Rick Dobbertin's 1985 Pontiac 23

Chapter Two: Finders 24
The Chris Ito Collection 26
Back Room Roadster 30
Frank Feruandez' Mercury 32
Rob Reisner's *Invader* 34
Deuce in the Shed 37

Chapter Three: Keepers 40
The Family Tub 42
Fred Steele's Sedan 44
Jim Griepsma's 1934 46
Dwain Rogers' Deuce 49
The Surf Panel 52
The Sharp Forty-One 54
Jim Kitchen's Model A 56
The Himsl Brothers 59
Deuce Done 62

Chapter Four: Lost and Found 64
Orv Elgie's Vicky 66
Jack Chrisman's Sedan 69
Orv Elgie's Delivery 72
Bueno's Bird 74
Dick King's Roadster 76
The Cunningham Forty 79
The Tribute Chev 82
Ray Goulart's Olds 84

Chapter Five: From the Yellow Pages 86
The Dresselhaus Deuce 88
The 'Dago Deuce Vicky 91

Little Yellow Roadster 94
The Stuckey Forty 96
The Titus/Southard/Cohen Roadster 99
Lupe Serrato's Sedan 102
The Lepesh Pickup 105

Chapter Six: Buried Treasure 108
Murphy Tiffany's Deuce 110
The Unknown Roadster 113
1933 in the Basement 116
Deuce in the Loft 118
The Craigslist Coupe 121

Chapter Seven: Race Cars 124
Mrs. Swallow's Midget 126
The *Mach IV* Mustang 129
The *Magwinder* 132
The Chevy 88 135

Chapter Eight: Missing Mercs 138
Steve Gonzales' 1950 140
Merc in Repose 143
Charlie Lopez' Merc 146
Jimmy Doyle's Bailon 1952 149

Chapter Nine: A Bit Different 152
The Barris *Bearcat* 154
Creighton's Mystery Bug 156
Lil' John's Corvette 159
Marlan's 'Vette 162
Low-Buck C-Cab 164

Chapter Ten: Collectors 166
Dick Martin's Deuce 168
Dave Dias' Pickup 171
The Marasco/Sharp Pickup 174
Sidney Allen's First Deuce 177

Chapter Eleven: Recently Departed 180
Marasco's New Pickup 182
Guy Ruchonnet's 1934 184
The *Flashback 1957* Chevy 187

Afterword 190

Introduction

Apparently you find hot rod archeology as much fun as I do. If you hadn't responded so enthusiastically to the first *Lost Hot Rods* book, I wouldn't be writing this second one. Thank you.

Obviously I must assume that you have read that first volume, so I shouldn't repeat things from it. If, by some chance, you discovered this book on the shelf and haven't seen its predecessor, I strongly suggest you get the first one as well, so you can start at the beginning.

However, let me recap just a bit, since there's been so much talk about "barn finds" and "vintage tin," and other similar subjects that aren't quite related to what this book is about. Finding a truly rare, collectible car hidden away in a dusty barn somewhere out in Middle America is about as likely as the storied roll in the hay with a beautiful farmer's daughter in that same barn. It's a romantic ideal that played far more often in Howard Hughes' B-movies at local theaters than it ever did in real farmers' barns. So, in the exceedingly rare instances when someone does find an original, dusty, and perhaps patina'd 1963 split-window Corvette, a 356 Porsche, a Hemi 'Cuda, or even a classic Duesenberg stashed among the hay bales somewhere, it makes a great story. It's a rare occurrence; in fact, it's almost bizarre. There have even been a few old hot rods or custom cars found in such places. But I think I could count the instances of such actual hot rod barn finds on two hands. There's only one in this book.

My first (and major) point is: If you go looking in farmers' barns anywhere across this country for rare, classic, or even moderately collectible cars, you're just not going to find much. If anything, besides an old tractor, you might find a clapped-out pickup or two, maybe the family's station wagon from the 1970s, or maybe even Great Aunt Tilly's funny-looking four-door bathtub Nash sedan. The thing is, searching for barn finds isn't very rewarding, and therefore not that much fun.

Similarly, searching barnyards, farm fields, deserts, woods, or creek beds for what we used to call vintage tin is just as unrewarding and frustrating. It's all gone. What there was left of pre-1950s original coupes, roadsters, or other cool potential hot rod material has already been rounded up by various collectors and now awaits resale (often at romanticized prices) in their warehouses or lots. On the other hand, if you're looking for decent, original cars or trucks from the 1950s or 1960s to build into cool rods or customs, there's plenty of that to be found. I call it the "New Vintage Tin." But that's another story that I've written about elsewhere. They are not lost hot rods. You're not going to find what we're talking about here sitting alongside rural highways in Kansas or Texas.

That's the second, but critical, point: We're not talking about rare, unmodified, collectible cars, or about original, old, vintage tin that can be built into something neat. If you find an old Corvette, or GTO, or even a Ferrari or Cord or something like that, it's exciting; it might be lucrative, and there's probably a good story about who owned it and how it got saved or stored. Any old car has some history. But such cars don't have the personality a rod or custom does. In fact, if a classic or collectible car has been modified or altered at all, that usually devalues it. It's a sin.

I personally think that finding old rods, customs, and hand-built race cars is a lot more fun. That's what this book is about. Maybe it's a once-famous car that appeared on the cover of a magazine or won a big trophy at a major car show, and you've often wondered, "Whatever happened to...?" Perhaps it was a local rod or custom that you remembered from the drive-in or drag strip back in the day. In several cases it's a T-bucket project, a chopped Deuce coupe, or a 1955 Chevy that got started years ago, but never quite got done. And there are plenty of such cars that enjoyed fifteen minutes of fame in the last ten or twenty years, then—poof—just seemed to vanish.

What these cars have in common, besides the fact that they all have become lost in one way or another, is that every one of them is unique. Every hot rod, custom car, or drag machine has been built by an individual who had his or her own ideas about how it should be done—what the perfect hot rod should be. Even if that person paid professionals to do some or all of the work, the owner still told the builders what to do. It was his or her vision, perhaps dream. In many cases, they even gave it a name. So, not only are no two of these cars the same, but each one has its own story, its own personality, and a unique history. That's what makes hot rod archeology so much fun. We're not just finding a cherry Model-T coupe or 1930 Model A sedan, but maybe Joe Cruce's *Tall T* or Ed Roth's *Little Jewel*. That's exciting, and it usually makes for amazing stories.

The third thing that distinguishes lost hot rods from barn finds, and makes the search much more rewarding is: You don't drive into the country to hunt for them on farms. You find them in the garage right next door, or down the street. To prove that point, in the first book I started by finding 25 examples right in my own neighborhood, within a half mile of my house. These ranged from magazine-featured Deuces, to 1957 Chevy projects, to Model As and Ts that had been stored in garages for decades. I only showed pictures of some of them because there were so many. And guess what? They're all still there.

The point is that most hot rods get built in urban or suburban garages or shops, not on farms, so that's where you're going to find them—lots of them; tons of them. That's another big reason why searching for lost hot rods is so much fun—there are so many to find. Nobody throws an old hot rod away. And if it becomes outmoded, it's probably not worth trying to sell. So it gets stored away, probably in a back corner of a garage or shop, so it can get rebuilt some day, or passed down. They become family heirlooms or are simply forgotten.

A final thing I should reiterate is that I don't approach the hunt for lost hot rods as a financial opportunity. Or even as a shopping trip. I'm not looking for cars or projects to buy. That's not the point. In my case it's a moot point, because I can't afford that sort of shopping anyway. But that doesn't lessen the fun. I'm more motivated by the "whatever happened to...?" factor, as well as the excitement of uncovering lost treasure. That's why I call it archeology. As I said in the first book, it's more akin to catch-and-release fishing. And what makes it so enjoyable and rewarding is that the stream is so well stocked.

In the first book's Introduction, I talked about how I became fascinated by hot rods as a youngster, and how I (and my like-minded friends) checked open garages, peeked into backyards, and searched back lots and alleys for any signs of hot rod activity or raw material. I knew every hot rod and dragster in town, whose it was, and hopefully where it went if it changed hands. I still had that impulse when I first happened into this business, and became a cub editor at *Street Rodder* magazine in 1973. When I was introduced to owner/publisher Tom McMullen, and found out that he was the guy who built that wild, blown, flamed 1932 roadster that was on the cover of *Hot Rod*, my immediate question to him was, "Where did it go?" I was surprised not so much by the fact that he didn't know for sure, but that he didn't care. He was on to new endeavors. That's the way rodding was then. That's how so many rods got lost.

When I finally convinced him to build a new version of his roadster (after a couple of offbeat projects), he wanted it to be completely updated—full independent suspension, digital gauges, four-cam engine, wire wheels, etc.—nothing like the original car other than body and paint. But I was more interested in finding the first one, which I did, in a storage shed in Riverside, California. With the paint stripped from the body, but not the hood, it was pretty complete, less engine. I showed what I found in an "Auto-Biography" on the car in the June 1975 issue. But it was another two decades before someone acquired the car to accurately restore it to its famous 1963 *Hot Rod* cover configuration.

That was the first lost hot rod I went and found and showed in print. I thought the first was the Tommy Ivo T—a hot rod I idolized as a kid—but I just looked it up and I didn't find it until 1977. It was then sitting in Hy Rosen's garage on jack stands, with engine pieces strewn around it, but otherwise complete in Barris candy-red paint. I showed pictures of it in my editorial in the November 1977 issue of *Street Rodder*, along with a "last seen" photo of the Grabowski T, asking, "Why aren't people searching for, finding, and restoring these historical hot rods?"

I must have been ahead of my time. It took another 20 years before the *Ivo T* got restored. But I want to point out that I started doing hot rod archeology stuff a long time ago, and have been urging other rodders to do it, too. Over many years, I have enthusiastically published pictures of well-known, but long-gone rods, customs, or race cars that I or one of my readers discovered. It makes me even happier to finally see many of them restored. Some of each are in the following pages. I'm so glad you like this stuff as much as I do. Happy hunting!

Search and Find

I have never written a mystery book, but this one is the closest I've come. Archeology is technically defined as the scientific study of found human artifacts. The emphasis is on finding them in the first place. That's the sleuth's job. That's the detective part of the detective novel, and it can be plenty intriguing, mystifying, and fun to figure out in itself. And if all that these books accomplished was to uncover long-lost rods and customs, telling the twists and turns, the hot and cold clues that finally led to the discovery, it still makes for plenty exciting reading. Most of these stories are amazing, if not nearly incredible.

In fact, some of them were literally incredible. They either weren't true, were dead-ends, or—most frustrating—were good leads that owners just wouldn't let me see or follow up, for one reason or another.

While working on the first book, I had no trouble finding all kinds of lost hot rods—way more than I could fit into that book; consequently some of them appear here. In fact, I thought that book may have had too many cars in it. So, this time I've tried to limit the number of finds so that I can show and tell a little more about each one. It wasn't easy and I didn't fully succeed. I still found more cars than I could squeeze in. Maybe there's a *Lost Hot Rods III* in the future. We'll see.

But I was still frustrated by the number of cars I actually located and wanted to include, but couldn't. Some of these involved certain mysterious aspects. However, I was more surprised this time around, and only slightly less frustrated, by how many cars I uncovered whose histories couldn't be fully accounted for. In some cases, I know the vehicle was in a magazine, or at a car show, or raced on a dry lake on a given date in the past, but the current owner got it second or third hand—possibly unaware of

Chapter One

its former exploits—and nobody remembers or recorded its status for one, two, or three decades in between. Even a few cars that have been with the same owners or families for that amount of time have mysteriously been lost, or even stolen, and later recovered with few clues about where they went. I show you some of these as well.

And, as you know, hot rods, customs, and especially race cars are constantly evolving entities. Trends and styles in rodding, especially in the 1950s and 1960s, changed as rapidly as clothing, dance steps, and teenage jargon. Not only did the owner of a given car want to keep it up to date, but any new owners along the line wanted to somehow rework the custom car to reflect their own styling and personality, to make it "his" car (yes, unfortunately there were hardly any female builder/owners of these cars back then). So when my archeological search uncovers a cool old rod or custom, it might be very hard to tell what forms and what fame it might have had in the past.

By the same token, many cars that become known in a given form at a specific time also had a life as a rod or custom long before that. One classic example is the Chrisman Brothers bronze, chopped, rear-engine Model A *Speed Coupe* that set numerous records at Bonneville and was featured on the cover of *Hot Rod* in the 1950s. It was significantly reworked by Barris with pearl paint, gull-wing doors, and pontoon front fenders as the *Dobie Gillis* TV prop, and magazine cover car, in the 1960s. Fortunately, it was perfectly restored to its original condition by its original builder, Art Chrisman, in the 1990s, when rodding finally realized that history and restoration are elements that should be valued and pursued at this point in our hobby/sport/whatever the heck it is.

This brings up two points relative to this book. The first is that, although being a car archeologist is intriguing and mostly a lot of fun, I also consider myself a hot rod historian, and this is a bit more serious. Neither is an exact science, but history tries to be. Finding a lost rod or custom is gratifying in itself, archeologically. If I can also accurately trace the history of this vehicle, either because the same person who built it 40 years ago still owns it, or the current owner has traced its lineage with some verifiable accuracy, so much the better. That's doubly satisfying for me, and hopefully for you too.

In this day of hot rod and race car restoration, it's also more important when a term such as "provenance" can be connected to such cars without its being considered an oxymoron. On the other hand, I was surprised by how many of these found cars either had huge gaps in their histories, little known history before the current owner, or even perhaps questionable credentials. This is the mystery I'm talking about. But rather than letting it be a frustration, I suggest that it adds intrigue to the plot, just as it does in a good mystery novel, and as it often does in an archeological dig. Where, exactly, did these artifacts come from? Why did someone make them the way they did? What do the various handmade parts and pieces mean, and are they clues about the car's history? That's why finding lost hot rods is more fun than finding any factory-built cars. And I hope you agree that this element of mystery adds to the fun, rather than creating frustration.

The second point is only loosely connected to the first, but something I need to address. In a number of cases where I did locate cars that have been owned by the same person for decades, perhaps going back to well-known magazine covers or major show wins, you might be upset or chagrinned to learn that this person significantly rebuilt and updated this car at some point in the past. I'm not just talking about changing wheels and tires or the car's color. I'm talking about changing the early Ford driveline for a TPI Chevy 350/350, or cutting wheel tubs into the body and rear frame for a narrowed 9-inch rear on coil-overs. Maybe they changed all the chrome accessories for brushed billet aluminum in the 1980s and painted everything else pastel pink with a red heartbeat graphic down the sides. That might sound sacrilegious or even sickening today for a car that won America's Most Beautiful Roadster or appeared on the cover of *Rod & Custom* in the mid 1950s.

But you have to understand, first of all, that this is the essence of hot rodding for anyone who has been in it since those days—to constantly modify and improve your car with the latest tricks in looks or performance that keep your hot rod hot or your custom cool. Second, the plain fact is owners can do whatever they want to with the car. That's another tenet of hot rodding. In my opinion, the fact that such cars still exist, in many cases with their longtime owners, and that you can track them down and trace them back through their significant histories, makes them worthy of inclusion here. I hope you agree.

Woulda, Coulda

I traveled close to 20,000 miles tracking down leads on lost hot rods for this book, maybe more. This includes banzai runs to Arizona, Utah, Northern California (it's a *long* state), and one 4,025-mile, two-week loop through Colorado, Oklahoma, and Texas that came within 20 miles of Louisiana. But you can only get so far on a freelance budget. So, one of the bigger frustrations of this book was trying to get information and printable photos of dozens of cars that I know exist in far-flung corners of this country, and even around the world. I really want to thank those who—oftentimes after several emails back and forth—did send me excellent material that appears in subsequent chapters. In other cases, I got what I got. But even if the photos are edgy, the stories are great.

One real frustration is a bulging, aging folder I keep of many lost hot rods that I know exist but, for one reason or another, I don't have photographs of how they look today. Some of these cars I've known about and have been tracking for decades. Others are ones I discovered in the course of working on this book, thought I had good leads on, but then evaporated (you know, like those fish you get on the hook that somehow slip off). In several cases I've corresponded back and forth many times with owners, who've either promised me photos that never materialized, or who simply refused (which is understandable). In other cases it might have been someone who knew someone who's cousin had the car, for sure. Well, maybe. And, unfortunately, there were several more that I woulda and coulda included here, but I simply ran out of room for them in this book, or they were "found" and published in other places before I could include them here, which is also fine. More for you to enjoy.

But what I decided to do in the first chapter is show and tell you about several of these "lost" rods that got away (to extend the fishing metaphor). I may not have real-time current photos of them, but I know where they are and what their story is, so that's almost as good, right?

This brings up one point that I should reiterate from the first book. Seeking a specific "whatever became of…?" lost rod is much more difficult than serendipitously finding one. Think of it this way: If some well-known rod or custom has been long gone, and lots of people have looked for it with no results so far, the chances are good that it no longer exists, or that some hoarder has it who won't reveal its identity or location. On the other hand, nearly everywhere I went looking for lost rods, someone said, "Well, if you're looking for those kinds of cars, I know where there's one," or "Yeah, my uncle Bob has one of those," or "There's an old shop in town that has a couple of those in the back room." They're probably not famous, but they're often cool cars with great stories. And if you know what you're looking for, you can find some buried treasure, too.

Three More Things

First, hot rod hoarders. There's a TV show about this long-known syndrome, and you're familiar with the term. There's a fine line between collecting and hoarding. Some readers might feel this description hits a little too close to home. Actually, true hoarders are more likely oblivious to the fact they have the disorder. You need to be aware that this condition exists, and it's been the

Top: It didn't dawn on me until now—my own car is a perfect example of my main message: You don't find lost hot rods in barns; you find them in neighborhood garages. This is exactly what I found in the two-car garage of a house in Orange County, where it had been sitting for ten years. The best part? This one was for sale. **Bottom Left:** Getting the Hydro rebuilt took some doing, but that's about all it needed other than cleaning and detailing. The big Olds ran good and strong, but then it caught fire. Can you tell this was the 1970s? **Bottom Right:** After the fire I rebuilt it like this, with a hot Chevy six and a 4-speed. I offer it as one example of a lost hot rod that got found and didn't get thrown back. This does happen. Would I want to go find it again? No thanks.

same way for decades. There are even some famous hot rod hoarders, whose historic rods or customs exist intact today because of it. I won't name names.

However, be advised that some—perhaps many—of the lost hot rods you might find squirreled away in garages, shops, or backyards, whether it's one car or several, are there because someone wants to keep them there. They're not for sale (at least not at any reasonable price), they'll probably never get worked on or rebuilt, and you might watch in frustration as some simply deteriorate. Worse are the owners who leave such cars sitting where people can see them, as if tantalizing them or daring them to ask if they're for sale, only to say "No!" You probably know such stories. If not, be prepared. Don't get mad. Look elsewhere.

Second is what I call the "First Car Syndrome." I've written about it before, so I'll be brief. What gene is intrinsic to car people and gives them this strong impulse to find their first car? Sure, if you like cars, you're going to have fond memories of your first one. You probably went on your first date in it, and did plenty of other first things in or with it. But admit it, for the vast majority of us our first car was not what we really wanted. It was either some clunky four-door passed down by an aunt or grandparent, or else it was the best we could afford with little money at age 16. In my case I was stuck with it because it wouldn't sell. But most of you moved up to something better as soon as you made some bucks. Even if you didn't, why go searching for some old car just because it represents teen memories? Given that it was nothing special, if not a piece of junk, it is very likely gone by now. You still have the memories, right? My advice is to go find the car you *wish* you had when you were 16.

Third, speaking of my own cars, I have had a few that qualify as lost hot rods that I found and was actually able to buy and rebuild, including a 1927 T Altered with an injected Chrysler Hemi and a 1960s Woody Gilmore Top Fuel dragster. And there is the early Cadillac-powered 1932 Ford roadster I recently completed. I had planned to show some of these in the first book, but I ran out of room, and the same is happening here. So here's just one, a 1932 Chevy coupe that had been converted, from a 1950s street rod of unknown history, into a 1960s drag car with a big-cammed, bored-out Tri-Power 394 Olds, a stick Hydro, and Inglewood slicks. This car had blown one of the gears in the Hydro and was parked, wishbone tow-bar still attached, in the corner of a suburban garage in 1964.

Ten years later, after the birth of street rodding, one of my fellow club members was looking for a "non-Ford" rod to build. He heard this Chevy was for sale, but passed on it. I bought it for $450. It was 1974. I had just become editor of *Street Rodder* magazine. I had to get a bank loan to pay for it. And it wasn't a 1932 Ford. Many of you know the story of that car because I wrote about it in the magazines.

I just learned that someone in Ohio now has it, and it's still basically the way I sold it. If I had it today I'd paint it orange again, put the Olds back in it, slicks, straight axle . . . seriously. But I'd rather move on to new projects.

And finally, on the subject of moving on, there was another recent flurry of internet excitement over a supposed sighting of something that looked like the long-lost, and very aptly named, *Uncertain T*. I discussed this in the first book, but it's pertinent here. I think it fascinates in the same way as an unsolved murder mystery.

But I gotta tell ya (again): If this one hasn't been found by now, given its uniqueness and publicity, it's either gone or in the hands of some perverse hoarder who is keeping it well hidden. Lots of similar Ts were built in the 1970s (none nearly as good). They're false leads. If you love this car so much, clone it. Or build something like it, only better. But searching for lost hot rods that can't be found is like a day of fishing without a nibble. It's good exercise, but it's not much fun. Move on.

Okay, all of you claiming Uncertain T *sightings. This is how the car looked in its final form—heavy gold metalflake paint with super-wide Indy rear tires on similar Buick wire wheels. If it doesn't look like this, you've probably found something else, which, of course, still might be something pretty neat.*

The Al King Chevy Caper

The story of this car reads like a Sam Spade dime novel. In fact, the mystery begins with what kind of car it is, and what the original owner/builder's name was. Further, in the first book I showed one photo of this car, along with several other cars. I stated that these vehicles—some of them well-known magazine-feature cars—had all disappeared and seemed nowhere to be found, despite my vigorous efforts to locate them. So I asked the readers of the book to contact me if they knew the whereabouts or any clues to the location of any of these cars. I had hoped to do a whole chapter in this book called "Follow Ups," showing lost cars from the first one that readers across the country might have found. Well, this is the only one.

Let me back up a bit. I've been collecting photos of early rods, customs, and lakes/drag race cars since the early 1970s. Somewhere along the line I found (or was possibly given by one of my hometown friends) an envelope that had some color pictures of this car in it. I knew it immediately. It was built by a guy who owned a body shop in Corona, California, where my family is from. The body shop faced on a side street, behind a Richfield gas station on the main drag through town. When I first saw this shiny, two-tone green, unusual car parked there (sometimes at the shop, more often at the gas station), on my way home from school, I was too young to pay it much attention. But a couple years later I was bit hard by the hot rod bug started reading car magazines and building models, and customized my bicycle.

I remember riding by King's Auto Body (at 513 Sierra Vista St.) to take a closer look at what I thought was somebody's Herculean attempt to make a sports car out of a good 1955 Chevy. The workmanship was excellent, but it wasn't a hot rod. And with its Continental kit, wide whitewall tires, funky wheelcovers, and aqua-green paint, it was nothing like the Larry Watson–style customs that we loved in 1959–1960. Besides, Mr. King, who built it, was an older guy who didn't cruise town or take it to car shows. It just sat there at the gas station most of the time. I was afraid to talk to the guy.

I had no idea this was actually a wrecked 1954 Corvette. King had hand-built the body mostly from 1955 and 1956 Chevy parts, sliced and diced it every which way, adding 1956 Dodge wagon taillights and a 1949 bumper at the rear. If I had known then that it had a six-cylinder engine and Powerglide transmission (even with the Corvette triple carbs), I'd have been even less impressed.

I was consequently quite surprised to find out, years later, that this car had been featured on four pages in the June 1958 issue of *Custom Cars* magazine. The black-and-white article, titled "The Body Beautiful," listed the owner/builder as Al King, and called him a "professional customizer." As far as I know, this is the only custom car he ever built. King's Auto Body (I found an ad for it in the back of my 1963 high-school yearbook) was strictly a collision repair shop. Nobody took their cars there for any custom bodywork. Further, the envelope I had with the color photos had "R. King, 1954 Corvette" written on it. Then somebody crossed out Corvette and wrote "1955 Chevy" over it. For some reason I thought the guy's name was Richard King, and that's what I called him in the first book. For a long time I also thought the car was a shortened and sectioned 1955 Chevy. (Actually, I just found out from someone in the Corona library history room that the owner of King's Auto Body was Elvert R. King.)

Here's where the real mystery starts though. As I said in the first book, I happened to see a car sitting on a knoll right next to the 60 freeway in the small town of Glen Avon, near Riverside, in the late 1980s. I recognized it immediately because it was exactly the same and appeared to be in excellent condition. There was a For Sale sign in the window, but I was on my way to an appointment somewhere farther east, and figured I'd stop on the way back to check it out. When I returned that afternoon, the car was gone, and nobody in the area knew anything about it. I actually went back several times looking for it, showing people pictures of the car, but nothing.

Al King used 1955 Chevy front sheet metal, sectioned and stretched 8 inches to fit on the 1954 'Vette chassis, and a pancaked hood. The roof is a cut-down 1956 four-door hardtop, and the doors/side windows might be 1955 Nomad. Everything is hammer-welded and leaded.

Chapter One: Search and Find

Then, several months after the book came out, I got a call from Cal Turner in Arizona. He said somebody told him there was a picture of his car in my book. I have no idea how he got my phone number, and he didn't have a copy of the book himself (still doesn't). But I could tell he was talking about the King car. When I told him about seeing the car for sale in Glen Avon in the 1980s, he said, "What?" He didn't know anything about it. It took me a while to get the story. Here's a synopsis.

Cal lived in Rubidoux and worked for an electrical contractor in nearby Riverside. One day in 1960 he was driving his company truck on a service call in Corona (about 15 miles away), and saw the Chevy sitting next to King's shop. He wasn't a rod or custom guy, but for some reason the car intrigued him, and he stopped to take a closer look.

King came out and Cal said, "Wow, I like this! How much you want for it?" King said, "Two thousand," and Cal said, "Sold." That's the story according to Cal. So the car left Corona in 1960.

Cal said he drove it "like a regular car" for several years, but he had company trucks to drive daily, so it got little use. He didn't take it to shows or anything like that. In fact, he said it was kind of a hassle to drive because everybody wanted to know what it was and ask questions. "I couldn't stop for gas without getting pestered," he said. "Most people thought it was a T-Bird."

For some reason he didn't explain, he swapped the 1954 Corvette six, complete with all accessories and transmission, as a trade-in on a stock 2-barrel 1963 283 at Baumann's Auto Wrecking in Riverside. I have a hunch the three carbs were a problem to keep tuned, and he wanted the newer aluminum 'Glide transmission. After installing it himself, he said he drove the car occasionally, but then decided in 1968 to store the car in a locked two-car garage at a rental house he owned in Rubidoux, right next to the 60 freeway. When I asked why he didn't keep it in his own garage, he said, "I didn't have one at my house."

So that's where the car sat for the next 20 years—more or less. Things are sketchy. Cal said an older couple lived in the house and were iffy on rent. The neighborhood was going downhill. Members of the Crips and the Bloods gangs were moving in from L.A., and some sort of turf war was going on. Cal obviously didn't go check on his stored Chevy very often.

The next thing he knew, he was at his own house in Rubidoux, moving out in 1989, and saw his Chevy drive by down the street. A friend was helping, and Cal said, "Hey that's my car!" They jumped in the friend's pickup and followed the Chev to a gas station, where Cal accosted the driver, placed him under citizen's arrest, and called the cops. Amazingly, the driver co-operated, said it wasn't his car, and called the owner, who soon arrived. Cal said both of these guys were taken away by the police, the car was returned to him, and that was the end of it. No court and no follow-up. Strange.

Of course Cal has no idea when exactly the car was stolen from the garage, or by whom. It must have been right about the time I saw it for sale next to the freeway, because the car was still in excellent condition then, and the thieves were probably trying to make a quick buck. It also explains why nobody knew anything about the car when I asked later. When Cal got the car back, it had a gang tag spray painted on the roof (it's still there). But he's pretty sure the person claiming to be the owner, who showed up at the gas station, wasn't the one who stole it.

It's a moot point, because Cal then moved the car to a better-protected, locked, and enclosed rental storage unit. He kept it there until 2004, when he moved to Arizona and built a large garage on his property to store not only this car, but also half a dozen Corvairs and Volkswagens in various stages of disassembly. Cal was 77 years old when I went to Arizona to see the car again and photograph it. He claims he "fired it up last January," and started a little bodywork on it some years ago. The car is in surprisingly original condition other than the engine, especially given what it's been through (some of which I can only imagine).

I have to wonder how it has weathered as much as it has since I briefly saw it 20-some years ago. But that's also a moot point. This is one fish I wouldn't throw back. I'd love to restore it the way I saw it when I was 13, with a three-carb, chromed, dual-exhaust six back under that pancaked hood. So I asked Cal what he thought it was worth. He hesitated, then said, "$90,000." I said, "No, really, what's the least you would take for it." He said, "Fifty grand." Well, at least we know this one survives, such as it is, miraculously. File this one under Hot Rod L.A. Noir.

Cal said he took a body-shop class, and the work below the taillight is the result. The trim ring is in the car. You can see graffiti from the 1980s on the roof and trunk. Although this garage has a locked door, birds and rodents apparently get in through the rafters.

Joe Bailon's *Candy Bird*

In my book *The American Custom Car*, I say that the *Candy Bird* might be Joe Bailon's most famous custom. He built it for Joe Castro in 1958, and it appeared on the covers of many magazines at the time. Besides the characteristic tubular-bar grille and bumpers, quad headlights, multiple scoops with chrome teeth, and handmade side pipes, it was of course painted by Joe in his original Candy Apple Red with gold scallops, plus Tommy the Greek teardrop pinstripes.

I was quite surprised to see this car parked in the spectators' lot at one of the L.A. Roadsters' Show and Swap meets at the Great Western Exhibit Center in the latter 1970s, and took the photo seen here. I mentioned this in the April 1989 issue of *Rod & Custom*, saying I hadn't seen the car since. A couple years later (February 1991) I received, and published, new photos of the white 'Bird, looking exactly the same, from Avery King in Southaven, Mississippi, saying he was going to restore it.

Somehow, by the time the *Custom Car* book was published in 2001, the *Candy Bird* was back in Northern California, and I have a couple photos of Bailon doing some work on it. It apparently got as far as a dark primer coat and new, original-style chrome nerf bars on the front.

So I recently called Joe at home in Auburn to ask where the restored Jim Doyle 1952 Merc might be, and if he knew what happened to the *Candy Bird*. You can see the Doyle Merc on page 149, but for the whereabouts of the 'Bird he referred me to Bob Falco, who has a collision and custom shop in Monroe, New York. Bob has been in contact with the current owner of the car, who lives in Philadelphia. He said he is the same person who sent it to Bailon's about 15 years ago, but had it shipped back in the primered condition, and has kept it the same way since. Falco was hoping to restore the car in his shop, but says that current economic conditions are probably forcing the owner to put the car up for sale by the time you read this. So the car exists in relatively original condition, but its future is definitely uncertain.

Top: The Candy Bird *as built for Joe Castro by Joe Bailon in 1958, painted hallmark Candy Apple Red. The taillights are inverted 1953 Lincolns. Bottom Left: This is how the 'Bird arrived at Bailon's in Auburn, California, sometime before summer 1995, still in white. That's original owner Joe Castro posing with Bailon (with hammer). Ownership is uncertain at this point, but it only got as far as full primer, early whitewalls, and new nerfs before it left. Bottom Right: In a back lot of the L.A. Roadsters show around 1978 I was surprised to see the 'Bird, painted white with rubber bumpers in place of the nerf bars.*

Chapter One: Search and Find

Harry Luzader's Deuce Coupe

Harry Luzader's metallic aqua-green Deuce coupe is my all-time favorite 1932 five-window, hands down. Many of you seem to agree. The car was beautiful, flawless, and still set numerous national records and won major drag meets.

When we were re-launching *Rod & Custom* magazine in 1988, we set up a booth at that summer's NSRA Street Rod Nationals to announce the fact and hopefully sell subscriptions. The guy in the next booth had a small company from Pennsylvania selling stainless-steel hardware, and sometime during the weekend he mentioned that the person who acquired the coupe from Harry Luzader lived in his neighborhood, and that he had the complete car, in pieces, in his garage. He said he had taken the car apart to slightly narrow the rear frame and inset the wheel wells for larger rear tires. This person said he could get me photos of the car, as it sat. I said, "Yes, please."

It wasn't until mid 1995 that an *R&C* reader from the same area of Pennsylvania sent me a photo of the coupe as last seen in public at the Nats East in Timonium, Maryland, in 1976, along with the name of the guy who owned it, John Dominick. John had watched Luzader build the car as a kid, bought it from him in 1972, reinstalled the original steel doors and fenders, repainted it the same color, and installed a dropped axle, street tires, and a tamer engine. I published this photo and info in the October 1995 issue of *R&C*, and you can read and see more of this famous coupe in the big book, *Deuce*, from *The Rodder's Journal*.

I contacted Dominick, who owned a large body and paint repair business in Pitcairn, Pennsylvania, at that time, and have remained in touch since then. I actually called him several times recently, hoping to finally show the buried treasure that still sits in his home garage just as it did in 1988. In fact, I even called the guy from the same neighborhood who first told me about it, and asked *him* to finally take and send me some photos. Nope. Dominick has his hands full running his business, and he's not handy with a camera. Plus he has a red, chopped, full-fendered 1932 coupe and a 1965 Stingray to drive. He'll put the Luzader coupe back together when he's ready. And I'll wait.

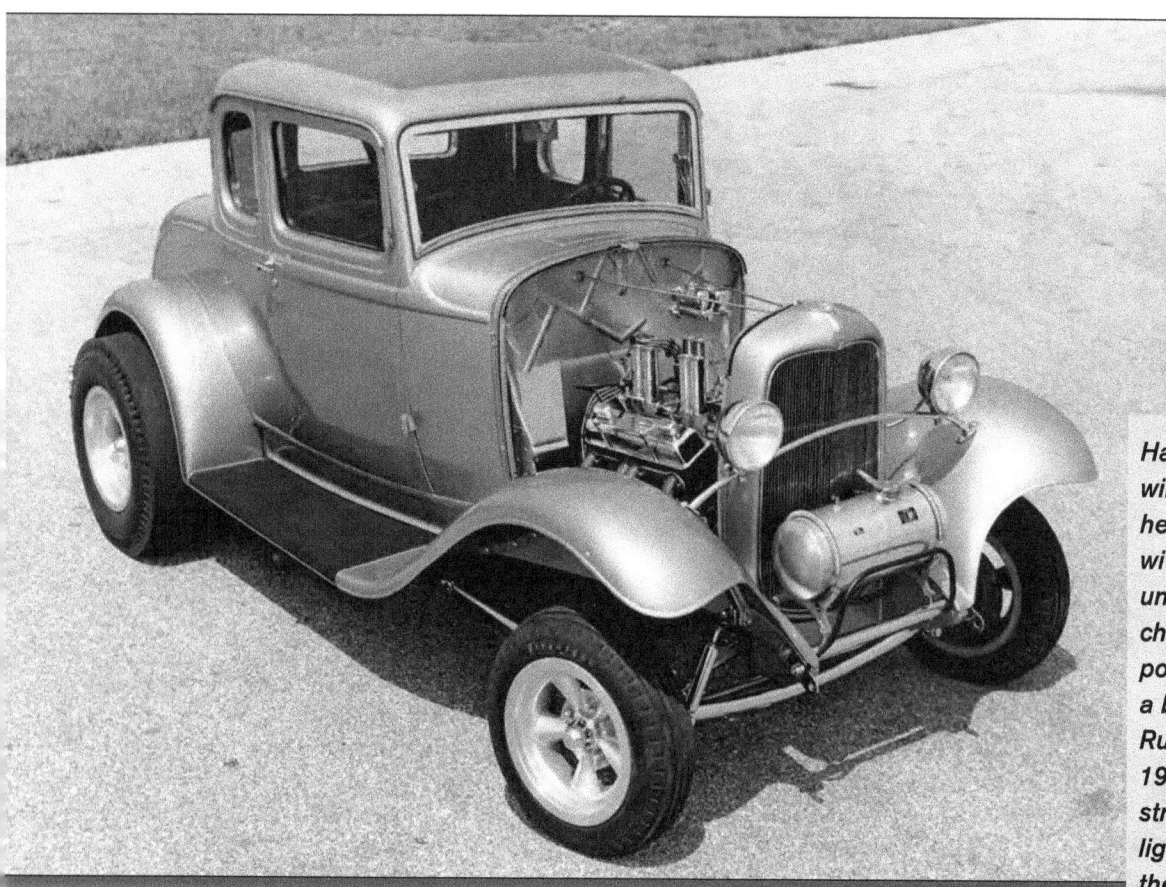

Harry Luzader built his five-window Deuce to race, but he finished it like a show car with hand-rubbed lacquer under the fenders, a fully chromed undercarriage, polished mag wheels, and a black button-tuft interior. Running C/ or D/Gas in the 1960s meant he needed street equipment such as lights and a radiator, and the lower classes required the extra weight. Its performance matched its looks.

The *American Graffiti* Merc

Chapter Eight is called "Missing Mercs." One I had really hoped to show in its present location and condition is the quickly chopped 1951 that played a significant role in the film *American Graffiti*. The two photos shown here are a rare look at it in color, when it was put on display at Universal Studios Tours not long after the film was made (circa 1976). It sat outside like this for a few years and deteriorated.

Sometime in the 1980s rocker/rodder Brian Setzer somehow acquired it, had the body straightened, repainted, and pinstriped. He re-chromed the bumpers and even installed tuck-and-roll upholstery. Then, in the August 1991 issue of *Rod & Custom* we showed two photos of the car in this condition, minus the Olds Fiesta wheelcovers, submitted by reader Robert Saueressig of Plainview, New York, who said he had purchased it from Setzer in 1987.

After more detective work, I finally located Steve Saueressig, who operates a towing/repair business on Long Island, and who said his brother Robert passed away in 1994, leaving the Merc to him. In fact, he said he had collected about 15 cars, including two 1957 Chevys and an Oldsmobile he had recently restored for his mother. He said the Merc has been sitting outside and has weathered considerably (it still has no side windows), but he seemed eager to restore it. I put him in touch with Glenn Shimmin of Coleville, Washington, who has built an exact clone of the car, which he has been displaying along with Mike Famalette's original *Graffiti* 1958 Impala as seen in the first *Lost Hot Rods*. I also asked Steve several times to send me photos of the car as it is today, which he several times said he would. But he hasn't.

Put this one in the Future Very Uncertain file.

As seen on the Universal Studios Tour in 1976, the Graffiti Merc still had some shine to its paint, but rust on the bumpers. Note that it has no side windows. The crease in the side probably happened during filming; it can be detected in some scenes. It sits high because it was propped on 4 x 4-inch blocks.

Chapter One: Search and Find

Eddie Dye's 1929 Model A

Certainly one of the finest track roadsters ever built, in league with the Bill Niekamp and Dick Flint cars, is the 1929 Model A built and painted by the Ayala Brothers for Eddie Dye.

It was featured on the (black and white) cover of *Hop Up* magazine in March 1952, but the story inside neither shows the Evans-built engine nor mentions the car's color (thought by some to be deep maroon or purple, by others black). The car's history after that is spotty, at best, and convoluted. I can only give a brief capsule here.

The beautiful nose, hood, and belly panels (later learned to have been formed by Whitey Clayton, not the Ayalas as stated in *Hop Up*) were sold at a swap meet and acquired by Jim Fuller of Santa Barbara, who built a 1929 roadster similar to Dye's (but with opening doors and black paint) to put them on. Meanwhile the Dye car was given a 1932 grille, a Model A windshield, and gold paint. It even appeared in a teen flick of the early 1960s. It was discovered by young rodder Tom Branch, who enjoyed it a lot as a neat old found rod before figuring out its true identity.

This car was then purchased by Pebble Beach collector/restorer Don Orosco, who convinced Fuller to loan him the original nose and other panels so his crew could make exact duplicates. The last I saw, this project was mocked up in bare metal as Orosco was completing the Lloyd Bakan 1932 coupe. Well . . .

Remember the billet-wheeled Bob Pierson 1936 coupe shown in the first book? It was bought by Jim Bobowski of New York, who partially restored it with wide whitewalls and DeSoto bumpers to show in the custom car exhibit at the 2010 GNRS in Pomona. Restoration continues on this car. And, in a further follow-up to the first book, Jim called me recently to say he had just acquired the remains of the Gil Ayala T-Bird from Dan Cuellar, and plans to return it to its second candy-red form.

What's this have to do with the Eddie Dye roadster? It turns out Jim's father, who lives in Florida, recently bought this car from Orosco, in uncompleted form, and is currently looking for the best shop to restore it fully and accurately. I suggested my son, Bill, as an excellent candidate for that job. We'll see what happens.

Photos of the Eddie Dye roadster are quite rare, and no color ones seem to exist. The Ayalas welded and leaded the doors, the wheel wells, and the cowl to fit a DuVall windshield. Whitey Clayton (who did the Niekamp car) formed the blistered and louvered hood, track nose, and what Hop Up says are full belly pans. There's a rolled pan in back, 1950 Pontiac taillights, and an Auto Butchers plaque, but no license plate at this point.

The *Charlie's Business Coupe*

I'd love to do a whole book just on lost drag cars. It's truly unbelievable how many still exist. Race cars of any kind become obsolete after a season or two. And an obsolete race car is worth less than a 1970s Cadillac. So who keeps them—especially dragsters, which are not easy to store?

This one, technically known as a Competition Coupe, was preserved by Charlie Mewes, who was a member of the crew when it was featured on two pages—looking exactly like this—in the roto section of the September 1961 *Hot Rod* magazine as the Sumner and Burt "A/Charger." The only reason I'm showing it here with one photo of it hazing the hides at Fremont in the mid 1980s, is because I simply ran out of space in this book.

When the first Nostalgia Nationals were staged at Fremont in 1982, Mewes partnered with engine-owner/driver Pierre Poncia to resurrect the car. Towed and push-started by Mewes' matching early Ford pickup, the *Charlie's Business Coupe* blazed the tires the length of the track on heavy loads of nitro, often lifting the front wheels at half track and other similar antics. It looks wicked and usually ran likewise. Not only was it a fierce competitor in its day, but this car is a true veteran of nostalgia drag racing, from its beginnings. It didn't miss any of the meets at Fremont.

In fact, Pierre (who inherited the car from Charlie a few years ago) has rebuilt it a couple of times, and ran it as recently as two years ago at a Bakersfield Reunion. Better yet, the car now sits in his Redwood City, California, garage next to the chute-pack-bodied front-engine dragster that appeared in *More American Graffiti* as Milner's nemesis, the *Hunt Bros. Team Car.* Pierre was involved with this car in the 1960s, and has beautifully restored it. So neither of these cars is actually lost. I know right where they are. I wish I could show and tell more. Maybe next time.

I chose this relatively tame photo of the Poncia-Mewes Fiat coupe running at Fremont in the mid 1980s because you can see the car. Normally the body was engulfed in tire smoke the length of the track, often with the front wheels in the air. This car is wild, and it lives to run again.

The *Modern Grecian*

John Saltsman of Rialto, California, recently finished a full-custom, chopped-top, bat-winged 1949 Studebaker pickup that he'd been slowly building for at least two decades. Besides a 1959 Chevy decklid as a bed cover, and taillights handmade by Gene Winfield, one of its unique features is a pair of frosted oval headlight covers just like the ones you see on the front of this hard-to-identify custom car from the late 1950s. In this pearl-yellow and candy-green form it was known as the *Modern Grecian*, originally built by Barris from a 1948 Studebaker four-door—of all things—for Earl Wilson in 1952, and then reworked like this in 1959. Besides the chopped top and other extensive bodywork, it had four fiberglass bucket seats that swiveled around a TV set that pivoted in the middle of the car. It was the epitome of kitsch.

Where did Saltsman get the matching headlight covers? They were a spare set made by Barris that John found in the trunk of the car when he owned it in the late 1980s. If you have copies of *Rod & Custom* from that era, check pages 34 to 35 of the October 1989 issue to see how the car looked then. It was surprisingly complete, including the full interior. John got the car from his uncle, Bob, who bought it from longtime Barris employee "Tubbs" after it had been damaged in a towing accident in the 1960s. Bob installed a Chevy 327 driveline and restored the car (in white and green paint) to show in the Midwest between 1968 and 1971. Then it sat outside for several years before John acquired it.

After its brief appearance in *R&C*, John got the car running, installed new floors, redid much of the bodywork, and restored more of the kitsch, including Tinker Bell tailfins and turbo aluminum wheel covers. In this form, still in gray primer, he drove it to several events, including Paso Robles. However, he said, "Someone from the East Coast, maybe New York, maybe New Jersey" kept calling, wanting to buy the car. With his pickup project pending, and his highly respected transmission business needing capital, he acquiesced in 1993. Neither John nor I have seen it since, though John says he's heard several reports that the same person still owns it, now painted pink. I have no photos to prove it. If someone out there knows, tell me.

George Barris gave me this classic shot of the Modern Grecian. I love the colors. Check out the turbo wheel cover.

20 Lost Hot Rods II

Steffon Hoppel's 1939 Ford Coupe

Steffon Hoppel has good intentions. He also has a rare and unusual but highly memorable hot rod 1939 Ford coupe that many remember from a three-page feature in the August 1958 issue of *Hot Rod* magazine. Steffon is also President and CEO of his own Fabrication Specialties company in Louisville, Ohio, which doesn't leave him enough time for several varied motorsports pursuits.

The car in question was built by Bill Commane from Van Nuys, California. It was a 1939 coupe craftily updated with 1940 DeLuxe front sheet metal and rear fenders/taillights, painted subtle black, with full trim in place. The only clue that it wasn't a flawless stock restoration were white-painted wheels.

But under the hood was a huge surprise: 332 inches of GMC inline six, with three carbs, a hot Winfield cam, and Vertex mag, followed by a Cad-LaSalle transmission and no less than a hidden Halibrand quick-change rear. The engine, built by Manny Ayulo, had to have a stroker crank and, though it had handmade tube headers, it only had a single exhaust with two truck mufflers. Inside was a pair of simple, black, lightweight Volkswagen bucket seats. Indy legend Eddie Kuzma was credited with the bodywork. This, as a caption plainly stated, was known as a "sleeper." My friends and I loved it, and it undoubtedly had something to do with my later gravitation to GM inline six engines.

Hoppel isn't quite sure how it got to Ohio, and it went through two owners who did some serious drag racing with it before his father bought it. Steffon says they have tales of how it blew away unsuspecting Corvettes in its day. He said he has some early photos, plus he fully intended to get the car out of the garage (after 27 years), clean it up, and take new pictures of it. That didn't happen. I understand—deadlines work both ways. So we had to settle for a couple of iffy small snapshots he emailed. But you can see that the car still exists, in incredibly original condition, and looks like it needs little more than a good cleaning, detailing, and tune-up to be back on the road, as shiny and sneaky as ever.

Given the radiator, this car might have had one of Ford's first inline sixes originally, but not 332 inches of triple-carbed, overhead-valve, Manny Ayulo–built GMC, followed by a Cadillac LaSalle stick and a Halibrand quickie. Other than some dust and those red horns on the firewall, this car looks exactly the same as it did in Hot Rod *in 1958.*

Sy Gregorich's *The Victorian*

Sy Gregorich, who bought the car new in 1955 and took it directly to the Alexander Brothers' shop in Detroit for nosing, decking, and Merc wagon taillights, kept going back for more custom work (1953 Stude pans front and rear, frenched lights, rounded hood, and white pearl paint with candy-red scallops), says *The Victorian* was not only the A Brothers' first serious custom job, but Mike Alexander's favorite. I know it's my all-time favorite mild custom (meaning it's not chopped, channeled, or sectioned).

After completion in the form seen here, it was featured in the September 1960 issue of *Car Craft*, and then selected as a "10 Best" custom of that year. After a candy wild-cherry repaint, Sy sold the car to *Orange Crate* and Portland hot rod car lot owner Bob Tindle in 1962, who sold it to Buddy Parazoo before it appeared in *Hot Rod* in November 1963 with Astro wheels. It then disappeared until Bob Neuman of Grand Rapids, Michigan, bought it from a *Hemmings* ad in 1969, with the hood, side trim, and paint missing, but the bodywork and custom interior still intact.

That's how the car was last seen in a brief mention in *The Rodder's Journal* Number 29 in 2005. Neuman had taken it to a custom shop in western Michigan, where a new hood was modified to fit the opening, but little else, as seen in the rear photo here. I recently called Gregorich to see if he knew what had become of the car. He said virtually nothing. It's still in the same shop, in the same state, while Neuman and the shop have both been working on other projects. At least this one is being preserved.

Meanwhile Gregorich, a very lively 77 years old, said he has built about 100 rods and customs over the years. But he recently sold his house in San Diego, which had a seven-car garage, and moved into one that has none. So finally he put the tastefully customized, mag-wheeled, bright-red 1956 Thunderbird, which he also bought new and which won a Top 10 award at the recent Goodguys Del Mar event) up for sale. He just shipped it off to a new owner in Norway.

We both hope to see *The Victorian* restored sometime soon.

Left: After two or three visits to the Alexander Brothers in Detroit, Sy Gregorich's The Victorian *looked like this when it hit the magazines in 1960—clean, crisp, and understated. Above: After a stint on Bob Tindle's hot rod car lot in Portland, Gregorich says the car was even seized by the government at one point. But now it's back in Michigan, like this, awaiting further restoration.*

Rick Dobbertin's 1985 Pontiac

I stated in the beginning that hot rods don't have to be old to be lost. Where are the America's Most Beautiful Roadster (AMBR) or Ridler (named in honor of early Detroit Autorama promoter/publicist Don Ridler) winners from 5, 10, or 15 years ago? I wish I had more room in this book to dwell on what I call "The Recently Departed." But here's one classic example.

Rick Dobbertin's twin-blown, dual-turbocharged, nitrous-injected 1985 Pontiac J2000 took the Pro Street movement of the 1980s to the limit, literally. If Pro Street was defined by tubbed rear wheel wells and steamroller-size (but treaded) wide rear tires tucked inside the sheet metal, Dobbertin's had just enough room for the *de rigueur* pair of wheelie bars, squeezed side-by-side, between them. They were as wide as they could get.

First featured in the October 1986 issue of *Hot Rod*, it was chosen Hot Rod of the Year in the December issue, with Gray Baskerville proclaiming it "beyond belief," and stating, "We can't divine what direction the 'Pro Street' syndrome will take; still, we cannot help but think that Rick's righteous Poncho will be leading the pack." It did. Nothing topped it. And Revell immortalized it with a 1/25-scale model kit.

So where's the actual car? I contacted Dobbertin when I was researching the first *Lost Hot Rods* book in 2009, and he said, "I sold it to a guy [collector Chuck Parsons] in Chicago a few years ago. He also bought *Orbiter* and is buying my old Nova." At the time Rick was heavily involved in a project called *HydroCar*, which was a car/boat that was supposed to sail around the world, or something. He said he'd send me photos of the J2000, but all I got was the one small picture you see here. I've heard nothing of the car since, but I have to assume it's still in the same collection. It was the icon of a significant, if sometimes silly, hot rod era.

Rick Dobbertin's 1985 Pontiac J2000 Pro Streeter, circa 1986.

Finders

There are lots of ways to find old hot rods and custom cars. I offered plenty of tips and tricks in the first book. But I also said that one of the best ways to learn how to do it is to read all these stories about how other people did it. There are similarities and patterns. But it seems every story has its own unique twists and turns. That's what makes them amazing.

Also, there are certain people who seem to have a knack for it. This is harder to explain. Some actually do it for a living, or at least as a sideline, so they have plenty of time to devote to the search, plus lots of connections. Others hole up in dark rooms, eyes glued to their computer screens, and scan every available site where they might be the first to bid on anything that looks remotely intriguing. That's not what I consider fun, but it works for some.

Chapter Two

The Chris Ito Collection

A graduate of the Art Center College of Design in Pasadena in the mid 1980s, Chris Ito spent 15 years working at ASC in Detroit with Larry Alexander (of the A Brothers) building factory prototypes and other special projects. Then he moved to his present position as director of design for Peterbuilt Trucks in Denton, Texas, where he's been for the past ten years. If that didn't keep him busy enough, he has also designed several recent award-winning hot rods, including Bruce Ricks' Ridler-winning 1956 Ford convertible, the *G-Force 'Cuda* for Alan Johnson, the *NewMad*, and the 1934 roadster that nearly won the 2010 AMBR for Steve Frisbie.

There are also more cars in Chris' collection than shown here, and they change regularly as he finds new ones. So how does this Finder do it? When you review the following stories, you see each one is different. Luck is a common factor. Having a network of friends who know what you're looking for—and having the wherewithal to purchase the right cars when you find them—is another.

The Rodwell 1932

I didn't really get to know Chris until he showed up at the 2009 GNRS in Pomona, where there was a special display for cars that had been on the cover of *Street Rodder* and *Rod & Custom* magazines. He was with a little red, channeled, blown-flathead-powered 1932 three-window that I knew quite well but hadn't seen in nearly 35 years. That's when Dick Rodwell drove it from Salt Lake City to Del Mar, California (after rescuing the 1950s rod from a junkyard and rebuilding it exactly as you see here) for the first NSRA Nats West, and I immediately fell in love with it, photographed it, and put it on the cover of the October 1975 *Street Rodder* magazine.

So did Chris Ito (fall in love with it) when he saw that cover, but he was still in junior high in Oregon. But he kept that magazine. Many years later a student from Salt Lake City happened to contact Chris to ask guidance about a career in automotive design. Chris asked if Dick Rodwell was still around. "Sure," said the student, "Dick is a very active rodder in the area."

"Whatever happened to his little red 1932?" was Chris' next question. "I might know someone who knows where it is," was the answer, and two days later he called with a phone number. That person knew who bought the car from Rodwell in 1975. He called him a "hoarder," said he had lots of cars and none of them ran, but he offered another phone number. Chris called, told the guy how much he had always loved that particular car, and of course the hoarder said, "No." So Chris kept calling him for two months. Somehow he finally convinced him, and the guy said, "It's going to you."

Not only did Chris get the car (in 2003), but it was still the same, the price was decent, and it even had the same tires on it. The only thing missing were the red Kelsey wires with widened chrome rims, but Chris has since located them too. The original chrome on the blower, carbs, headers, and even the 1939 transmission

Above: Other than steel wheels in place of painted and plated Kelsey wires, this is exactly how this car looked on the cover of Street Rodder in 1975. The front axle is an original Bell tube. **Right:** About all I know of the engine is that it's a 1948 Ford with a S.Co.T. blower and twin 97s. All the chrome, including headers and oil pan, is from 1975.

all polished up, as did the rest of the car. The wood-grained dash and black-velour/vinyl interior is excellent. A lucky find? Maybe, but certainly an excellent one.

The Blue 1932

The short version of how Chris got this car is, "A friend told me it was on eBay, and no one else bid on it." The longer version is more complicated and mysterious, but dig this: Chris had to sell a 1934 three-window coupe to find this one. The buyer lives in Ontario, Canada, and his father said he thought he remembered the chopped and channeled, Olds-powered 1932 three-window from the London area in the 1950s, and produced a small photo of it (dated 1956) in gray primer, sitting in the pits at the Cayuga drag strip (see back cover). Pure coincidence!

The person Chris got the car from, on eBay, worked for R-M Auctions and had acquired it from a family after it sat for 35 years. He knew nothing of its history. Chris said all he could learn was that a guy named Ken Wilson, who was described as "a sort of Indiana Jones of hot rodding," from Chatham, Ontario, Canada, got the car in the 1960s and turned it into a show car. He blended its 1950s heritage and late-1960s-to-early-1970s trends such as button-tuft upholstery and wood-trimmed interior accents. It had a blue Plexiglas roof insert, no front brakes, a fully chromed Olds rear end, and a dead cylinder in the 1954 Olds 324.

Chris started by soaking the engine in Marvel Mystery Oil to un-stick the valves and solid adjustable lifters, rebuilt the three 94 carbs, re-plated the rear end, built better-looking headlight stands, and swapped some Keystones for 1960s polished E.T. mags. With a 1939 Ford transmission and open drive, he said it runs well and is much safer to drive than when he received it, "It needs some carpet, but otherwise it's done."

The Cockroach

This car is unreal, especially to be found in this condition. It's called *The Cockroach* (for unknown reasons), it's a 1931 roadster on 1932 rails (partially chromed), and it was sprayed 78 coats of candy-copper lacquer fogged in gold by Ed Lepold, according to an old show sign. The current upholstery in the car was done by Dickie Wright in the mid 1960s. And 90 percent of the chrome is original too.

Chris' research says it was built by Jim Cooper, from O'Fallon, Illinois, beginning in the late 1950s and finished by the mid 1960s. Although it was drag-raced, driven on the street, and shown extensively, Chris can find no mention of it in any magazines.

Where it was for four decades is unknown, but the Cooper family obviously preserved it well. Someone Chris calls "a flipper" was able to buy it, along with several other cars, from the Cooper family around 2006. He (or someone else) replaced an earlier Nailhead Buick engine and 4-speed transmission (the chrome clutch linkage is still there) with a 425 engine

Left: In contrast to the Rodwell coupe, this three-window has the classic Eastern look with its chopped top, un-chopped grille, lowered rear, molded fenders, and even the light blue paint. But this one's from Eastern Canada, not the United States. **Top Right:** The candy-cane plug wire covers and red plastic fuel lines are 1950s show kitsch, but the chrome firewall and frame covers are hardcore. **Bottom Right:** The 'glass buckets, black upholstery, and wood accents smack of a later-1960s update. Check the blue Plexiglas roof.

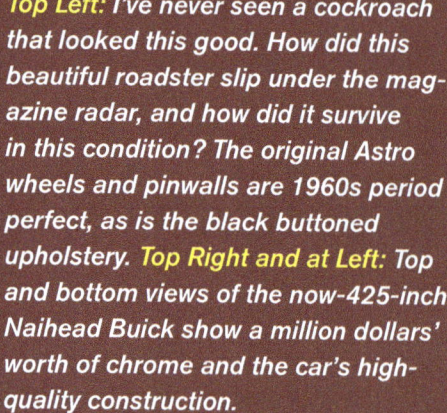

and T-400 automatic. After getting the car running, he took it to an auction in Pebble beach in 2007, and then it went to auction in Dallas.

The person who bought it in Dallas, knowing that Chris was a local rodder who loved such cars, called him and said, "I have a car for you." How could Chris argue? He said he got it in 2007 or 2008. The Astro dished wheels on the car now are original to the 1960s, but Chris found the similar-vintage whitewall slicks. For some reason the 1955 Chevy rear and radius rods were painted red, so he had them chromed to match the undercarriage. But the rest of the car is just as Chris received it, and apparently just as Jim Cooper built it by 1965 or so. Chris says it was very well-built then, and it's an excellent driver now; he's taken it on several 100-plus-mile trips so far. He hardly has to add, "It's done, and it's a keeper." We can all heartily agree.

The Rebel Forty

Yes, this chopped and channeled 1940 coupe with a sectioned hood and raised fenders was originally built in the 1940s, but few (including some of its owners) know its pedigreed history. In fact Chris didn't know what it

Top Left: I've never seen a cockroach that looked this good. How did this beautiful roadster slip under the magazine radar, and how did it survive in this condition? The original Astro wheels and pinwalls are 1960s period perfect, as is the black buttoned upholstery. Top Right and at Left: Top and bottom views of the now-425-inch Naihead Buick show a million dollars' worth of chrome and the car's high-quality construction.

was when he bought it, because there were few clues to its story. He found it on Craigslist.org only because a friend told him it was there. He could see that it might have originally been built a long time ago, but it had this red-with-ghost-flames paint job, it sat high, it had handmade running boards and black-painted bumpers, and it wore some 1970s wheels and tires. Plus, the photos were bad. The ad said it had "movie history," but we've all heard that before. Chris watched the ad, with the price continuing to drop, for three months. "I got a screaming deal on it," he said.

I traced and told the full story of this car in the February 1993 issue of *Rod & Custom*, along with several early photos, but it got squeezed into a few columns in the "Roddin'" section. It was built by Larry Nicklin in Los Angeles beginning in 1948, and finished in beautiful black lacquer with 1949 Plymouth bumpers. He drove it to Art Center College, where he got an automotive design degree in 1952. At some point he painted the car

You probably can't see the pearl-ghost flames over the Porsche-red paint in these photos, but Chris plans to change it. The first things he did included removing the running boards, adding the ripple bumpers, and of course the wheels and whitewalls.

coral, then left it in his mom's garage when he got a job in Detroit. Realizing he'd be working there for some time, he told his mother to sell it. A Hollywood bit actor got it for $400, and next thing it was one of the cars seen prominently in *Rebel Without a Cause*, notably in the "chicken run" scene. It also appeared in *Hot Rod Girl*.

Nicklin went on to an illustrious design career in Detroit, unaware of his coupe's movie credits, and he built a significant classic-car collection. The coupe's history was unknown until Jack Thomas of Bakersfield, California, bought it in 1979, removed the hood, dropped in a 6-71-blown Chevy and 4-speed, and cut out the rear fenders for big tires. Later, learning the car's story, he reinstalled a flathead engine and the hood, but painted it red and left it more like a rod than a custom. Having moved to the state of Washington, Thomas is the one who finally put it on Craigslist.org and sold it to Ito. This car obviously has some unique provenance, and Chris continues its restoration—probably black, or maybe coral. We'll see.

The Street Digger

What in tarnation is this? Can you believe it's a blown and injected, front-engine, full-canopy, yet fully street-legal dragster? You better believe it. This is Chris' latest acquisition, and he's plenty excited about it. The car is amazing, but so is its story. I can't tell all of it here, but I'm sure you'll hear all of it when Chris finishes rebuilding it.

Mike Minette of Dallas, Texas, hand built this car beginning in the latter 1960s when front-engine diggers were king. He built the 160-inch frame from round tubing, but made it wide enough in the rear for two seats. He fabricated the tubular A-arm independent front suspension (with rack-and-pinion steering), plus a 1966 Corvette IRS using Mopar torsion bars. Next he made his own plaster molds to form the fully-enclosed fiberglass body—his first attempt at such work.

The engine was a 1967 'Vette 427, fitted with 8:1 pistons, a fully functional 6-71 blower, and Enderle mechanical injector running gasoline. The transmission was a Torqueflite. A radiator and electric fan was hidden in the nose. After years of work, Minette finished the car in black paint. With lights, wipers, and license plate, it was not only street legal, but he drove this car, towing a trailer, from Dallas to the 1974 NSRA Nats in Tulsa!

It made the cover of the August 1974 issue of *Car Craft*, which is where Ito first saw it when he was 15. It was also in *Popular Hot Rodding* and *Hot Rod Yearbook* No. 13. "I just went crazy over this car," he said. "It was one of the two most influential cars of my youth" [the other being the Rodwell Deuce]. He still has the magazines.

More than 25 years later, Ito moved to the Dallas area. He was checking out a very nicely built Z-28 at a local cruise night, and the owner mentioned that Mike Minette had done the chassis and suspension. Bingo! Ito had forgotten Minette was from Dallas. He asked the guy if Minette had a street-legal dragster. He said, "No, but he has a street-legal Outlaw sprint car, with a wing and injectors." Wow! Chris excitedly called Minette, who unfortunately replied he hadn't seen the dragster in 20 years and had no idea where it was.

So Chris looked for and asked about this unique car for 8½ years with no luck. Then, one day the same dealer from Dallas who had sold *The Cockroach* to Chris called to ask what he thought a rod-cum-dragster he had found was worth. After a few questions, he figured it was the Minette car. Some oil company in Houston had it, painted it yellow, then let it sit for 15 years. The engine was blown up, but it was otherwise complete. It took Chris a while to actually get the car, but he finally did. He said getting it was "kind of a sentimental thing." But the best part was getting to know Minette, who now is helping Chris round up parts (including some from "big-name cars" from the past) to build a new 454 stroker for it.

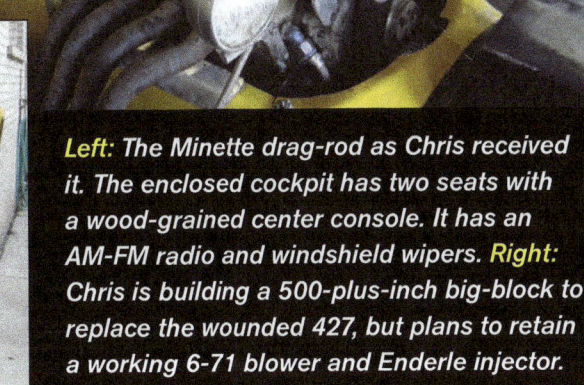

Left: The Minette drag-rod as Chris received it. The enclosed cockpit has two seats with a wood-grained center console. It has an AM-FM radio and windshield wipers. Right: Chris is building a 500-plus-inch big-block to replace the wounded 427, but plans to retain a working 6-71 blower and Enderle injector.

Back Room Roadster

When you're a writer, you always keep notebooks and files full of tips, leads, and story ideas. You also continually have people telling you about stories, articles, or books they say you ought to write. This one falls in both those categories. I leave the people involved anonymous because the primary one asked me to.

This goes back many years, to when someone who's a big name in the automotive aftermarket industry used to throw a big Christmas party attended by many other names in the industry. Somehow I was included. And each year—only at this party—I saw this one affable guy who was VP of sales for a company that made a certain type of performance engine parts, and he always said, "You need to do a story on all the hot rods my boss has, if he'll let you. He's got dozens of 'em, stashed in garages and containers." The boss (the owner of the company) was never at the parties, and I had my doubts that he'd let me see (let alone publicize) his hot rod stash.

But I kept a note in my potential story file, and finally decided to call. The owner, Ken, seemed quite affable and eager to share his stuff. He said he'd been paring down his collection, due to his advancing age, but when he started telling me about the cherry 1932 Ford roadster he'd found in a neighbor's garage, I figured it was something that should be in this book. Besides, it all fits right in with the mystery theme.

When I met Ken at his office, the first thing I saw was a fully dressed flathead V-8 in one corner, complete with a 4-71 GMC blower topped with three carbs and a hand-fabricated finned aluminum oil pan. On three of the office walls hung dozens of rare flathead heads, and on the fourth were shelves lined with similar intake manifolds. Then, among all these goodies were photos of various cars Ken had built and owned over the years, both rods and customs. One was a 1927 T touring with a Riley dual-port four-cylinder, and another was a sectioned 1937 Ford pickup with an overhead-converted flathead V-8. Ken said he did all the work on these vehicles, from metalwork to mechanicals.

However, he said that arthritis had been making it difficult for him to get on a creeper to crawl under cars, so he'd been thinning his fleet. From 20-some at one point, he was down to about half a dozen, most of which were back in a corner of the warehouse behind his manufacturing plant, including the Deuce roadster he had told me about. We went to look.

Besides the gennie-looking blue 1932 with black fenders, there was a partially finished 1929 closed-cab pickup with Chevy power, a 1929 roadster in primer with a set of Dixon F-heads on a 1948 engine, a coffin-nose Cord made from a 1941 Hollywood Graham, and a complete Studebaker Avanti. The 1929 roadster was a car that Ken pieced together himself, using a set of repro 1932 rails and a Brookville body. Done in early 1950s style, its highlight is a 265-inch 59A with a Potvin cam and Dixon heads. The heads are being reproduced in very limited quantities by someone in SoCal, whose father ran a set on

Left: When we got to the back corner of the back room, and peeled back some car covers, this is what we found. Note the hood in the box next to the running board. **Right:** I keep saying, don't look in farmers' barns; look in your neighbor's garage. This is exactly what Ken found eight blocks from home, just a few years ago.

Lost Hot Rods II

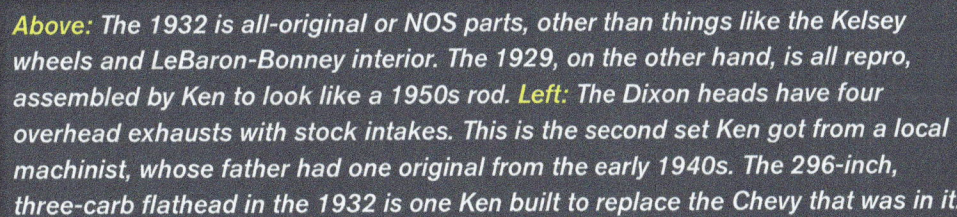

Above: The 1932 is all-original or NOS parts, other than things like the Kelsey wheels and LeBaron-Bonney interior. The 1929, on the other hand, is all repro, assembled by Ken to look like a 1950s rod. Left: The Dixon heads have four overhead exhausts with stock intakes. This is the second set Ken got from a local machinist, whose father had one original from the early 1940s. The 296-inch, three-carb flathead in the 1932 is one Ken built to replace the Chevy that was in it.

what was claimed to be the first Deuce to run over 100 mph at Muroc before the War.

But Ken's Graham/Cord is more typical of the types of cars he has accumulated over the years. Being in the performance parts business, he has always been in contact with people building all kinds of hot rods all over the country. In fact, the blown flathead in his office came from a builder in Canada. I'm not sure how he heard about the Graham, but someone had already started to convert it to a Cord, using original front fenders and a poorly handmade hood. Ken enlisted a talented metalman to work the hood into better shape, while he swapped the Pontiac OHC six that was in it for a small-block Chevy with a Gale Banks twin-turbo setup. Unfortunately, he says, further work on these cars may be difficult.

But the 1932 roadster is the lost hot rod I mainly came to see, and it's ready to cruise whenever Ken wants. The story of how he found it is the classic, "hey, I've got one of those in my garage" scenarios. Ken didn't even have to go look for it. It kind of came to him.

Ken's neighbor from across the street started a renovation project on his house, and hired a handyman/contractor who lived in the same general neighborhood to do the work. After a week or two, this guy couldn't help but notice a variety of vintage rods going in and out of Ken's driveway. It wasn't long before he came over and said—yep—"I've got one of those in my garage." When he told Ken it was an original 1932 Ford roadster, of course he had to go see. Ken said it was about eight blocks away. Although it looked mostly gennie on the outside, it had a small-block Chevy with a 1939 transmission and 1932 rear. There was an old dropped and filled axle in the front, with 1948 brakes on 1939 spindles. The wheels are 16-inch bent-spoke Kelseys. Ken said the guy had owned it for 30 years and had put lots of NOS parts on it. What he didn't say was how he talked the guy out of it, but I assume it involved a non-refusable offer.

When Ken got it, the main thing he did was replace the Chevy with a 296-inch 1948 Merc engine he built using a Canadian block, Isky cam, and Edelbrock heads and three-carb intake. That's about all it needed.

Chapter Two: Finders 31

Frank Fernandez' Mercury

The reason I'm including this gorgeous candy-red 1940 Merc convertible in this chapter is because Bob Barnes told me about it. He's the Finder. In fact, he led me to a couple of the lost cars in the first book. How does he do it? First of all, he's been a member of the L.A. Roadsters club since 1967, and he's still driving the same 1934 Ford roadster he got in 1965. He's been heavily involved in street rodding since well before there was an NSRA. To say he has a lot of good contacts is a major understatement. Also he loves to buy and sell hot rods. I'd show you some of the great lost ones he's found, but they never stay in his garage long enough to photograph. And on top of that, he runs a chrome shop (Verne's Plating in Gardena, California). So every day he's talking to people who are building everything from Pebble Beach classics, to lowriders, to rods and customs.

That's how he met Frank Fernandez. He came in the door about ten years ago with a lot of pieces from a 1940 Mercury convertible, and Bob could tell right away that this car was a piece of history. Frank and his chopped Merc should really be in the next chapter, because they're "Keepers."

But before I get into the story, let me introduce another thread that runs through this book. I'm not even sure what to call it. Coincidence is a word that comes to mind. It might not be immediately apparent, but there are several cases in which one car or owner is somehow connected to another by happenstance. In this case it's a total coincidence. Just when Frank was buying this custom Merc in 1953, my wife, Anna, was going to kindergarten at the school where I took these photos. It was a half block from her house, which was exactly 2 miles from where Frank lived. So even when I first met Anna, nearly 20 years later, this beautiful early 1950s custom was parked in a garage right in the same neighborhood, and I had no clue. It wasn't really lost, because Frank knew where it was. But nobody else did—then.

Here's the story. In March 1953, Frank saw this burgundy 1940 Mercury with a chopped padded top appear on the lot at Moran Cadillac at the corner of First Street and Pacific Coast Highway in Hermosa Beach. He couldn't miss it, because he lived just a block up First Street. The car was beautiful, so he pulled in for a closer look. The salesman said a customer from Palos Verdes had brought it in. He had the car built for his son, probably in 1949 or 1950, but the son was drafted and sent to Korea, where he was killed. The father didn't want the car. But Frank did. He paid $400 for it, and it was like new.

The only problem was that nobody knew who did the work on the car. Frank didn't ask at the time. It wasn't important. There was no Carson tag inside the top. Years later Frank showed the car and his early photos to Eddie Martinez, and he guessed it might be an Ayala job.

Left: Frank removed the guards and an override bar from the 1940 Merc bumper, and painted the headlight doors, but everything else is the way it was in 1953, including the spotlights and the suspension. **Right:** Frand and I don't know who leaded the rear fenders and splash pan to the body, nor inset the taillights in the 1946 Ford bumper guards. But Paco Lopez sprayed the candy-red paint and Santy of Hawthorne recovered the original chopped, lift-off top of unknown origin.

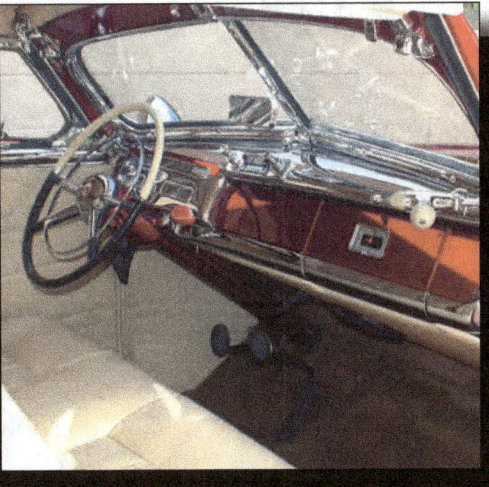

Left: Everything got liberally coated with candy red, and Joe Reath liberally hopped up the 1947 Merc mill that came with the car in 1953. *Right:* Although Frank updated the upholstery and carpet materials, the chrome dash and Ford accessory wheel are original. The red plastic on the dash is similar to that on the Barris Zaro Merc, but apparently it was a fairly common modification back then.

Then Frank took it to one of George Barris' Culver City car shows, where George looked it over and, surprisingly, stated it wasn't one of his. So that part remains a mystery.

But that doesn't bother Frank much. He's had it long enough that he just considers it *his* car. He drove it pretty regularly until 1963, when the usual priorities of family and career relegated it to the garage (though Frank proudly says that he always kept it in running condition). Beginning as a draftsman/designer, he worked his way into management at TRW aerospace. But after raising his kids and building a couple of houses, he finally decided in 2001 that it was time to rebuild the Merc. Now, looking at the 1950s photos, some of you might wince that Frank didn't restore the car exactly as it was. But understand that he kept it that way for nearly 50 years. He wanted to keep the car essentially the same, but a little newer and nicer.

Frank took the car to A-1 Universal Body & Paint in Gardena, where Paco Lopez pulled and stripped the body for the candy-red paint, saying it was the best sheet metal he'd seen on a car that old, with absolutely no rust. The original transmission and Columbia 2-speed rear in the car were still fine, but Frank took the "bored out" 1947 Merc engine that was in the car when he bought it to no less than Joe Reath for a full rebuild including porting, polishing, balancing, plus a Clay Smith cam, stainless valves, Offy heads and intake, Fenton headers, and Mallory ignition. Frank rebuilt the three 97 carbs himself. Bob Barnes did the fresh plating at Verne's, while Santiago in Hawthorne redid the Carson-style top and redid the upholstery in a Lexus material selected by Frank's wife. Since completion, the car has won Best in Show at the nearby Signal Hill car show a couple years in a row, so that tells you something. Plus Frank, at age 78, is fully enjoying driving it again after preserving it all these years.

Left: Frank took this great Kodachrome photo in 1956, showing the original fine metallic burgundy paint, possibly Chevy Ruby Maroon. The Chevy was his younger brother's, while the taillight belongs to Frank's brand-new 1956 T-Bird. *Above:* This 1956 interior shows the same dash and steering wheel, plus red horizontal binding in the top's headliner. The maroon and white upholstery was in the car when Frank got it, with no clue as to who did it.

Chapter Two: Finders

Rob Reisner's *Invader*

You want lost AMBR Oakland award winners? How about one of the few to win twice (1967 and 1968), and certainly the only one with two running, driving engines? Here it is, in Marietta, Georgia. It's Bob Reisner's *Invader*, which had an aluminum body hand-built by Don Borth, red-candy over white-pearl paint by Joe Anderson, red velvet lay-down interior by Joe Perez, and no less than two 389 Pontiac GTO engines, two B&M Hydros, and two Jag independent rear ends. And, of course, an amazing story.

It starts with a mystery. The 1970s was a weird era, especially for car shows. It was a time of rolling outhouses, bathtubs, telephone booths, stagecoaches, and you name it. Well, Reisner, with various partners, became a promoter during this era, gathering lots of these zany show machines and trucking them around the country to car shows. Another person heavily involved in this activity was Jay Ohrberg, previously known as "Mr. Roadster" and later the builder of the *Pinnochio* dual-engine 1932 highboy roadster. The story gets muddled through the 1970s and 1980s, but as far as I know, the *Invader* was lumped in with these other show machines for a couple of decades. I'm not sure where they were or who exactly owned them. Then I heard that Ohrberg had about 30 of them, and was taking them on a World Tour through France, Germany, Sweden, Japan, and who knows where.

I heard about it one morning in the late 1980s (I think), when someone handed me a Xeroxed sheet of paper listing all these wacky "cars," saying they were on the dock in San Pedro, for sale, "as-is," to pay shipping (and/or other) unpaid fees—"Bring cash." That day. Between bathtubs, barber chairs, and at least two "World's Longest Limos," the only car that caught my eye was the *Invader*. But, of course, I didn't have any cash.

Enter Ron Martinez, then living in the San Fernando Valley of L.A. Ron was a life-long hot rodder and closet car collector, mostly of 1950s and 1960s Corvettes and muscle cars, with a rod or custom thrown in. Other than his car-buddy close friends, few knew that Ron also pursued a long and successful career as a TV producer for Universal, Paramount, Warner Brothers, and Viacom for 30 years, working on shows such as *Murder She Wrote*, *Knight Rider*, and *Sabrina the Teenage Witch*, just to name a few.

And Ron knew Jay Ohrberg, and he had cash. He snapped up the *Invader* and a couple others. Unfortunately, they hadn't fared well on the cruise from Korea. Ron said the *Invader*'s chrome was not only heavily rusted, but the car had come loose in its container and had been accordioned front-to-back and side-to-side. Ouch! Fortunately, I don't have photos.

So, in his typically quiet style, Ron took the car to young, under-the-radar, but quite talented paint and metalman Scott Guildner, and basically said, "Fix it." Scott not only started hammering and massaging the aluminum body back into shape, but he also disassembled the car to send all the chrome out for re-plating. Ron said they took the Pontiac engines to some local

Left: Bob Reisner's *Invader*, seen in Oakland in its original form, won the AMBR big trophy outright in 1967, and then tied for it with Joe Wilhelm's *Wild Dream* in 1968. *Above:* You wouldn't know this car got trucked around the United States for a couple decades, then shipped around the world, before being dumped on a dock, basically as "salvage." Ron Martinez saved it, and he and Scott Guildner beautifully and accurately restored it. Note the bluing on the headers; yes, it runs and drives.

Bored to 400 inches, the Pontiacs were basically stock, other than M/T cross-ram intakes, but Ron added "wilder cams to make 'em sound better." Each has a 4-speed hydro transmission. The custom IFS uses twin Jag coil-overs and disc brakes.

rebuilder in the Valley, and Ron found "some old guy who lived in a wrecking yard" who knew how to expertly rebuild the two Hydro transmissions. Of course they also found things like rusty water inside the Jaguar differentials, instead of gears, but Ron knew a Jag expert who could fix them. Surprisingly the Joe Martinez upholstery, minimal as it is, was still in usable condition. Then Scott finished it with fresh white-pearl and candy-red paint, and reassembled everything.

Of course it runs and everything works. You can tell it's not the most comfortable thing to drive. But the lead photo for the feature in the July 1967 *Hot Rod*, when it was on the cover, shows Reisner driving it down the boulevard. And I was there that day, five—maybe ten—years ago when Ron took it to the L.A. Roadsters show in Pomona, pulled in line with the other roadsters, and drove it in to collect a pewter mug. Everybody's jaws dropped. He did the same thing at the NSRA Nats in Louisville in 2010.

Ron retired a few years ago and now lives in Georgia, where he has about 24 cars in his warehouse. Besides what's left of Nye Frank's *Pulsator* streamlined dragster, shown here, and a much-better-preserved *Wine Truck* (which now belongs to someone else), his other lost hot rod I want to show you is the former Jim Ewing 1929 hiboy roadster. Any red-blooded hot rodder knows Super Bell–founder Jim's chopped, orange, track-nosed 1934 coupe. In fact, I included it at its present home in Maryland in the first book.

But far fewer remember the simple, traditional, 1929 on A rails that Jim built in the late 1970s. Featured in a couple of magazines at the time, it has a Chevy II four-cylinder hooked to a 1939 Ford transmission and a Culver City Halibrand quick-change rear. With black paint and a bright red interior, it rides on a set of Eric Vaughn's Real Wheels, and of course has a Super Bell dropped I-beam and brakes.

No big story or mystery about this one. Ewing put it up for sale at the L.A. Roadster show in 1983, and Ron bought it. Besides keeping it in excellent condition, he chromed the rear radius rods and added two carbs to the motor. What else could it need? It's a perfect little rod, and now you know where it is.

A happily retired Ron poses with the cool A roadster he bought from the late Jim Ewing nearly 30 years ago, and has obviously kept in pristine condition.

Chapter Two: Finders 35

*Top: The aluminum body was formed by Don Borth, who also made the one for Mickey Thompson's streamliner. It took much straightening to get back in this shape. A chromed Jag IRS has two differentials connected by a center axle.
Bottom Left: The original windscreens, teak dash, and Joe Perez–stitched reclining seats are in surprisingly good condition. Bottom Right: Nye Frank's* Pulsator *AA/FD with two injected Chevys, driven by Bob Muravez, not only won Best Engineered Car at the 1965 NHRA Winternationals, but was perhaps the only full-bodied streamliner to hit 212 mph. With treads on the back and skis on the front, somebody converted it into the* Ice Kutter *show car. It's still as Ron rescued it from the dock, in condition similar to that of* Invader. *Restoration is planned.*

Deuce in the Shed

This is the best "Found" hot rod in this book. I just wish I could have been there when they opened the garage door on this dusty Deuce. No one had a good camera, so you have to squint to see the details in the small photos. But it is an amazing scene.

The reason this car is in the "Finders" chapter is because Alex "Axle" Idzardi told me about it some time ago. Axle is the guy who found the long-lost Barris 1938 Ford custom shown in the first book, as well as the organizer of the annual Suede Palace at the Grand National Roadster Show in Pomona, plus the significant "Customs Then and Now" display there in 2011, among other things. He's very good at finding lost hot rods. He was hoping to acquire this one. I was hoping to show it in the first book, but things didn't work out that way. Thankfully, however, the car has finally come out of decades of hibernation, and you can see it here.

It was actually Axle's good friend Jim Bouchard who knew about the Deuce. Jim is a relatively young guy who has a rod-building shop in San Jacinto, a small desert community at the base of the mountains about 100 miles southeast of Los Angeles. Jim grew up in the adjoining small town of Hemet, and his parents and well-known painter John Carambia's parents—all avid hot rodders—lived on the same street. Jim "Bones" Noteboom also lives in town and figures into the story. It gets quite complicated. Here follows my effort to sort it out.

Glenn Miller is the guy who owned the Deuce. I interviewed his daughter Melanie and her husband, Bobby, to get some facts. Miller apparently ran Muroc with a 1936 Ford in the 1930s. He got married in 1936. He then started a truck repair business in Wilmington, next to Long Beach, and eventually got the contract to maintain Shell Oil trucks. Nobody's quite sure, but Miller got the Deuce sometime between 1951 and 1953. What we are sure of is that Miller got into crackerbox boat racing heavily from 1946 to 1959, first with flatheads, then with Chevy engines, and his *Li'l Stinker* boats won three or four national championships. Bobby worked in Miller's big truck shop starting sometime in the 1950s, and said the 1932 just sat in a corner, exactly as it looks today. He said the only time he saw it run was when they moved to a larger shop in 1959; Miller got the coupe running and drove it over. Bobby said it sounded wicked. But it never ran again.

Back to Jim Bouchard. Miller retired and moved onto a large rural piece of property in Hemet around 1980. He and his wife lived in a mobile home, with a large tin-shed shop behind. Jim's grandmother lived next door, and Jim watched as Miller's property filled with gas pumps, an old gas truck, porcelain signs, derelict boats, and plenty of other stuff. He didn't know what was in the shed, but there were rumors about an old hot rod.

Left: If you're a lost hot rod hunter, you couldn't ask for a better catch. This is exactly what the Wiltons found when they opened Glen Miller's tin shed door about a year ago. It took all day to dig the coupe out, but that's all they took.
Right: The Deuce sat right here for 30 years and in Miller's truck repair shop another 30 before that. The tag on the license says 1953. You can see the body is cherry.

Five years later, 16-year-old Jim was driving his rodded 1946 Ford coupe, and this "nice older gentleman" he met at the 7-Eleven store started asking questions about it. To shorten a much longer story, the guy was Glenn Miller, he came to see Bouchard's shop, and they became friends. He finally invited Jim over to see "his stuff," and Bouchard invited Bones to come along. When Miller opened the shed's roll-up door they saw a partially covered orange 1965 Mustang, machinery, welding equipment, stacks of aluminum castings (Miller made Chevy timing covers for boats), and an unpainted, chopped, but pristine Deuce coupe layered in dust and cobwebs in the corner. Jim said the shop, as well as the whole property, was stacked with stuff, with small paths to walk through it. They were amazed. Bones immediately offered Miller $15,000 for the coupe, but Jim said he was kind of taken aback, and simply said, "No."

There's way more story than I have space to tell. Miller continued to visit Bouchard's shop. Bouchard's and Carambia's dads (both hard-core rodders) finally went to see Miller's place in 1996, and somebody offered $20,000 for the Deuce. Still no.

In 2000 Miller died, followed shortly by his wife. Some of the stuff disappeared from the yard and a young renter moved in. I'm skipping details, but Bouchard had worked for a utility company in Hemet and still had one of his shirts. Wearing it, clipboard in hand, he visited the property, told the renter he had to check wiring, including in the shop out back. Yep, the Deuce was still there. From the renter, he got the name and number of Miller's daughter, who lived in Orange County.

Over the next ten years they kept the secret of the Deuce in the shed fairly quiet, but called the daughter, Melanie, pretty regularly. At first she seemed overwhelmed by it all, saying "I don't know what this stuff is worth." Later, I think it was Alex who told me he offered $25,000, but Melanie told him she'd been watching the car auctions on TV and figured the 1932 was worth twice that. So . . .

Enter Dave Wilton, Jr., who also lives in Orange County, and is involved in off-roading. He was friends with Melanie and Bobby, and they mentioned that there was an old fiberglass-bodied dune buggy out at her father's property in Hemet. He was also interested in a boat or two. So Dave and a friend took a day to go out and look. The dune buggy and boats turned out to be junk, but what they saw in the tin shed looked intriguing.

Dave's father, who had retired to Northern California after selling a semi-truck parts company, was an early Ford enthusiast with a restored 1929 A pickup and Vicky, and was running a small business making Lincoln brake conversions. He was a rodder in the 1950s, and Dave, Jr. thought he might be interested in this old 1932 coupe. He sent photos. His father was.

In fact, when Dave, Sr. came down to see it, he said, "I want the car," and obviously made Melanie an offer she didn't refuse (I have no idea how much).

Alex, Jim Bouchard, and I were all quite surprised to learn of the sale when we saw photos the Wiltons put on

Left: *With roller tires on the front and some dust blown off, this is how I found the three-window in Dave, Jr.'s garage. The top is only slightly chopped, and it has a filled grille shell, slightly dropped headlight bar, nicely dropped axle, and juice brakes. There are virtually no dents, and the only rust is on the surface.* **Above:** *Don't know what the pedals are, but everything else is gennie 1932 three-window, including the mohair. The dash has a stock speedo and a Stewart-Warner amp gauge. Window frames were perfectly cut and finished.*

the internet when they picked the car up. Dave, Jr. let me come over and take photos shortly after, when he got it to his garage in Fountain Valley. A week later he trailered it to central California, where he met his dad, who took it up to his home in Paradise, California. I asked Dave, Sr. what his plans were for the car and he was quite emphatic that he was going to clean it up, get it running, refurbish the mechanicals, but otherwise keep it just the way it is.

So is this a happy ending for the story? It is for the finders but not for the longtime seekers. For them, this is a big fish that got away. For the Wiltons, this is a prize catch. I'm glad they let me share it.

Top: As found, the 59A flathead had three 97s on an Evans intake, Offenhauser heads, tube headers, and even once-chromed water pumps. Daughter Melanie said they found a receipt, "1 full-race flathead, $225," but no other particulars.
Bottom Left: The only things missing on the car were the 1939 taillights and, strangely, the rear spreader bar. Note the leadwork in the corners of the roof. Wilton said he found an L.A. newspaper dated 2/1/44 inside the leaded trunk lid.
Bottom Right: Whoever chopped the top was good; check the door fit and the gaps. The goodies are just part of what was stashed in the trunk, including Evans manifolds, exhaust dump tubes, front shocks, and a new aluminum flywheel with complete clutch—stuff that never got done.

Keepers

Some of the hot rods in this chapter were long lost before the original owner and builder found and restored them to their original form.

In a couple of cases where the original car is lost to oblivion, the former owner has cloned it. A couple more have recently been re-acquired by their original owner/builders after a long absence.

But most of these "Keepers" are truly that—hot rods that have been owned, built, and nurtured by the same person (or family) for decades, either in the same basic form, or in a variety of guises and uses, over the years.

Chapter Three

The Family Tub

When it comes to hot rods that have been kept in continuous use by the same family, in pretty much the same unaltered condition, I think the Hynes' 1925 Model T Touring is probably the king of the keepers. Yes, Isky built his T roadster a few years earlier, but it hibernated in a back room for a very long time, and is now sequestered in a museum. This yellow tub has never been in a museum, it's never quit being driven, and it's never even had a top in all that time. And the reason it's jacked up in Rod Hynes' garage now is only because Rod was charging up an 8,000-foot mountain pass on the last Pasadena Reliability Run (2009) when the well-used early Ford ring-and-pinion expired. It'll be back on the road as soon as he finds the right parts.

Ironically—or not—Rod's father, Tom, was parked at the Rose Bowl for one of the first Pasadena Reliability Runs, with a car full of cohorts in their crazy hats, when freelance photographer George Essig took their picture and Wally Parks put it on the cover of the March 1950 issue of *Hot Rod* magazine. To this day nobody knows exactly why. Yes, it made an eye-catching, different kind of cover. But the car was nowhere to be seen inside the magazine, the cover proclaimed it had a V-8 under the hood (not at that time), and the only I.D. of the car, on the contents page, was that the owners were members of the Road Dusters club of the Mojave Timing Association, denoted by the plaque on the front. That same plaque is still there.

It wasn't until four months later that Tom Medley fully photographed the car, and it was featured on a two-page spread in the July 1950 issue, complete with a Rex Burnett cutaway. If you can find a copy, or if you look closely at the cutaway shown here, you can see that nearly everything on the Touring, from the Model A frame rails with tube crossmembers, to the bracing inside the body, and most mechanical details, are still exactly the same. The only big difference is that the Miller single-stick OHC Model A four banger with twin Winfield carbs in the car (then) is now replaced by a potent little 1938 V8/60 flathead; the third one that's been in it so far.

Tom "Red" Hynes started with a 1929 roadster that he built in 1941–1942. Rod said he put the lighter 1925 "bathtub" body on it in 1946 partially with intentions of round-track racing, but also because he got $40 for the A body and the T was only $15 at the junkyard. The *Hot Rod* feature claims the whole car weighed just 1,480 pounds, and it's probably the same today too. The best line in that story, likely penned by Medley, was, "Yellow body of car and bright red wheels are accented by owner's red hair." Son Rod's long red locks keep that true too.

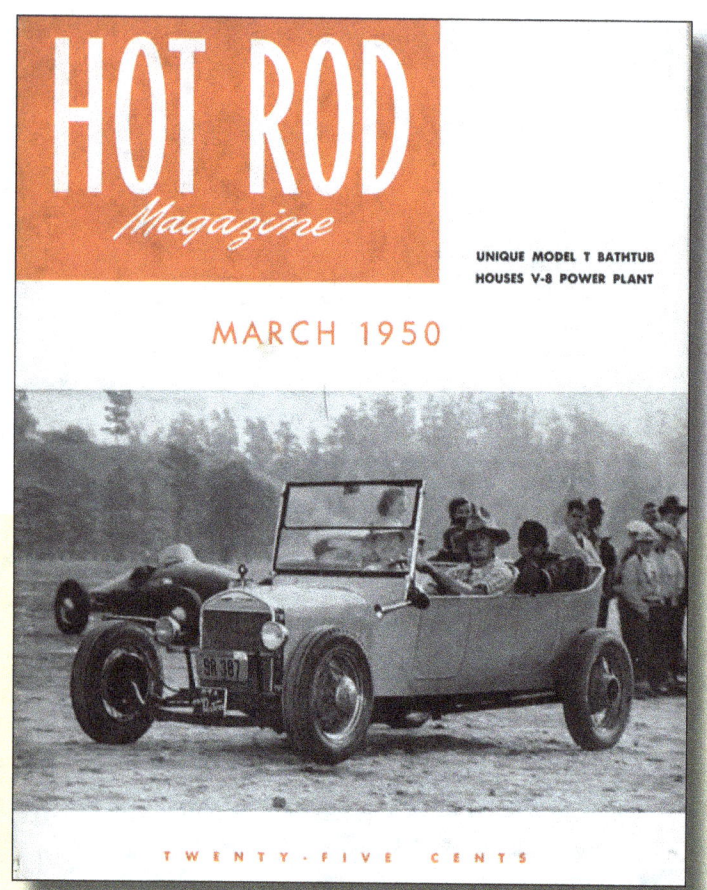

Left: Tom Hynes sits behind the wheel of his T tub in his floppy hat at the Rose Bowl for the Pasadena Reliability Run. The street-legal belly tank in the background still exists today, too. **Right:** No one knows why the Hot Rod cover and the eventual feature were separated by five months. Possibly to make up for it, the two-page spread included 11 photos plus this Burnett cutaway. Other than the SOHC Miller-head four, the car is nearly identical today.

Rod, born in 1952, says that the yellow tub was sort of like "my older brother, always part of the family." In fact, it was the only car in the family until Tom won a 1950 Chevy in a poker game in 1954. But he still used the tub to drive to work daily for another ten years. The four was swapped for the first V-8/60 in 1951. This was replaced by a big 296-inch flathead in 1954, which gave way to a 265 Chevy in 1958, then back to another 296 flattie in 1961. That flattie broke and was replaced with a Pontiac Tempest four with three Stromberg 97 carbs in 1964. Besides driving to work, Rod said his dad raced it regularly at Santa Ana, Saugus, San Fernando, and Colton on the weekends. Some engines wore out, some broke, but all were adapted to the early Ford driveline.

Besides the *Hot Rod* coverage, the tub was also featured in a gratuitous drag race in the L.A. River scene—driven by none other than Norm Grabowski—in the 1958 Mamie Van Doren B movie *Girls Town*. Rod said, "Someone called and offered $50 a day. Dad said 'Sure.'" Thank God this wasn't the hot rod they rolled. (For more on this, with photos, see "Hot Rod River Racin'" in *The Rodder's Journal* No. 11.)

Meanwhile Rod, infused with hot rod genes, learned to be a machinist and started building and racing Fuel Altereds (with 1923 T bodies, of course), as well as whittling aluminum connecting rods for Childs & Albert to earn a living. He was one of the stalwarts keeping the Fuel Altered flames alive (literally) through the 1970s and 1980s, and which he continues today. So when the tub was finally getting tired, Rod's younger brother Martin, an environmental engineer then living in Colorado, volunteered to restore it, which he did between 1982 and 1985. Not only did he repaint, re-plate, and reupholster it, but he built a new V-8/60, including porting and relieving the block, fitting lightened ForgedTrue pistons, and building new headers.

I remember seeing the car at some Midwest event at that time, and riding in it with Marty to a location to take new pictures for *Hot Rod* magazine, but I don't think they were used. At least I can't find them. Then Marty got a job as maintenance engineer for McMurdo Station, spending six months each year at the South Pole, so Rod became the caretaker of the family T in California (Tom passed away in 1987). It might be laid up for the moment, but that won't last long. This bright yellow hot rod tub has been on the highway, in this form, since 1946, and it's not near retirement age yet. It's a keeper.

Above: The tub currently resides in Rod Hynes' Tehachapi, California, garage, next to the bare chassis for his Fuel Altered, another potential T project, and his dad's complete, bright red 1938 Ford pickup in a corner you can't see here. *Top Right:* The first V-8/60 came from a Louie Senter midget in 1951. Tom put another one in during the 1970s, and son Marty rebuilt it in the 1980s with Edmunds heads, handmade headers, and three 81 carbs. *Bottom Right:* As soon as he finds a good ring-and-pinion, Rod plans to have the banjo back together and the tub back on the road, as usual.

Chapter Three: Keepers

Fred Steele's Sedan

Fred Steele of Maynard, Massachusetts, has been called a lot of things I can't print in this book, but as a founder and past president of the Tyrods car club, major domo of its annual Old Timers' Night, long-time member of the L.A. Roadsters club, and many other things, "East Coast Hot Rod Legend," or at least "Patriarch," is not a stretch. But you have to know Fred. If you ask him a direct question, you might or might not eventually get a direct answer, but you get a good story. Fred's done enough interesting stuff he doesn't need to make things up. I've known Fred a long time, and I think we have a mutual admiration for each other.

I asked if he could send me some photos of the purple, chopped 1928 Model A sedan that he's had since 1958. I got a thick envelope with 30 prints in it, including pictures of a 1959 Lincoln convertible he's had since new, his wife, his granddaughter and her pedal car, a friend's nice chopped 1950 Merc, and so on. Pictures of the A sedan included an NOS running board chromed in 1957, wheels made from Model A wire centers adapted to widened 15-inch rims, specific decals in the windows, the Columbia 2-speed rear end, etc. So what you see here is basically what I got.

I don't know who chopped the top, painted it, or other such details, but Fred built this car between 1958 and 1960, telling me once that he patterned it after Jack Chrisman's sedan (see page 69). I think the engine is a 265, but it might be an early 283, backed by what Fred calls a Lincoln transmission.

But the truly amazing story about this car—the reason it's here—is that in 1961 Fred drove it all the way from Boston, Massachusetts, to Tijuana, Mexico, to have the white truck-and-roll upholstery installed . . . and it's still there. He said it cost $100 and took a day. I'm sure the tale of that cross-country trip, in this hot rod, at that time, is even more amazing, but so far I haven't gotten Fred to tell it. Maybe one day. I wish there were better photos to show it. To quote Kurt Vonnegut, "So it goes."

Fred has owned dozens of unique rods and customs over many years, ranging from a white T-bucket roadster (that appeared on a Ventures' record album cover in 1964), to Deuce roadsters, T-Birds, a chopped Buick Riviera, and a

Top: I think Fred said the custom wire wheels were made in the 1970s, but they're by far the newest parts on this much-chopped 1928 A sedan, otherwise built between 1958 and 1960. *Bottom:* The purple paint is plenty old, but Larry Hook added the 1950s-style striping. Window decals are historical in themselves. Taillights are perfunctory.

Lost Hot Rods II

bright-yellow chopped 1950 Mercury that he rebuilt from a wreck. He then drove the Merc 9,000 miles across the country—stopping in Tijuana for another white upholstery job, this one costing $150—and it was featured in the seminal August 1977 "Chopped Merc Issue" of *Street Rodder* magazine. He still has that car.

But we were all surprised when he sold his signature hot rod—a very chopped, very channeled, very purple, four-carb flathead-powered 1932 roadster—to Ross Meyers shortly before it appeared in the "75 Most Significant" Deuce display of 2007. Why? Fred said, "It was time to thin the herd." Storage was a problem and he didn't need all those cars in his retirement years. He's keeping the 1928 sedan because, "It starts and runs easier; it has a top and windows for East Coast weather; it's more comfortable; and it has a back seat to throw a grandkid or a cooler in. Besides," he adds with a twinkle in his eye, "the roadster was worth way more money." Yes, Fred's always been good at business. Say hi when you see him at a Northeast rod run. He'll probably offer you a cool one from the ice chest in the back seat.

Above: **This is about as much of the TJ tuck-n-roll as you're going to see. It was done in 1961. Note the chrome window frames.** *Top Right:* **The reliable 2-barrel small-block has been there 50-plus years. Fred says the steering is from a 1952 Ford pickup.** *Bottom Right:* **Notice the Merc door handles, a Moon gas pedal, early Stewart-Warner gauges, and a nice 1950 Ford Crestliner steering wheel. The dash appears to be Zolatoned. Other stuff? Your guess.**

Chapter Three: Keepers

Jim Griepsma's 1934

This one is more of a show than tell. Jim Griepsma not only still has his well-known *Hot Rod* cover-car 1934 coupe, but he also has lots of pictures of it. In fact, he even still has his first car, a custom 1941 Ford coupe with a blanked-out center grille, skirts, spots, and shaved nose and deck that he got in 1949 when he was 15½. Now in his son Curtis' garage, it was deep Honduras Maroon to start with, but they had Gene Winfield paint it deep candy red in 1997.

I had heard rumors for several years that Griepsma and his coupe were around. I think it was Bones Noteboom who said he was in the Lake Isabella (Kernville) area in the mountains east of Bakersfield, California. But nobody around there knew him, and nobody had seen the car since the late 1950s. I kept asking, but nobody had a clue. Finally, after some diligent sleuthing and internet searching (fortunately it's not a common surname), I made phone contact with Jim. It turns out he lives *way* up in the hills northeast of Bakersfield, behind a couple of locked gates, on rutted gravel roads on a small, secluded ranch where he raises llamas. The coupe had been stored there for years, in its late-1950s condition. But just a couple of years ago he had taken it to a large body shop in downtown Bakersfield that did some custom work, to finally have it restored and updated.

From what Jim was telling me on the phone, it sounded like the plans for the coupe were a bit nebulous, and I wondered what he meant by "updated." He said the shop (City Body Works) had redone most of the body, which was in primer, but had to finish the rear wheeltubs. The frame was still original to the 1950s, but needed the rear portion narrowed to fit the new 9-inch rear end. Hmm. This sounded potentially ominous. Was this classic hot rod going to be turned into an 1980s space coupe or something?

As I mentioned earlier, hot rodding in the 1950s was all about updating cars. So Griepsma was continually doing it to his coupe—to the point that most pictures in the December 1956 *Hot Rod* feature spread showed it with a flathead engine, but on the cover it had a fully dressed Chrysler Hemi as well as fresh flames on the fenders and striping on the body. Jim said he got the car as a channeled three-window on a 1934 frame in 1953, one year out of high school. Using the well-equipped shop on his family's dairy farm in Artesia, he chopped the top himself and did all mechanical work. However, he had Ed Schelhaas (who did custom work on Larry Watson's *Grapevine* and other Renegades club cars) bob the rear fenders, roll the rear pan, and fill the dash.

He said the flames on the fenders were Barris' idea, who may have had something to do with getting the car on the *Life of Riley* TV show (in one

This is how Jim's coupe looked on the cover of the December 1956 Hot Rod. *Jim said they had the coupe at the Burbank studios about three weeks, and that William Bendix was a "super guy," the kid was "so-so," but the wife was "real . . . um . . . bad."*

46 Lost Hot Rods II

Jim built the car, originally with a flathead as seen here, in the obviously neat and well-equipped shop at his family's dairy. Later, Jim opened his own four-stall garage in Bellflower, which he operated until he retired to his mountain ranch.

episode), as well as on the cover of *Hot Rod* magazine. But within a year Jim took the car to Barris' twice, first to have a three-piece hood made (with a scoop and more flames) plus one of George's horizontal-bar grille inserts for the sectioned 1932 shell. In 1957 he took the car back "for fancier paint." He said George stripped it, and was doing things like fairing-in the door hinges (which Jim hadn't requested), when the fatal shop fire occurred. Fortunately Jim's coupe was in an area that didn't burn, but it was in pieces, unpainted, and it just never got put back together.

Yes, Jim has all the pieces. Even the bobbed fenders. The current plan is to paint it a brighter yellow, put the same Hemi back in, and reassemble the car much like it was on the *Hot Rod* cover in 1956, but without the funky flames and with a somewhat narrowed rear end. When I saw it at the body shop and took the pictures (page 48), things were at a standstill. Which way it goes from here remains to be seen. But it's still here.

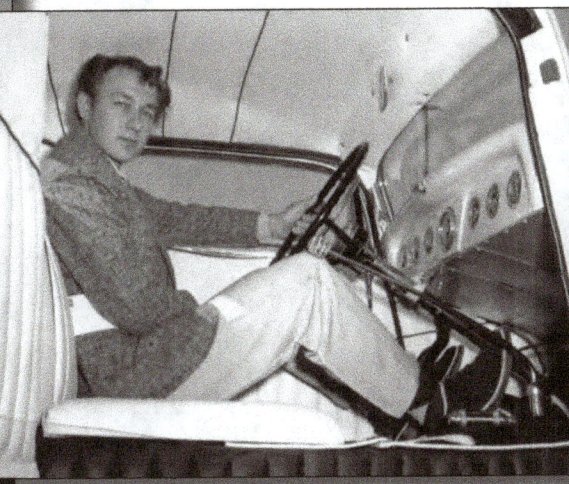

Above: Barris painted those flames; Jeffries did the striping. The cars in the background mostly belong to fellow Renegades members. Jim had one of the few rods in the mostly-customs Long Beach club. Right: The tuck-and-roll is cool, but young Jim is cooler. Yes, those are blue suede shoes, with argyle socks. The seat sat right on the flat floor.

Top: This photo's not the greatest, but this was the coupe's final form—with a scooped and flamed hood by Willie Sutton and a Barris bar grille—seen at a school-yard car show before Jim took it back to Barris for "fancier" paint. *Middle:* This is how I found it at City Body Works in Bakersfield. The body is straight and primed. The wheel tubs are partially installed, and the untouched frame lies under the body. *Bottom Left:* The Barris hand-built grille, still in good condition. *Bottom Right:* This is Jim in his garage at his small ranch today. That's the chromed, four-carb Hemi just as it came out in 1957, and—yes—those are the same pegboards seen in the early garage photo (page 47), which now cover three walls and hold even more tools.

Dwain Rogers' Deuce

To call Dwain Rogers' 1932 hiboy a "keeper" is a bit of a stretch, since the car was out of his possession for 24 years. But he found it twice; once in 1972 and again in 2001.

I became aware of Dwain when he was shown sitting in a bright-red Deuce hiboy roadster on the fifth-ever cover of *Street Rodder* magazine, September 1972. But he said he built that one from a channeled body with bad floors and fenderwells, and he actually had it sold when the cover shot was taken. So, with cash in pocket, he and a buddy jumped in his lace-painted Nova and drove from Texas to the L.A. Roadster show to find a better one. Through a few leads, he actually found a complete, original, running 1932 roadster hidden under a tarp in the back corner of what he called an old rodder's garage in Monterey Park. He paid $2,500 for it, which was "a little expensive for the time," but it had no dents, no rust, all original sheet metal, and he started it up and drove it out of the garage. Not only that, but he rented a tow bar, hooked it to his buddy's Nova's back bumper, and towed it 1,200 miles home with no problem. Plus—get this—the friend bought an Olds-powered 1932 Tudor at the Roadster swap, and *drove* it home, following Dwain.

Dwain had the fenders off his new roadster the day he got it home, and he knew exactly how he wanted to build it—just like Tom McMullen's with a few exceptions. The exceptions included a healthy two-carb flathead in front of a Muncie 4-speed, with a chromed 8-inch rear hung on 1936 radius rods and buggy spring, with red Kelsey wire wheels. After painting the body black, Dwain spent 17 hours drawing and taping flames as close to McMullen's as possible. However, he didn't care for Roth's thick white striping, so he spent another two months learning how to pinstripe them himself in yellow. All this is still on the car today. In fact, at the 1973 NSRA Nats in Tulsa, it won Best Homebuilt Paint, as well as the Best Nostalgia trophy presented by the Early Times of SoCal. Not bad.

Within two years he further emulated McMullen's 1932 by dropping in a 265 Chevy, adding a Moon tank in front, and five-spoke American mags. It made a couple of magazine covers in 1975. However, by 1980 Dwain needed capital to start a non-automotive business, sold the Deuce to someone in Galveston, and dropped out of the rod scene. The roadster next went to the Pate, Texas, swap meet, got bought by Don Ferguson, Sr., in California (who probably put a flathead back in), and went through several more owners.

Then, in 2001, Dwain picked up a copy of *Street Rodder* magazine and happened to be reading a six-page article on the Richard Munz car collection in Wisconsin. In the back of one of the photos, in a basement stall, he saw the flamed Deuce hiboy. A caption mentioned it had belonged to Don Ferguson, so Dwain knew it was his old car.

Dwain wrote Munz, asking if he could buy the car back. Munz answered that he "didn't usually sell cars" and, besides, the last owner had first buy-back rights. But Dwain is persistent. He continued writing for three years. Munz finally called, saying, "How do I know it was your car?" Dwain sent several convincing construction photos. Finally Dwain and Richard met at the 2005 L.A. Roadster show. By chance the "first buy-back" guy was there, too, and Dwain got him to tell Munz he could sell the car to Dwain. But still no.

It wasn't until a full year later, Dwain said, that Munz unexpectedly called him and said, "I'll sell now." So that was it. He won't say what it cost, but Dwain finally got

August 1975. Dwaine patterned the flames as closely to McMullen's as he could.

Chapter Three: Keepers   49

This is the same roadster in Dwain's Temple, Texas, driveway today. He recently added the wheels and tires, replacing caps and rings that were on it, but everything else is as he built and painted it in 1972. Note the same black California plate is still on the car.

his old roadster back that he'd built himself from that gennie original, in 2006. Besides making an aluminum panel to mount a whole dash-full of early 2½-inch Stewart-Warner gauges, the only other change was to swap steel wheels for a fresh (old) set of 16x11 and 15x4 magnesium American wheels with appropriate big and little rubber. This one might not have been a keeper the first time he had it, but it certainly is now.

Left: Nope it's not a barn; it's a garage in Monterey Park, California, 1972. This is what Dwaine found under a tarp. Then he got in, turned the key, fired it up, and drove it out. I wish I had a better photo, but the car's amazing. *Right:* That's Dwain driving his friend's Nova, towing the gennie Deuce back to Texas. And the friend is taking this picture through the windshield of the Olds-powered Deuce Tudor he just bought in California to drive home. That's doubly amazing.

50   Lost Hot Rods II

Dwain got the dropped and drilled front axle at the L.A. Roadsters swap a week after he got the car. You can barely see the chromed Ford rear on 1936 split 'bones under the back. It doesn't look it, but all this paint, chrome, and upholstery is now 40 years old.

Left: I'm not sure which interim owner put the flathead back in, but it's an .080-over 1949 block with Offy heads, Edelbrock intake, and handmade headers. It's still backed by a Muncie. **Right:** The tan upholstery is circa 1970s, but the curved-glass Stewart-Warner gauges, Bell wheel, and floor shift aren't.

The Surf Panel

You might recall an article in issue No. 9 of *The Rodder's Journal* called "Surf Rods." One of the several surfboard-carrying hot rods shown was a brick-red-primered 1930 Ford panel truck with a 1960s-era 9-foot-3-inch Ole surfboard sticking out of one of its back doors. That was in 1998, but a couple years ago when I was signing copies of *Lost Hot Rods* at AutoBooks in Burbank, California, Mike Hilborn came up and plopped some color photos on the table and said, "Remember this? It's in my garage." Of course I recognized it, because it looked essentially the same.

The photo in the magazine, taken from the rear, showed wide whitewalls on unpainted steel wheels, a nice white-covered roof, a hint of an overhead V-8 engine, and things like one bent rear bumper, a license plate wired onto the other, an off-angle trailer taillight, and a similar off-angle left-front wheel. Very typical early 1960s surf wagon stuff. It got you, your buddies, and your boards to the beach and back; not much else required.

In Mike's photos the red oxide primer had weathered and the nice white top was gone, but I could see some shiny-black wire wheels with small chrome hubcaps, newer (if mismatched) tires, a 1932 grille shell, seal-beam-converted headlamps, and a bright-yellow-painted, nicely detailed Pontiac engine with Weiand finned aluminum valve covers, a chromed generator, and a pair of AFB 4-barrels.

Well, here's the story. He bought the panel in 1959 at age 15½ for $50, and drove it home to Torrance, California, with the stock A engine. In Mike's words, "I was turning wrenches and had the car bug. My panel was to drive to high school and go to the beach surfing. The original engine didn't last very long, so my folks financed a rebuilt Model B from Ford Obsolete in Long Beach with dual down drafts and new tires. But a Model B still wasn't very fast, so next was a flathead V-8 with a 1939 box. In 1962 I got out of school and the need for speed was lurking. Every guy in town was running a Chevy, so I went to a junkyard on Vermont, asked what they had besides Chevys, and they pointed to a 1957 Pontiac. I put in the 347 with the 1939 transmission, and added a Sig Erson cam and Tri-Power." Then Mike's cousin, a transmission expert, built a 4-speed Hydro that's still in it.

The panel hit all the SoCal surf spots until Mike got drafted. Then he got into boat building, which took him to Fiji and New Zealand, among other places. The truck got parked and stored in 1967, mostly inside, mostly by his parents, for the next 40 years. After some years in the desert in Palmdale, the parents and the panel migrated to

Top: Mike says this was at the Redondo breakwater, 1963, which explains the brand-new, black California plate wired onto the bumper. The surfboard was a new foam Ole, replacing his former balsa log. Bottom: Mike (in hat) and friends roll the panel out of his parents' red barn for the first time in 40-some years. He said the Inglewood slicks still had 1967 air in them but the white top must have blown off somewhere on Pacific Coast Highway years ago.

52   Lost Hot Rods II

the beach community of Ventura, north of L.A. Mike also moved there in 1999, and in 2007 one of his neighbors, who knew he had the panel, took him to a small, artsy car event called The Primer Nationals.

Mike took one look, and said, "It was the right time, right place, and I had the right vehicle." During the next year Mike and some of his neighbors and friends got the panel out, replaced a cracked engine block with a 1959 389, got it running again, and drove it to the next event. In fact, he's taken it back each year, adding, "Every year after the Primer Nats I take it apart and fix something." Right now he's working on a new top. But he really has no plans to take it anywhere else, or to fix it up much further. "I guess I just like it this way," were his final words.

Top: The Pontiac now has a 389 block and a factory intake with dual-quad AFBs. *Middle:* The next project is a new top, but full restoration is not in the plans. *Bottom:* It now sits a little better on black-painted Cadillac wire wheels.

The Sharp Forty-One

If you haven't heard or seen the name Greg Sharp, you must not have been reading any hot rod or custom car magazines for the past 30 years or so. Greg joined the L.A. Roadsters even before that, when he acquired Dave Marasco's beautiful 1929 roadster pickup (see pages 174 through 176). He's also been writing articles at least that long for the magazines, mostly on topics relating to rod or custom history. He not only has a magnetic memory for everything pertaining to the subject, but he has amassed a sizable photo collection, leading to his being respected and relied upon as "the hot rod historian" by many less-knowledgeable magazine editors (including me). After retiring from a full career as an LAPD motorcycle officer, he was hired as Curator at the NHRA Motorsports Museum shortly after its founding 16 years ago, where he continues working more than full-time today.

That's the main reason this stunning, bright-yellow 1941 Ford pickup has joined the ranks of lost hot rods, though it certainly is a keeper. I used to see Greg everywhere, at rod events and on the highway, in his yellow truck all through the 1980s. Then—poof—it disappeared. Here's what happened.

Greg said he's loved Forty pickups since he saw Pete Paulsen's at the Renegades car show in Long Beach in 1959. He got this one from Early Times member Del Austin at the Model T swap meet there in 1976. It was cream, had a dropped axle, louvered hood, and a 327 hooked to the stock driveline. After four years of breaking transmissions and rear ends, he took the 327 to his buddy Don Cummins (as in Larsen & Cummins) and the truck to (fellow L.A. Roadsters member) Magoo's, where it got a Turbo 350, 8-inch Ford rear, and a Corvette Yellow paint job. Greg drove it that way to LAPD's Venice Division, about 50 miles from home in La Mirada, daily throughout the 1980s, plus to car events on weekends.

What he didn't know was that, shortly after rebuilding it, Monogram asked me to help redesign a few of its 1/24–scale model kits, and I used Greg's truck as the pattern for their *Forty Hauler*, not only sending photos of his pickup, but actually building a model of it that was used on the cover of the box.

But by the end of the 1980s, Greg decided to give the 1941 a well-deserved rest, getting something more economical to drive to work. Then, one morning in the early 1990s, he fired it up to take it to the Early Times swap meet. It ran for a minute, then popped, and Greg saw smoke coming from the hood louvers. The electric fuel pump quickly fed flames on top of the engine, as well as on the garage floor under the truck. He pushed it out, and got the flames doused with damage to the engine,

Above: Here's how it looks today, tucked away in Junior's storage facility. Note the shaved bumpers (by Birdman) and the Greek-style striping (by Itchy Otis). It's still Corvette Yellow. *Left:* I took this photo of Greg in his freshly rebuilt, bright yellow 1941 at Forty Ford Day in Anaheim in the early 1980s. Minus the sidemount spare, Monogram used it as a pattern for its *Forty Hauler* model.

Lost Hot Rods II

firewall, and paint on the hood and cowl. It could have been much worse, but in Greg's words, "It was pretty demoralizing, so I shoved it back in the garage where it sat while I decided what to do."

It sat about five years. Then Greg retired from the LAPD, started working at the NHRA museum, and Pete Chapouris opened his large new shop in Pomona, with Pete Eastwood and Jim Jacobs among the initial employees. Greg said he took the truck there for repair. And, as these things always do, one thing led to another. "The cab never came off the frame, but that's about all that wasn't done." It got a Mustang II front suspension, a new 300-hp crate engine with an Art Chrisman–tuned AFB 4-barrel, a parallel-leaf rear suspension, and finally a whole new repro bed. But such work takes time and money. This one took a lot of both, especially time.

Greg is particularly proud that so many of his heroes have worked on this truck. Kent Fuller did the louvers. Chuck Porter gave him the Appleton spotlights. Sherm's Plating (Don Tognotti) did most of the chrome. At some point it moved to Junior's House of Color, where it got more metalwork and paint, striping by Tommy Otis, the spots installed by Junior and Dick Jackson, and 1941 Studebaker taillights contributed by Kurt McCormick. Finally Joe Perez said he "outdid himself" on the 1962-style pearl white much-pleated interior with yellow piping (my favorite part). By 2002 it was finished enough to win its class at the Grand National Roadster Show (in San Mateo that year). But there are just a few niggling things Greg wants done, so it's been sitting in Junior's "warehouse" (actually the former Art Chrome custom shop in Hollydale) ever since. And that's where I took these photos. Not lost, but not seen . . . quite yet.

Above: Instead of ashes, you see typical detailing by Junior and Bill Larzelere under the hood. Mattson's built the radiator and firewall fluid tanks. *Top Right:* You can't see how P-Wood filled the dash for Mooneyes gauges, but feast your eyes on all that gorgeous pearl-white tuck-and-roll by the incomparable Joe Perez. *Bottom:* Besides the Appletons, Greg's customizing bent shows in the 1941 Stude taillights, 1949 Chev license guard, and the wide whites and Merc caps.

Chapter Three: Keepers

Jim Kitchen's Model A

"I encountered Jim Kitchen's pearl white 1929 hiboy roadster at the first lakes meet of the 1978 season. The first time I walked by it, parked near the starting line and covered with a fine layer of El Mirage dust, I assumed it was one of the competitors. It certainly looked the part with its Halibrand mags, tall-profile skinny tires, roll bar, front-mounted Moon tank and pressure pump, and its Enderle-injected Chevy engine. It looked just like a couple dozen other oldtimers competing that day, except that it was fitted with cycle fenders, headlights, and license plates—all required for the SCTA Street Roadster class. But this oldtimer didn't come out to race that day. It had actually been *driven* up the Cajon Pass, over the bone-jarring rut of a dirt road to El Mirage, and across the dusty lakebed just to watch."

I wrote the above in 1978 when I first photographed this car for a feature in *Street Rodder* magazine that ran in January 1979, including a lead shot of Jim blazing the tires on the weed-choked remains of the Colton drag strip. That article ended with Jim saying, "I haven't changed a thing on this car in 15 years, and most of it is older than that. But now it's right back in style." Well, Jim was way ahead of the return-to-retro style in 1978, but he kept, and regularly drove, the roadster just like this until 2000. Then he decided to finally tear it apart and make it back into a real race car, with a new chassis and enough modern upgrades to make it serious, but still maintaining its basic look and heritage.

This venerable A-Bone was built as a street roadster by Bill Freeman in Riverside, California, in the early 1950s. But by 1953 the father-son team of Leithold & Leithold (also of Riverside) stripped the street stuff, lengthened the frame, dropped in a hot flathead Ford six, and started racing it at the Colton drags, El Mirage, and even Bonneville by 1954. A plaque on the dash says it ran 127 mph at Bonneville in 1955, possibly with an overhead GMC six, which was installed about that time.

The light-blue roadster had a big Jimmy inline six with five carbs when young Jim saw it the first time he went to the Colton drags, not far from his home in San Bernardino, in 1958. He said it was running 99 mph, and racing new Corvettes. Finally it broke 100. It was the only car he remembered from that first day.

It ran a best of 104 mph with the GMC, but by 1960 the Leitholds painted it red and switched to a six-carb 283 Chevy V-8. They raced all over SoCal. When it was advertised in the March 1962 *Drag News* for sale for $1,000 cash, it had headlights, the same fenders, full black upholstery, a Cyclone quick-change, and 367 trophies. Jim bought it. "I always loved that car," he said.

He swapped the full-race 283 for a brand-new factory "fuelie" 365-hp 327 in 1963. After blowing too many 1939 Ford boxes, he adapted a Cadillac Hydro to the torque-tube/Cyclone rear. Then, employing Kitchenesque logic, he figured the FI engine should have real fuel injection on it, so he bought and installed a brand-new set of Enderles, along with the requisite pump, Moon tank, etc. This was his daily driver until he got drafted in 1964.

During the 1970s he shortened the frame when it cracked, and added a suicide front end and mag wheels. Scotty's Muffler did the work. Then, by 1974, he swapped in a new Model A frame and painted the car pearl white. It stayed that way for the next 26 years, and got driven plenty.

When he rebuilt it for Street Roadster class lakes racing in 2000, he had Al Simon fabricate a heavy, dedicated frame from 1/4-inch steel plate, along with the necessary cage and suspension. The braced 9-inch Ford rear

Jim Kitchen has owned this 1929 Ford roadster since 1962, looking much like this. The mandatory cage unbolts. The aluminum hood scoop is hi-tech, but it works. Note the minimum signage on the gennie body.

actually sits above the frame, and a Super T-10 4-speed replaces the old Hydro. Running a Steve Batchelor 301-inch small-block with Hilborn injectors and a Crower roller cam (plus many other tricks), it set the D/SR record at 190-plus mph at Bonneville in 2002.

So, of course, they built a 371-incher for 2003 and set the C/SR record at 199+. But lordy, you can't stop there. With more tweaks and tricks, Jim got in the Two Club at 201, eventually setting seven records, including two at El Mirage (one current).

However, it's been 12 years now and chasing Bonneville records just gets more expensive. When I asked Jim what his plans are for the car, he said, "Well, it's basically retired." Then, hardly pausing, he added, "I mean, we'll just run El Mirage for now. We've got the C record at 193.9, and I think we might go for the D class." He was up there the following week and ran close to 200 on a really bad course.

Top: The right-side pipe indicates the Leitholds were still running the Ford six at this 1955 Colton drag meet. Later they switched to GMC. The frame is lengthened 6 inches. *Bottom:* The airport was operating, but the strip was abandoned when this photo of Jim's street rod was taken in 1978. The front mags came off Scotty's roadster. The Enderle injectors were real. The fenders are the same. Jim drove it like this for 37 years.

Chapter Three: Keepers   57

Top: This is how the car looked in Jim's driveway in 1999. The unusual decklid louver pattern dates to the Leitholds. *Middle:* Same roadster, same driveway, today. Now it's back to a Street Roadster class racer. Behind it is the 1928 Mercury Torpedo Saloon that Jim pieced together 20-some years ago. In the garage is his 1954 Plymouth coupe on a 1982 El Camino chassis with a healthy 354 Chrysler Hemi. Jim has fun with cars. *Bottom:* For the race engine Jim switched to Hilborn injectors and lots of other hi-tech stuff (some not attached in this photo). The Weiand valve covers are the same, though.

The Himsl Brothers

Where do I start with this one? Art and Mickey Himsl have owned more hot rods than I can count. In fact, each of them has owned one of these cars, at one time or another. Plus Art has painted, flamed, or pinstriped so many famous rods, customs, and motorcycles that I couldn't begin to name them. He's the hot rod Rembrandt of our generation. A visit to Art's home in Concord (25 miles northeast of San Francisco), where these cars were photographed, is worth the trip. It's a cross between a transportation museum and a mini-Disneyland, including the multi-scale model train layout that circles the "poker room" above the shop. When I got there, Art was showing little brother Mickey the new flying saucer he was building. You get the idea.

Mickey's T

Let's start with Mickey's T, since it came first. This car, made from the front half of a 1927 T touring, was actually thrown together by a guy named Larry Selmer for the 1959 Oakland Roadster Show. By that I mean he had part of a T body, most of an A frame, and he borrowed most of the rest—engine, driveline, axles, suspension, wheels and tires—from his sprint car buddies. And he stuck a 5-gallon paint-thinner can on the back for a gas tank. It was definitely a kooky little car, and young Mickey Himsl fell in love with it. But after the show Selmer had to give all the parts back, leaving little but the body and frame.

Three years later, Mickey traded a complete 1929 A "phone booth" pickup he had built for that body and frame and $700. First Mickey built a big, stout 308-inch flathead for it, adding chrome sidepipes, an all-new chrome suspension, slicks on mags in back, and spindle-mount 12-spokes up front. Then Art chipped in with chartreuse and violet Metal-flake lacquer on the body and frame, copious pinstriping, and he even stitched what tuck-and-roll there was. Mickey chromed the gas tank, adding a coiled fuel line, and the car became *The Moonshiner*. In this form it made the cover of the June 1963 *Rod & Custom*, with a great cutaway drawing by Pete Millar in the three-page feature inside. Mickey said he "showed it all over" during the 1963–1965 seasons.

What's more amazing, though, is that he also said he drag raced it "all over" at the same time, setting the D/Altered record at three strips, running in the 12s at 113 mph on gas. Can you imagine? "Well, I had to add a roll bar, scattershield, and safety hubs," says Mickey, as if that

Seen in one part of the driveway of Art's amazing home/shop/model train layout is Art's original Dodge-plus-T touring and Mickey's clone of his T-bucket.

Chapter Three: Keepers   59

Larry Selmer's version of the Moonshiner T was built specifically for the 1959 Oakland show, using parts borrowed from sprint car buddies. The channeled body was blue, the engine and suspension yellow, with little chrome. Midget wheels in front and giant slicks in back added to the definite kooky look.

Art's Tub

made it safe. But then Art reminded him how much street racing they did with it, because people couldn't believe the little flathead T was that fast. But it was. It weighed 1,425 pounds, with driver.

What became of it? Good question. In 1966 someone offered to trade a black-lacquer, full-fendered, Buick V-8-powered 1932 Vicky for it, straight across, and Mickey of course couldn't refuse. Later, he traced the T to a guy who owned a pizza parlor in Fort Bragg, who had it for 20-some years. Then—poof—the owner and the T both disappeared with no trace. Since he couldn't find it, he decided to build this duplicate, combining the simple blue paint and tailpipes of the first version that he loved, with plenty of chrome. Starting in 1996, he had it done in time to show it at the 50th Anniversary Oakland Show in 1999. Having let the first one go, he figures he'll keep this one.

Art's tub has a similar, but different, story. First, it's the cab of a 1916 Dodge roadster pickup he found in a field for free, mated to the back of a 1927 T touring. He started building it in 1963, making a frame out of aluminum channel and using a Dodge front axle. By 1967, painted in faded candy tangerine with multi-hued flames, he put it in the Oakland show, where it won the Sweepstakes award (classed as a Rod Phaeton, it wasn't eligible for the AMBR, according to Art).

More significant, however, in 1968 it was invited to be part of an art show at the San Francisco Art Institute. This was, as far as I can determine, the first time a hot rod was shown in an art gallery. In fact, Art remembers they had to remove the rear tires and chromed Olds rear end to get it through the doors on dollies. The show, titled Contemporary Folk Art: The Hot Rod Aesthetic, included Himsl's tub, and two choppers painted by him, among more typical art hung on the walls. The curator was Phil Linhares, a longtime hot rod enthusiast and art curator, and it drew significant attention as a first in the art world, including a major article in Rolling Stone magazine.

But things were happening quickly in the late 1960s. Art, Mickey, and their brother Joe were charter members of a new club called East Bay Rods, and they were driving their show cars on

Above: Mickey got the body, frame, vertical Model A steering, and the gas tank. Art did the 'flake paint, striping, and even the tuck-and-roll. Mickey added plenty of chrome, but also a hot 308-inch flat motor.
Right: As seen at Oakland in 1967, Art's abbreviated tub used the front half of a Dodge and the back of a T touring. The unique front axle is also Dodge (with midget wheels and no brakes). The polished frame was aluminum channel. And the Corvette engine used a cross-ram intake.

the highways to Roadster Roundups. Pretty soon they were calling this "street rodding." At the same time Art and Mickey teamed up to create the free-form, aptly named the *Alien*, which won the big AMBR trophy in 1969 (followed by Andy Brizio's *Instant T*, painted in Art Himsl "ribbons" the next year). During this time, though it's hard to believe, Art traded his Touring to Mickey for a complete Dragmaster chassis for a Model T. Mickey said he only had it about a year, and then sold it to, ". . . some kid who was a buddy in the army. This guy put a 4-71 blower on it, and was doing wheelstands, which cracked the aluminum frame."

What exactly happened to the tub after that is unclear (another mystery), though it somehow got painted yellow, with a tall tan top. Then someone either put a new frame under it, with a Jag independent rear end, or was in the process of doing so. During about 20 years of this time the car was in Mickey Galloway's shop, or in his possession. Finally, in 2005, Art heard the car was for sale, in pieces, so he decided it was time to get it back. It still had the original body and front suspension, with a new steel frame and the Jag rear, so that's what Art used to restore the car the way you see here—pretty close to its 1967/1968 version.

Will he keep it this time? Probably. There's plenty of room in the "museum." But when I was there to take these pictures, he was putting the finishing touches on his latest roadster with a Buick Straight-8 engine and a handmade silver body painted with a zillion rivet heads to look like an airplane. You never know what Art might do next.

Top Left: Mickey has built lots of Model Ts over the years, so he had lots of parts to recreate his first one. He decided on the blue/yellow/red paint scheme, with the chopped windshield and tall tailpipes because he liked Selmer's version so much, but he added considerably more chrome. This wheel/tire combo is one of several he has for the car. *Top Right:* This 59A runs four 97s and Edelbrock heads, with plenty of brightwork. Mickey added front shocks this time, but still no front brakes. It never had 'em; and at 1,400 pounds, doesn't really need 'em. *Bottom Left:* The main difference from the first version of Art's tub is the Jag rear, which he kept but reworked to sit much lower than it was when he got the car back. Polished-aluminum covers mimic the original frame in front. The paint's similar, but Art never does the same thing twice. *Bottom Right:* This time Art added spot discs on the front, and an Edelbrock inline dual-four intake on the Chevy engine. That skull ornament on the radiator is the same as the one on Isky's car.

Deuce Done

I had planned to have a chapter in this book called "Follow-Ups," or something like that, to show updates, progress reports, or other news about lost hot rods shown in the first volume. But, besides the discovery of the Al King Chevy seen in Chapter One, the only other car with news to report is this 1932 coupe. And it has made significant progress.

Tony Moise's Deuce was seen only as a small, uncaptioned photo in the first book. Tony and Chuck Hulsizer owned the TE-440 dragster with the blown Chrysler Hemi that was wrapped and stored in Chuck's back yard. The first book mentioned the dusty Deuce in Tony's garage, saying he was finally restoring it. Well, here it is and here's its story.

I took the forlorn-looking "before" picture in 1987 when I first met Tony and he took me to Chuck's to uncover the dragster. It has a broken windshield, unpainted sheet metal, and a flathead sitting askew in the frame. But, from the front, it looks like a pretty straight, cherry 1932 five-window that appears to have a filled grille shell, very straight grille, dropped axle, and juice brakes. Gennie fenders were hanging on the wall.

Tony grew up in Lancaster, which was one of the two small towns located in the high desert above Los Angeles, better known locally as the Antelope Valley, but famous among hot rodders as the home of the dry lakes, including Muroc, Rosamond, and the still-operating El Mirage. Lancaster is at the opposite end of this high-and-dry valley from El Mirage, where there's just enough water to grow some crops. Tony and his high-school pals who formed the Lancaster Coupe and Roadster Club (LCRC) in 1950 weren't into old-time lakes racing. They were into drag racing on new legal strips like a few that came and went in nearby Palmdale, or on the better one "down the hill" in San Fernando. Before the dragster, Tony put together a hot little 1929 hiboy roadster that looked and ran a lot like the Waters & Murray *555* and one called the *22 Jr.*, owned by another Tony.

But young Moise was also looking for a good car to build into a nice street coupe. He knew where one was. It belonged to "the 1932 guy," who had four or five Deuces sitting in his yard. The five-window coupe he had his eye on had the dropped axle in the front, full fenders, and was pretty nice, but it had come from the local alfalfa fields where it was an "irrigation car." The trunk and the rear pan were cut out to hold a small bed for hoes, shovels, and other farm tools.

Worse—wouldn't you know?—the guy wouldn't sell it. He was a collector. But, after lots of bugging, he finally told Tony he would get first chance if he ever decided to sell.

That took a number of years. Tony had graduated from high school, gone into the service, sold his roadster, gotten out of the service, gotten married, and started

Left: Tony Moise's Deuce coupe had been sitting in this corner for 27 years when I took this picture, and I seriously doubted that would change. *Above:* Same corner, same car. What a difference. Tony had to find a new deck lid and rear pan, and his old-school bodyman did some nice lead work. But all the rest of the sheet metal is gennie 1932 that came with the car in 1960.

Lost Hot Rods II

building the dragster with Chuck. He had even had his first son when "the Deuce guy" decided, in 1960, that he was going to college in Alaska(!), needed some cash, and was willing to sell Tony the five-window. It was still the same. Besides the axle and brakes in front, the rest was all stock. He threw in a 59A flatmotor, but it was loose in the frame. So Tony bought it, parked it in the corner of his garage, and there it sat for the next 33 years.

These stories can go one way or the other. This one has the happy ending. In 1993, finally retired, with the kids raised and gone, Tony decided it was time to build the little street coupe he always wanted. He didn't mess around. He knew at this point in his life he didn't have the shop, tools, or even the inclination to do all the work himself. And he could afford to pay someone else. So he started—get this—by selling the entire gennie frame and chassis, as well as the flathead engine, back to the same "deuce guy" he bought the car from!

Then Tony purchased a new frame from TCI, complete with tubular IFS, disc brakes, and coil-overs at all four corners. For running gear he went with the obvious 350/350/9-inch combination, using Edelbrock components on the engine. After stripping the mostly excellent body to bare metal himself, he took it to Johnny Weaver in Lancaster, who filled the top with a section from a 1965 Mustang roof, and finished the body using a minimum of lead ("old-school style," says Tony), before painting it GM Torch Red. Finally Tony took it down the hill to San Bernardino to have Ron Mangus stitch one of his excellent interiors, including the rumble seat "for the grandkids."

After waiting so long, it didn't take much time to get the project done. Using readily available aftermarket parts simplified the process. But the result is a really nice, all-original 1932 coupe that sits right, looks dynamite, and is ready to go at the turn of the key. Tony says he and his wife go somewhere in it almost every weekend, with grandkids in the rumble as often as not. In 2003 they drove it all the way to Louisville, Kentucky, for the NSRA Nationals. It has more than 50,000 miles on the clock so far, and counting. I wish more of the lost hot rods in this book had such happy endings.

Top: With hinges and handles, rubber running boards, stock hood, King Bees on a dropped bar, and Halibrand-style wheels, it has a perfect blend of resto and rod. That red paint really pops. And it sits right too. *Bottom Left:* Tony went with an aftermarket firewall for extra room; otherwise it's a typical 1990s well-dressed small-block. *Bottom Right:* Tweed was the thing when first-class stitcher Ron Mangus did the classy and comfortable interior. And, yes, the carpet's a little soiled because this finally finished little Deuce coupe gets well used now.

Chapter Three: Keepers

Lost and Found

This is the classic case of the "I wonder what ever happened to...?" hot rod search. As I explained earlier, trying to find a specific rod or custom—especially a well-known one that has become lost—is much more difficult than looking in likely places where you might discover long-hidden, but lesser-known early cars.

This chapter represents some real sleuthing on my part, either recently or some time ago. It also includes a few equally well known cars that I just happened to stumble upon through good luck—or because I was looking for something related, and these popped up as part of the deal. Even good detectives get lucky sometimes.

Chapter Four

Chapter Four: Lost and Found

Orv Elgie's Vicky

This was the first of Orv Elgie's lost rods that I had planned to find, because I thought I knew right where it was. He sold the car to Bob Nelson in 1975, and I thought he still had it. I knew Bob at the time, and I had earlier photographed his brother Jim's 6-71–blown GMC-powered 1929 Chevy sedan for *Street Rodder* magazine. Jim has had it since the 1960s and still owns it today. I'd have included it in this book except he drives it so much it isn't even close to being lost. I'm a fellow inline-six early-Chevy owner too, and I've known Jim for years (we're in the same car club) but I hadn't seen Bob in a while.

When I contacted Bob recently to see the Elgie 1931 Chevy, he said, "Oh no, I sold that to a guy who has a big warehouse in downtown L.A. that he turned into a car museum that looks like a 1950s drive-in movie theater." He didn't remember the name. But somehow I found the guy and saw his amazing collection (which is a story for another day), but he didn't have the Vicky. Bob had sold him a Chevy phaeton, in pieces. Bob said, "Oh, maybe it was the college professor from Fullerton." Bob's memory was fuzzy, and this happened a lot longer ago than I thought.

I called dozens of people. I got lots of hazy clues. But no one had seen the car in years. Yet I got the feeling it was in the area, near where I grew up.

I can't remember who gave me the name of Pius Abacherli. Several car people knew him; they said he had a collection of vehicles, and bought and sold a lot. But they didn't know where he was. They said his family had dairy farms in the Chino area. Again, it's an unusual name, so I started calling Information. I found one lady who said she knew him; he was a cousin, but she wouldn't give me his number and she didn't like him. Pius is a very nice, energetic guy who just turned 80. He now lives near Palm Springs, but he maintains the family homestead, which is a very small ranch in the very small town of Mira Loma, which is next to Norco, which is a suburb of Corona. That's where he and some other family members keep their cars and other stuff. It's kind of a museum in itself—and another story. See how this goes?

I can't recall exactly how I reached Pius. His business card has no address. It just has his phone numbers and "Wheeler Dealer." But we arranged to meet at the family place because that's where the Chevy was, stored in a cargo ship container. I began to wonder. When I got there, I wondered even more. The house was really

Above: The 1964 Corvette fuel injector on top of a 1967 283 is probably the most expensive part on the car. Orv started with a field-find $200 Vicky, then paid $350 for a nice 1931 Chev two-door sedan to get good fenders, doors, windows, etc. Compare that to 1932 Ford Vicky and parts prices, even in 1974. That's why Orv built a "non-Ford." *Left:* Orv did the wood dash, wrecking yard steering, A/C, pedals, and added 1970s-era stitching in brown 'Hyde and carpet. It's all as nice as original.

old, and there was old stuff everywhere, from tractors to pedal cars, weather vanes and gas pumps to hit-and-miss motors. Behind the house was a double row of tin sheds that held who-knows-what. A guy named John came out, and I immediately recognized him. He said he was the youngest of seven Abacherli kids, and Pius was the oldest. I had forgotten his name, but John had been in my class in high school. I hadn't seen him in 40-some years. He said he had a couple cars there he wanted me to see. Now I was really wondering.

Pius arrived in his truck in a cloud of dust, introduced himself, then went over to unlock the big double doors of a metal container next to a dilapidated wood shed. When he opened it I was amazed. There was Orv Elgie's 1931 Chevy five-passenger coupe looking just as good as it did in the September 1974 issue of *Hot Rod*. Gray Baskerville did one of his hallmark comparison tests between it and Wayne Henderson's black 1932 Ford Victoria in that issue. It was also seen semi-finished in color on the February 1974 cover of the *Rod & Custom* "Garage Scene" issue.

As we got it out to take pictures, Pius told me he traded four vehicles, plus cash, to Nelson for it "about 35 years ago." He said he and his wife drove it to their wedding in September 1979. The car was still just as Orv built it. The only things he'd added were beauty rings on the Chrysler wire wheels and driving lights on the bumper. He had shown it once at the Grand National Roadster Show in Pomona a few years ago. It was still in near-show condition. When we finished the photos he put it back in the container, and John showed me what was in some of the other sheds. But, as I keep saying, that has to wait for another time.

Right: This is the Elgie 1931 Chevy Vicky at the Abacherli ranch in 2011, looking very much like it did in Rod & Custom *and* Hot Rod *in 1974. Bottom Left and Right: Whereas he used selective chroming with shades of black under his 1937 delivery, there's no brightwork at all down here. This is called paint detailing, and it's very cost effective. It's also in very good condition considering its age.*

Chapter Four: Lost and Found 67

Top: Not only does this Chevy epitomize the non-Ford trend of the 1970s, but it's also a perfect example of the resto-rod trend of that era, except that rare Chevy accessory items were a lot cheaper (if harder to find) than 1932 Ford parts.
Bottom: Here's a teaser. After Pius showed me the Chev, brother John opened the next garage to show me this gorgeous Merc chopped and painted candy red by Bill Hines. Next to it was a perfectly restored orange and black-striped 1972 Plymouth Road Runner with a 440 Six-Pack and 4-speed. Elsewhere was his chopped 1955 Mercury painted candy blue by Rod Powell, among other goodies.

Jack Chrisman's Sedan

This is the car that made Von Dutch famous. When readers of *Hot Rod* magazine saw "Torrid 1929 Tudor" in the December 1954 issue featuring Jack Chrisman's heavily chopped, really fast, Honduras Maroon A drag sedan, the thing that shook them up was the gonzo grille insert brush-striped by Dutch. Not only was it one of his hallmark works, but this was the first exposure to Von Dutch for rodders across the country. Given the understandable clamor by readers, *Hot Rod* devoted an entire article to Dutch three months later.

This is also the car that launched the amazing, inventive, and nearly unmatched drag racing career of Jack Chrisman. Running on at least 75-percent nitro with a flathead built and tuned by his nephew Art, this car immediately set records at Santa Ana and Pomona, then went considerably faster when they installed a big Chrysler Hemi.

Of course Jack next jumped into Howard Johansen's twin-Chevy dragster, winning major events across the country to earn the NHRA's 1961 World's Points Champion trophy and the T-Bird shown here, being one of the first touring drag teams ever. Next Jack stuffed a blown, injected, fuel-burning, direct-drive big-block in the diminutive, white, tire-smoking Comet generally credited as the first blown, fuel Funny Car.

I can't begin to recount the tales of Von Dutch or the career of Jack Chrisman here. For the former, including a chapter on all the Chrisman cars, with Jack's wife Dee describing the night "the boys" decided to chop her Model A, I suggest my book *Von Dutch: The Art, The Myth, The Legend*. For the latter, I recommend *The Chrisman Legacy* by Tom Madigan, covering the whole family (though Jack's exploits deserve their own book).

There are two primary points I want to make here. First, this is the actual 1929 A sedan the Chrisman boys chopped, Dutch striped, and Jack drove, with nearly all the original body and sheet metal. It's not a clone, as several have stated.

Second, this car was definitely lost and found. At least, I had to do a whole lot of sleuthing to find it when I was researching my *Von Dutch* book. When I reported the discovery in the August 1993 issue of *Rod & Custom*, I noted that one person had known where it was all along, former NHRA Top Alcohol racer Dale Smart. Most of

Yes, this is the real Jack Chrisman–chopped 1929 Tudor, restored with the original body and sheet metal by Jim Travis for Jack's family. Longtime striper Dennis Jones carefully recreated Dutch's designs, including the flying eyeball logo on the rear panel.

it was hanging from the rafters of his huge industrial-ventilation company warehouse in Compton, California, ironically just a few blocks from the original Chrisman's Garage. Of course I was hoping to find the famous Dutch-striped grille insert or at least the flying eyeball he painted on the rear pan, but of course the grille art was long gone and, strangely, the piece of the pan where the eyeball had been was cut out.

I certainly remember riding on a forklift three stories up to inspect the body stashed at the top of a pallet

Top: *The family decided on a few modern updates to make the car usable today, such as radial white walls. The Von Dutch design on the blacked-out grille shook up rodders across the nation.* **Bottom Left:** *Art built this big 392 Hemi, just as he did the original, except this time he used dual 4-barrels rather than injectors to make it drivable. Getting it in the Model A required moving it back and dimpling the hood sides.* **Bottom Right:** *This interior is more like the way Smart found the car, but the roll bar, Bell wheel, and 1939 dash with Stewart-Warner gauges in a flat chrome panel are original to Jack's car.*

rack. It was complete and, if I recall correctly, still had much of the interior in it. The fenders, louvered hood, running boards, grille, and other body parts were even higher, hanging from the ceiling against a far wall. I took pictures, but they ran so small in the article you couldn't see much. Those photos aren't available to me today.

In the 1993 article I stated, "About 25 years ago, Dale happened to see the car—less engine—sitting in a driveway in the San Bernardino area, and was able to buy it (from the same 'kid' Jack sold it to). He didn't realize what he had until he got it home and started recognizing familiar parts. Unlike the gutted race version, the car had a full red and white tuck 'n' roll interior . . . the exterior was in red primer." That's what Smart told me. However, Jim Travis, who restored the car for the Chrisman family, says Nick Arias tells a different version about finding the car abandoned in a rock quarry in Irwindale years ago.

Regardless, sometime later Smart gave the car's remains to Jack's family (wife Dee, son Steve, and daughter Lana), with the stipulation it be restored in Jack's memory "the way he would have wanted it." They hired Travis (longtime L.A. Roadsters member, owner/driver of the SoCal 1934 coupe, and restorer of the Mickey Thompson four-engine *Challenger I*, among others) to do the job. He worked closely with Art Chrisman, who built the new Chrysler Hemi for it. Rather than the gutted, single-seat racer seen in the 1954 issue of *Hot Rod*, they decided on a street-drivable version with full upholstery and a more modern driveline. For full details on the restored car, I refer you to the copious story on it in the September 2002 issue of *Street Rodder* magazine. The photos seen here were taken at the NHRA Wally Parks Museum in Pomona. Hopefully it will still be on display there after you read this.

Top Left: You've seen plenty of more recent adaptations, but here's a photo, from my collection, of the actual flying eyeball Dutch painted on Jack's sedan in 1954. The tiny lettering says "Haus Von Den Flieger Augen." *Top Right:* Here's a surprise bonus. In 1993 Dee told me she still had the 1961 T-Bird Jack won as NHRA points champion in her garage, and how he had all the lettering rubbed off it by the time they drove it home from Indy. (To see George Hurst handing Jack the keys, check the November 1961 *Hot Rod*.) Here it is today in Lana's garage. This car is still absolutely original and pristine. *Bottom:* The red interior is factory fresh. The holder on the column has every registration slip, since 1961, in Jack's name. On the other side is a Sun tach, the only non-stock item.

Orv Elgie's Delivery

Looking at this simple, green 1937 Ford sedan delivery today, it's difficult to understand the impact it had when it appeared on the cover of *Rod & Custom* in early 1970. It's hard to imagine it having any impact at all. That's exactly why Orv built it, and that's exactly why it had the impact it did.

This, believe it or not, could be considered the poster child for the emerging street rod movement of that era for a number of reasons. Let's start with the obvious. It was different. In fact, until that time, 1937–1938 Fords were the orphans of hot rodding. They were the only years of early Fords rodders didn't want. That's why Orv chose it. "I did it to be different," he said recently. "It was one of a kind. Nobody liked them." Of course there was also a method to this madness; actually it was more of a necessity. You see, if nobody liked these old Fords, it meant they were the cheapest to buy. And that's all Orv could afford at the time. He traded a 1938 Chevy pickup for this one, in pieces. Then he did all the work on it himself, bit by bit.

Why a sedan delivery? "To be even more different," was Orv's immediate reply. "Plus the back has that nice curve to it; sort of streamlined. My wife said it looked like a ducktail." Orv noted that the 1936 delivery had the same shape, "But a 1937 was way cheaper than a 1936. Even the parts at the swap meet were dirt cheap."

What really made this unusual 1937 Ford a standout was the way Orv built it. Using nothing but early Ford and carefully selected wrecking-yard parts, plus his own fabricating skills, he rebuilt the chassis, driveline, body, and interior. He also painted and detailed everything, top and bottom, inside and out, including gloss black on the frame, wrinkle finish on the inside of the fenders and under the floors. He used just enough chrome plating (front and rear axles, springs, radius rods, etc.) to make it look like a show car.

Then he loaded it with his wife, six-year-old son (with a bean-bag chair to sit on in back), and their luggage and drove from SoCal to northern Toronto, Canada, to visit relatives. Then they stopped by Peoria, Illinois, to take in the first Street Rod Nationals on the way home. It was a 7,000-mile trip. "We stopped at a 25-cent car wash and cleaned the undercarriage. People couldn't believe we drove it," says Orv. It was voted Best Appearing Car. A year later the Elgies drove it back to the Nats in Memphis, and copped the Best Closed award.

This green 1937 delivery epitomized the new street rod movement by being a less-desirable, unusual, low-

Left: I'm pretty sure this is the first 1937 Ford to ever appear on a rod magazine cover. Wide tires sticking out of an elevated rear end was the hot setup for 1970.
Above: Sixth owner Tom Westrope has been a good caretaker of this delivery. His new (to him) paint job has been on it 30-some years at this point.

buck model; being completely home-built; and being a show-quality rod that got driven thousands of miles to cross-country events with the whole family riding along. I think this is the car that created the popularity of 1937 Ford street rods, including the swoopy three-window and roadster versions you see today.

The next logical question for me was, "Where is this significant street rod now?" Fortunately all it took was a call to Orv, who is now retired in Bend, Oregon, but still building hot rods. Orv said he had it at a show at the Cow Palace in late 1971, and promoter Harry Costa "bought it right on the show floor. He offered me more than I could refuse. I used it to buy our first house." Costa showed it for a year, then sold it to someone in Minnesota, who then sold it to upholsterer Dan Drum in the Bay Area of NorCal. Drum, naturally, redid the interior in a 1970s motif, including high-back seats replacing the T-Bird buckets and button-tuft.

Tom Westrope is the name Elgie gave me for the new owner of the 1937. Tom and his wife, Robin, live in a sprawling house with two big garages out back in Los Banos, California, where they've operated the Tee-Dee-Us Automotive garage for years. They've both been ardent hot rodders even longer. In fact, *Rod & Custom* did a six-page article in the October 1956 issue, showing how Gene Winfield installed a Chevy V-8 in young Robin's 1953 Bel Air, and she now drives a fully rodded 1953 Chevy convertible. Other cars in the Westrope garages include a Deuce three-window, a 1932 Woodie, a 1980s 1933 roadster, a 1948 Ford custom, and their son's 9-second 1969 Camaro.

Tom said he bought the delivery from Rick Stees in the Bay Area in 1979. By that time the olive green paint was in bad shape, so he had Steve Fernandez of Lodi repaint it in a slightly different shade, including pearl ghost flames. Fernandez also did the lettering and pinstriping now on it. The only other thing Westrope changed was to replace the Wide Track Pontiac rear end with an equally chromed Corvette IRS and a set of chrome wire wheels tucked inside the still-flared rear fenders.

With the same 340-hp 327 and Powerglide that Elgie installed in 1970, Tom figures he's put another 30,000 miles on it, and even picked up the Best Delivery award at the Western Street Rod Nats in Merced in 1985. Having owned it 30-plus years now, he says it spends more time in the garage these days. But that's where it remains; ready to run whenever Tom and Robin feel like taking it out for a spin.

Top Left: Besides the valve covers, not much has changed in the deep engine compartment. Jim Babb built the embossed brass radiator in 1971. Top Right: The wood-paneled dash is Elgie's handiwork, but the equally 1970-style interior was stitched by fourth owner Dan Drum. Bottom: Besides just being different, this nicely curved end of the 1937 delivery is what attracted Elgie. You can see the chromed leaf spring of the mid–1960s Corvette rear end, which was Westrope's other major change.

Chapter Four: Lost and Found   73

Bueno's Bird

Remember I mentioned "mystery" earlier? This radical T-Bird's story involves abandonment, theft, investigation, discovery, and enough twists and turns that I'm not sure even I have it straight.

When I spotted it in a back corner at the Goodguys event in Pleasanton, California, a couple years ago, looking like it had just been restored, I immediately recognized this fully customized, candy-painted 1956 T-Bird. At least I thought I did. Wasn't it on the cover of one of the magazines? No, it wasn't built by Cushenberry or Bailon. It didn't even have a name. Unfortunately, I didn't find the owner the day I saw it, so I had to do some detective work to track it down.

The current owner and finder/restorer of this T-Bird is Ron Bueno of San Leandro, California. He is the slightly younger first cousin of Jimmy Jimenez of Hayward (both of these are East Bay towns, near Oakland), who was the car's original owner. Ron still remembers Jimmy letting him drive it to high school when it was brand new in coral pink.

Jimmy then had it fully customized by Joe Ortiz. Ron said Ortiz was the Fire Chief of Hayward in the 1950s, lived in a small house behind the station, and did all his custom work right in the firehouse. ("They had to move the fire engine out so he could work.") Ortiz wasn't a big-name customizer, but he also built Chuck Maita's 1958 Impala and painted Rich Guasco's AMBR-winning Model A in Chicano Purple. That's the color he first painted this 'Bird, according to Bueno, with a white padded top and matching interior by Sahagon. And that's how it appears in one photo on the cover of the February 1962 *Car Craft*, when it was named one of "10 Best" customs of the year. Inside that magazine, as well as in Barris' book, *Kustoms of the 1950s*, however, the T-Bird is shown in its next-year version with a chopped windshield, no top, bullet headrests, and green metalflake paint with a new Sahagon interior to match.

But, like too many customs, its first life was short. Bueno says the next year "some guy from San Francisco volunteered to paint it in silver pearls and screwed it up." Discouraged, Jimenez said he parked it in a "chicken farm barn" in Hayward, where it sat, deteriorating. When the state needed the property for a road in the early 1980s, Jimmy ("Who just got out of cars," according to Ron) gave the T-Bird, including the pink slip, to two teenagers, Tony and Eddie, who lived next door, saying, "Just get it off the property." But teens in the 1980s weren't into custom topless T-Birds. The car sat outside and deteriorated more. Then someone stole it. Tony and Eddie didn't care.

Sometime between five and ten years later, Bueno, who is a contractor, was building a six-car garage on an acre lot in Castro Valley. In the back corner was a small, very low vehicle covered in tarps. He had to go look. One peek revealed the canted headlights of the T-Bird. Bueno asked the property owner whose car it was, mentioning it was his cousin's and had been stolen. No answer. The next morning the car was gone. Ron knew the person across the street, and he had seen the tow truck, and knew the driver, who towed it away. Ron called the com-

Left: This is more to show the eye-popping Chicano Purple candy/pearl color than the new white upholstery. **Above:** Recognize this custom? It was built by Joe Ortiz for Jimmy Gimenez in the firehouse in Hayward, California, in 1961, and then again in 1962. Bet you didn't know that.

pany; they revealed nothing. He called Tony and Eddie; they still didn't care.

Then, after another ten years, Bueno was at the Sacramento Autorama, and behind a car on display was a small sign reading "Cars for Sale." One was the T-Bird! The owner was Bob Ennis of Folsom (longtime owner of the *Hemi-Roid* 1939 Chevy seen in *American Graffiti*), and he said he had a "lien sale" title to the car, which he'd had about eight years. Ron didn't ask where or how he got it. He decided it was time to get the car back. The price was $9,500, but that included the B&M supercharged and fuel-injected small-block Ford engine and transmission you now see installed in the car. Bueno said okay and bought it.

The body and lead work was surprisingly still good—no cracks—but the car needed complete rebuilding, which Ron entrusted to Randy Lackey of Randy's Rods in Medford, Oregon. It needed things like new headlights, taillights, and bumpers, and Randy reworked the chassis with his own custom air suspension. For paint, he wanted the same Chicano Purple as original, so he sent Carlos Limas of San Jose up to Medford to help Randy spray it in a mix of candy and pearl. It's subtle yet dazzling. Finally, Mike Pacilius of Tri-Valley Interiors in Pleasanton trimmed it in white pleats with deep-purple carpet.

This long-lost 'Bird was just barely finished when I spotted it at Pleasanton. I'm glad I could track it down. But I'm more glad Ron Bueno—by luck or strange fate—was able to relocate and rebuild it. It hasn't been out of the garage since I took these pictures.

Top: **The** Car Craft **feature says the car is sectioned. Ron says, "Only in the back." Original taillights were 1959 Mercury; these are handmade. Other small changes include deleting the outside tailpipes. I'm glad this one was found—twice.** *Bottom:* **I don't know where the original engine went. This 312 modern Ford small-block, with Holley blower and EFI, came with the car when Ron found it (the second time); it was installed by Randy. Note the liberal use of candy-purple paint.**

Chapter Four: Lost and Found   75

Dick King's Roadster

Nobody seems to know who Dick King was. Certainly he must have some relatives somewhere, but it's a very common name, and I haven't been able to find anyone who can give me any hard information on this person or on the beautiful little track roadster he owned in 1951. I can't even say, ". . . he built," because I really don't know who did the work on this channeled 1929 roadster with a superb hand-formed aluminum nose.

Here's what I do know, according to *Hot Rod* magazine: The three-page report on the second Oakland Roadster Show in the May 1951 issue shows Rico Squaglia's T with the big AMBR trophy and states that the runners-up were Niekamp's previous-year winner and Dick King's 1929 A Merc roadster, also blue, which bore a strong resemblance to Niekamp's car. The car is shown in one photo with chrome wheels, early Ford 'caps, V-windshield removed, and—though stated as blue—what looks like polished bare metal on the nose, hood, and possibly cowl. A sign shows it was entry No. 106, and the caption says, "Dick King's roadster tied for first place in lakes car beauty contest." That's it.

Earlier, in the January 1951 issue, *Hot Rod* had a one-page feature on the Thunderbolts' car show in Sacramento, showing a similar full photo of the car, this time appearing to be completely painted in some light color, presumably blue. The captions says, "A rounded nose, louvered hood, and smooth belly-pan made Dick King's 1929 roadster one of the show's finer cars. Dick is a member of the North Bay Roadsters." Longtime Sacramento customizer Dick Bertolucci, who was there, says he remembers nothing of King, this car, or who might have built it. I don't recall the club name, either. It's a mystery and more mystery. But there were a *lot* of round-nosed track roadsters in the Oakland/Bay Area at that time.

The car is obviously well designed, superbly crafted, and looks like a cross between the Niekamp and Dick Flint 1929 roadsters. Despite its being classed a lakes car, there seems to be no record of it competing there.

And where this cute roadster might have been or who owned it between 1951 and 1984, when Barry Williams spotted it parked behind something else at the Pomona swap meet, is further mystery. It was painted gold, had a small-block Chevy in front of a holey firewall, what looked like a 1938 Ford windshield, and newer upholstery. The registered seller was Craig Criger, and a previous owner was listed as John Riggins.

Barry Williams was basically a sports car guy. But he had raced a Kurtis 500 with a Nailhead Buick in the 1950s. Then he got into Porsches, and ran a Porsche parts business (i.e., wrecking yard) with a partner. He was at the swap with Neil Emory's son Gary, and when they found the roadster, Gary strongly suggested Barry buy it (remember, Valley Custom built the nose,

Above: Is this the elusive Dick King? Is this El Mirage or that dry lake near Reno? The license dangling from the grille appears to be a 1951, the windshield looks nicely handmade, and the car seems to be at least partially dark primered. This photo was among Barry Williams' scant records. Right: Besides wheels and tires, this is how Williams found the car in 1984, as seen at Bill Oliver's garage/shop in Trabuco Canyon. Note the newer interior and what looks like a cut-down 1938-or-so Ford windshield. The body looks quite good, though.

pans, etc. on the Dick Flint car). So Barry did. As Gray Baskerville put it, in a classic line, "The sound of cash crying while Williams was buying sounded like a girl saying yes."

Baskerville found this under-the-radar rod and brought it to my attention. Williams took it to lesser-known shops to have it restored/rebuilt, starting with Bill Oliver's Rod Works in Santa Ana's Trabuco canyon. He refurbished the boxed and Z'd (rear) 1932 frame and running gear, installed a built 1946 Ford flathead, Zephyr-geared 1939 transmission, and 1940 rear end, and then chromed everything.

Meanwhile Bruce Henderson of Costa Mesa stripped and straightened all the sheet metal before Neil's other son, Don, prepped and painted it a light, bright blue. Finally A. L. Cooper of Huntington Beach rebuilt the interior using saddle-tan vinyl. Finished by 1990, Baskerville photographed it for a feature in the February 1993 issue of *Rod & Custom*, and I put it in the foreground of a nighttime cover shot at the old Harvey's Broiler. Shortly thereafter I was asked to assemble a show titled "Road Rebel: The California Hot Rod" at the new, enlarged art gallery at Art Center College in Pasadena. I included this 1929 as a classic track roadster, along with Roth's *Outlaw*, the Pierson Bros. coupe, Isky's roadster, Doyle Gammel's 1932, the Wally Welch chopped Merc, and other icons.

Top: This is how the restored car looked in the art gallery show at Art Center College in 1993. A new V-windshield was crafted like the original, and Don Emory's paint was flawless. *Bottom:* An inverted Pierce Arrow panel with Stewart-Warner gauges was a highlight of the original interior, along with a fuel pressure pump on the left and a Bell wheel. The seats look a bit like early Porsche.

Chapter Four: Lost and Found 77

But that amounted to this beautiful roadster's second 15 minutes of fame. Barry was not an outgoing guy. I never saw him, or the roadster, after 1993. He didn't drive it much, if any; he kept it stored with his early Porsches. When I went seeking it to include in this book, I found that Barry had passed away in 2009 and, not having any immediate family, the fate of his few cars was uncertain. Finally I connected with Vince Weatherby of Costa Mesa, who said that "Barry was like an uncle to me," and was trying to sell the car for a respectable price for the estate. He also let me photograph it where it was stored. However, given the economy and the relative obscurity of this roadster, it generated virtually no interest among buyers at Pebble Beach auctions, or elsewhere, and the last word I heard from Vince was that he had purchased the car himself, even though he's more of a Jaguar/sports car enthusiast. Now that it's been found for a third time, will we see this classic, original postwar track roadster again? That also remains a mystery.

Top: **This is where I found the car recently, stored with Ferraris. The nerf bars, lights, radius rods, etc., are original, as is the body. What you can't see is that everything under the car (axles, springs, shocks) is chromed.**
Bottom: **The 1993** Rod & Custom **feature says internals of the 1948 Ford V-8 were unknown, but it has Offy heads, an Edelbrock intake, and three 97s. A few modern components show that stringent restoration wasn't quite as important as function 20 years ago.**

The Cunningham Forty

What made this 1940 Ford sedan such a standout when it debuted in 1957? Two things. The first is obvious: it had one of the earliest and most brilliant candy-red paint jobs that actually looked like candy when printed on the cheap paper covers of 1950s magazines. So it got on plenty of covers, including the November 1958 *Car Craft*. Surprisingly, one of the car's owner/builders, Dick Falk, claims the paint wasn't really candy. The *Car Craft* story calls it a special-mix, ultra-red, lacquer finish.

The second isn't so obvious. But I think it's because this otherwise ungainly, rotund sedan was severely channeled (5½ inches), with the hood sectioned and fenders raised a like amount, plus farther lowered with a stepped frame—but the top wasn't chopped. This gave the car a striking, yet pleasing and balanced, proportion, much like Ron Dunn's 1950 Ford by Valley Custom. I can't think of another 1940 sedan done this way.

The Tudor was supposedly sliced and tacked together by excellent metalman Hal Hutchins of San Rafael, California (North Bay Area). Then Dave Cunningham of San Francisco bought it, installed a full-race, four-carb Merc flathead, and helped Hutchins weld the car together, including molding all seams. Hutchins then sprayed the candy-looking red and applied white pinstripes. Cunningham had the seat, doors, and headliner upholstered in brown with ivory squares, with a tarp over the back seat area.

A year later Cunningham took the car to Barris where it received sunken quad headlights, flared fenders with indented, aluminum-paneled coves, more body molding, huge nerf bars, and new candy-red paint with large white scallops by Junior. The engine and interior stayed the same.

After more covers (including *Car Craft* March 1960) and car shows, this car just disappeared from about 1964 to 1972. At that time Bill Roach bought it as "a shell," with no driveline, from Harry Costa. Dick Falk was doing metalwork and restoration in his garage at the time, and Roach brought the car to him. The plan was to build it into a show winner again, perhaps shooting for an ISCA national show championship. After sandblasting the body shell, Dick, along with Ed Fry and Pete Ogdon, reworked the body. They rolled the fenders and rear pan under, and built a full set of removable bellypans for it.

Next it went to Andy Brizio's rod shop to have a 302 Ford, C-4 transmission and 8-inch rear installed with plenty of Cobra accessories and chrome, plus front disc brakes on the dropped axle and T-Bird wire wheels. Then it went to the Himsl-Haas studio for new candy-red paint with variegated black in the fender coves, and finally to Kenny Foster's AA-Action Interiors for an incredible narrow-pleat upholstery job in pearl white.

This was of course followed by an intensive year-long tour of the national show circuit, more magazine covers,

Above: In 1957 Hal Hutchens sliced and molded the body, painted it candy red, and added the delicate white pinstriping. Bumper holes in the front fenders were left unfilled though. Right: Far too many 1940 Fords, coupes or sedans, got their tops chopped, which usually made them look worse. Channeling and sectioning the body made this one strikingly low, but retained pleasing proportions. I always loved the painted reversed rims with "baldy" hubcaps.

and so on. When he didn't win the championship, Roach drove the car to the NSRA Nats in Tulsa and then promptly sold it to Pete Ernani who owned an automotive/tire store in San Francisco. Pete's son Lenny recently told me how they "showed the car everywhere" for about four years, but always drove it, removing the bellypans to do so. He even drove it to high school and dates on occasion. "Dad always kept it spotless," said Lenny, but then it got pushed to the back of the garage. He kept it 15 years. Then in 1988 he took it to the Pleasanton event and put a For Sale sign on it.

Dick Falk, who lived nearby, saw it, went to get his wife, and came back to buy it. Having worked on it, he felt an attachment to it. The Falks drove it to numerous events for the next ten years, as-is. Then Dick decided in 1999 it needed freshening up, so he stripped it to bare metal, did his usual tweaking and fitting of body panels, reinstalled chrome reversed wheels with beanie caps, and then had Darryl Hollenbeck lay on the current ultra-brilliant candy-red paint job. Nearly everything else remained as it was in 1973.

Finally, after 14 years, one of Dick's so-called friends called saying he "Always loved that car" and wanted to buy it. This was around 2002. Dick set a price and both agreed. The next thing Dick knew, the car was crossing the platform at the Barrett-Jackson auction on TV, and a car collector named Gary Cerveny from Malibu had bought it. That's where it is now. And it seems to be in good hands.

Top: Other than this dazzling new candy-red paint done by Darryl Hollenbeck in 1999, the Forty remains basically the way Dick Falk and others rebuilt it for Bill Roach in 1972.
Bottom: This is how the Barris shop rebuilt it for Cunningham in 1958. Falk says Bill Hines did much of the new bodywork, including fender coves with textured aluminum inserts. Junior sprayed the candy red with pearl-white scallops. Note the chrome window frames, hinges, etc.

Bill Roach owned a Budget car rental agency, and the seats came out of a used-up Toyota. The tilt column and under-dash A/C are typical of early 1970s street rods.

Top Right: Kenny Foster, from Sacramento, was the king of rod and custom upholstery in the 1970s, and this photo shows why. It's as nice now as when he installed it 40 years ago. *Middle:* The 1941 Studebaker taillights were added in 1957. The big nerfs with tailpipes were added by Barris in 1958. To put the chrome reversed wheels back on in place of the T-Bird wires, Falk had to narrow the newer rear end. These photos were taken in Cerveny's mountain-top driveway in 2011. *Bottom:* Denny Craig installed the small-block Ford with Cobra goodies at Andy Brizio's shop; Jim Babb built the brass radiator. All this was done in 1972.

Chapter Four: Lost and Found

The Tribute Chev

This is a story about two different lost cars; one is a tribute to—or certainly inspired by—the other.

Bill Hoffman's 1954 Chevy coupe-turned-hardtop was first seen in *Rod & Custom* (April 1958) as the "Up and Down Custom." In the age before air bags this car blew minds because it sat right on the ground. If that weren't enough, this tasty custom had a full-race three-carb Chevy six and a gutted interior; and the copy stated it held six strip records around its Portland, Oregon, home. The article also vaguely stated the suspension was "adjustable" for racing, but didn't say how. Besides the obvious, and deft, removal of the B-pillars, nice custom work such as the frenched headlights, peaked hood, unnamed taillights, and neatly trimmed 1953 grille with extra teeth was hardly mentioned. It was the stance and the hardtop that cemented this car's image in our minds.

It appeared in the same form in the September 1958 *Car Craft*, but many of us missed the November 1959 *Custom Cars* feature, by which time it was fully engulfed in wispy flames by LeRoy Teeples, and had a full custom interior, "handmade" wire wheels, and even a trailer hitch. Then it was gone. Where did it go?

I recently located Hoffman, who said he flipped the rear spring shackles and swapped front coils to raise the car. It ran 98.6 at 13-flat in the quarter with a 261 six. He later towed his boat to the lake with the same engine. Then, around 1961, he put that engine in a 1939 Chevy to run Bonneville, put a stock six in the flamed 1954, and put it on Bob Tindle's car lot where it sold to a young lady for $2,200. Someone told Bill he saw it in a wrecking yard in Eureka, California, about five years later.

On the other side of Portland, young Russ Meeks saw Hoffman's 1954 on the streets and at shows. "I was greatly impressed by the car as a youth," he says. Russ eventually opened his own rod-building shop, and when he acquired a 1954 Chevy Bel Air to build as a personal project in 1972, he remembered Hoffman's car. He frenched the headlights, peaked the hood, and fabricated vertical taillights much the same. He also removed the B-pillars, but figured Hoffman hadn't gone far enough, so he whacked the whole top 3 inches while he was at it. He also molded the grille around multiple 1954 teeth, reshaped the dash, and made further modifications. He reworked the suspension and steering, and had a 3-71-blown GMC six to install, but that didn't get done. Russ did, however, paint the car white murano pearl, taped, and sprayed lots of flames in candy tangerine over gold pearl, like Hoffman's, and finally let Spike Parham start multi-colored pinstriping, beginning on the hood.

As happens, however, this project got put aside in 1974 and then finally sold, by necessity, to a buyer in Portland in the late 1980s. It had no engine, bumpers, or most of the stainless trim.

The next part of the story moves south to a small agricultural valley between Los Angeles and Ventura in 2005. Greg White of Santa Paula, a professional welder and custom car devotee, then lived in nearby Fillmore, and happened to see this chopped, wildly flamed, custom 1954 Chevy on a trailer behind the local 76 gas station with a For Sale sign on it. I don't know how it got there, but a guy in town had it about three years, installed a 454 Chevy, Turbo 400, and 8-inch Ford rear, but not much else, and his wife had just ordered it out of the backyard. Greg got the number, offered way less than the price stated, and the guy said okay.

It turned out the car had no papers. Plus, the way Russ worked, he had completed the inner and outer window frames on the left, but not on the right. Fortunately Greg can weld stainless, so he finished that, got the car running,

This was a 1954 Chevy two-door post. Russ Meeks not only cut out the B-pillar to make it a hardtop, but whacked the lid while he was at it. He also frenched and added many teeth to the 1954 grille. It had a stock 454 GM big-block when Greg White got it. He then added air bags to the updated suspension in the front.

reworked the front suspension (adding an airbag system), and got Rick Grindle to finish pinstriping the car from the hood back.

Besides bumpers, it took Greg two years to find and replace the rest of the stainless trim on the car, plus the four 1955 Mercury center taillight lenses needed to match Hoffman's. The car was also missing things like door latches, a hood latch, window risers, etc. It did have a headliner, and Greg had Santa Paula Upholstery cover the seat in tasty orange-and-white tuck-and-roll.

There's still plenty left to do on this car. It's amazing the paint is in such good condition, considering it has 40-year-old lacquer and who knows where-all it's been. But the best part is, unlike its inspiration, this wild 1954 Chevy custom has been found, finally put on the road, and is being fully enjoyed by the Whites as Greg continues to finish details as time and budget allow. That's how customs are built by us common folk, right?

Top Left and Right: Bill Hoffman's hard-topped 1954 Chevy lowrider was an obvious inspiration to Russ Meeks. Most people remember it like this, in white with orange rear-fender accent and a gutted race interior. But a year later it was covered in similar flames in red, yellow, orange, and blue candies, and had full, white tuck-and-roll upholstery. **Middle:** The paint's not perfect, but amazingly good for murano pearl lacquers applied in the early 1970s. Spike Parham added striping on the back half of the car, and Greg recently found four center sections of 1955 Mercury taillights to fit the openings formed by Meeks. **Bottom:** Greg recently got the seat upholstered in tasty 1950s style, but the door panels are painted chipboard for now. Meeks heavily reworked the dash; the large opening was to hold a row of eight-track tapes! Greg is contemplating a new design as work continues.

Chapter Four: Lost and Found

Ray Goulart's Olds

As I walked through Gary Cerveny's huge garage full of cars, ostensibly to see the Cunningham Forty, I stopped in my tracks at this candy-red custom 1950 Oldsmobile. "Where did you get this?" I asked, quite surprised. "We got it at an auction. My wife liked the color and the dash," Gary said. That's not a flippant answer. His wife has good taste.

Although it doesn't get the full credit it deserves, Ray Goulart's Olds is one of the best-designed, best-executed customs of the early 1960s. His brother LeRoy's long-lost lime green 1950 Ford, built twice by Gene Winfield and discussed in the first book, is better known. But Ray's Olds is not only completely owner designed and built, but it has miraculously survived in nearly exact original condition since he reworked it from a convertible starting in 1959.

Yes, the first thing he did was add the un-chopped roof from a 1951 Chevy Bel Air to make it a hardtop, adding a smaller sedan rear window. Then came the handmade oval grille, 1959 Impala headlights, 1958 Olds taillights in 1953 DeSoto fenders, flared fender lips, rolled pans, and so on. Inside, he split the seats into buckets, built a center console, added newer Olds space-age gauges and steering, and had it all trimmed in a black "biscuit" design. He'd already converted the Hydro to a 3-speed stick, but then swapped the Olds V-8 for a 401-inch Nailhead Buick mainly because he liked its looks! He had Winfield paint it candy copper, then gold-to-red 'flake, but it's been candy red the rest of its life.

Goulart sold it in the mid 1960s, and it's been through countless owners since. I first saw it, looking nearly like this, driving into the L.A. Roadsters show and swap meet at the Great Western Fairgrounds in the early 1970s. When I featured it in the October 1989 issue of *Rod & Custom*, it belonged to Jack Walker in Belton, Missouri, and still had Buick Skylark wire wheels. The only differences today are the chrome wheels with wide whites.

So who's Gary Cerveny? That's quite a story. You might recognize his name as the owner of the *Timbs Special*, that long roadster from the 1940s with the straight-8 Buick and swoopy tilt-up body that looks more like an airplane or streamliner. But when I asked, his immediate answer was, "Corporate pilot," as in freelance pilot for executive jets. But then he started talking about his work as a stunt coordinator and "second unit director" for movies and TV shows over the years, involving hairy

This 1950 Olds started life as a convertible. Ray Goulart not only welded on a 1951 Chevy hardtop, but performed all the other extensive, yet tasteful, modifications.

helicopter stunts, many with Gary at the controls. He likes that sort of stuff.

When I arrived at Gary's place, which is at the top of the mountains overlooking Malibu just off a remote section of Mulholland Highway, he was in one of his two large garages working with his father on a 1963 Watson Indy roadster powered by a Hilborn-injected small-block Chevy. They'd been racing it with other Indy cars on the big oval in Fontana. Gary said he has also competed in the Mille Miglia, as well as running the historics at Laguna Seca. Somewhere in the conversation he mentioned he had been an L.A. County Sheriff during most of the 1970s, mainly "for excitement."

Gary grew up in the San Fernando Valley, where he went to Poly High in Sun Valley. He said he drag raced at San Fernando, Lions, and Orange County, and belonged to a club called the Deacons of La Tuna Canyon. The club car was a Henry J with a six-carb Chrysler Hemi (a duplicate of which Gary has now). His own high-school ride, "Because I couldn't afford a 1956 or 1957," was a 1958 Impala with a Hilborn-injected 301 Chevy and 4-speed, running 8-inch cheater slicks on American five-spokes. It ran 108 on the strip, but even better on the street.

By the early 1980s he built an all-steel 1923 T-bucket with a round tank in back (which he still has), and somewhere along the line he built and campaigned a jet-powered I-H Semi, the *Screaming Eagle*, around U.S. drag strips, followed by a jet-powered motorcycle. Yes, he likes excitement.

He built his current home above Malibu in 1990. Unlike some of the palaces in the area, his could be described as two very large garages topped by living spaces, one for him and his wife, Diane, and the other for his father. "I originally built the main garage at 4,000 square feet to limit my collection to 25 cars. But I have 53 cars now," he says. It's a very eclectic collection, ranging from Bill "Maverick" Golden's 1963 Dodge 426 Wedge NHRA champ, to the *Hisso Special* 4-ever-4 dragster, to things like the Hudson Italia 1955 show car, a Kaiser Darrin roadster, assorted Shelby Mustangs and Corvettes, and so on. Diane noted that they acquired the Cunningham Forty in 2004, and the Goulart Olds in 2005. Gary says, "I have no intention of selling them. I don't sell many."

Given the number of vehicles he currently has to tend, drive, or race, there's no telling when you might see either of these famous candy-red customs. But at least now you know where they are, saved and safe.

Top: Elements like the radiused and flared wheel wells, small front fender vents, and thin bumpers predated similar factory designs by decades. I don't know who painted the current candy, but the car has looked like this since the mid 1960s. **Bottom Left:** Goulart built the buckets from the 1950 Olds seats, made the console, and formed the dash, which has blackface Stewart-Warner gauges. Note that working Appleton spotlights, the only 1950s throwback, are mounted in the doors, not the cowl. **Bottom Right:** The Buick 401 Wildcat engine with factory dual quads was one of Ray's last changes, but he added it more for its looks than the extra power.

Chapter Four: Lost and Found

From the Yellow

First off, the title of this chapter refers to the fact that each of these cars was featured in at least one of the rod or custom magazines of the 1950s or 1960s—magazines whose pages are at least a bit yellowed by now. Some were on the cover, some were only shown on one or two black-and-white pages inside. Nearly all have been rebuilt or restored, to more or less degree, over the years. But the important part, the reason they're being shown here, is that all still exist today.

Pages

Chapter Five

Chapter Five: From the Yellow Pages

The Dresselhaus Deuce

This turquoise 1932 Ford sedan built by young Ray Dresselhaus of Pueblo, Colorado, in 1962, has been surprisingly well preserved by Les James of Evergreen, in the Denver area. The car first appeared in *Hot Rod* in February 1963, comprising three "roto" pages and one full-color page, photographed by Tony Spicola. Photos from the same session ran as a two-page black-and-white feature in the September 1964 issue of *Popular Hot Rodding*.

I loved Tony Spicola's photography. He was a freelancer from Colorado who started shooting just about the time *Hot Rod* magazine introduced color inside. In fact, a full-page photo by Tony of Otto Rhodes' pearl-white F-100 pickup was one of the first two such pages to appear in *Hot Rod* in the August 1962 issue, as you saw in the first volume of this book. Typical of Tony's work, he included the car owner along with a good-looking girlfriend, he in a bright red shirt and she in red short-shorts. Besides adding people and bright colors, Tony also included strobe lighting in daytime shots to punch up the metallic, pearl, or candy colors (and chrome) of the time. One of his favorite photo locations was the red rock Garden of the Gods or, as in this case, a lakeside beach to lend plausibility for the woman wearing a (then) skimpy bathing suit.

I forget exactly how I found Tony, but I contacted him recently, hoping that he might still have files of this excellent 1960s photography. Unfortunately he doesn't. He's had quite a busy career since those days, including promoting and producing rock bands from the 1960s on, among several other things. Quite coincidentally, the only car he still had a few color photos of was the Dresselhaus sedan. Unfortunately, he was only able to send me low-resolution images, so they must be shown small here.

I found Les James through Russell DeSalvo of Pueblo, and it was Joe Haska (both men seen in the first book) who took me to his car shop. Les operates a large petroleum distributorship in Golden, where I photographed the sedan, and where he has ample space to build and store several car projects ranging from rods to relics. He currently has 12 cars, including a 1929 DeSoto that has run the Great Race five times. Next to this 1932 was a similarly colored Deuce Phaeton rod. Back in the day, Les started with an A-V8 1929 roadster and graduated to an A/Gas 1941 Willys racer in the 1960s.

Les said he saw Ray building this sedan, and then saw it displayed in the Sabers' car shows in the early 1960s. But then both dropped from sight. When he

Above: **The underside of the car was painted white with four full-length pipes and mufflers, plus plenty more chrome chassis pieces.** *Right:* **Too bad this great photo can't be larger. That's young Ray Dresselhaus with his show-winning Deuce in 1962, and that's Mary Lou Korholz wearing a smile and a Jantzen.**

answered a two-line ad in the local paper reading, "'32 Ford street rod for sale," in 1983 or 1984, he was quite surprised to recognize the turquoise Deuce, which was still the same except for slot mag wheels. Ray still owned it, and Les said even he looked pretty much the same! The car was in a storage unit. Something had fallen and put a good dent in one front fender and the four chromed exhaust pipes were rusted out. But the rest of the paint and chrome was so-so, and the frieze interior was in good shape.

Les straightened the fender first, using only a bit of lead as filler. Then between 1988 and 1990 he and Gary Koerner stripped the car to bare metal and repainted it, matching the original San Remo Turquoise lacquer. Les is proud to say there is no plastic filler anywhere in the car. At the same time they added a 350/350 combo to the gennie chassis, mounting a modern 8-inch rear on coil-overs and disc brakes on the existing chrome-dropped front axle. All the parts he removed are wisely stored high on a rack in the shop.

Although he says he's only put about 2,000 miles on it in the three decades he's had it, and he admits that "everything I've got is for sale. For a price." Still, Les states, "This is my favorite vehicle." He's had it longer than most. My hunch is that it will be in his collection quite a while yet.

Above: A 283 Chevy with three 97s and chrome Hedman Hedders was hooked to an early Ford driveline. Right: That green material was called frieze, common on 1950s couches (and show rods). It's all still in the car, including the headliner, but not the copper-plated dash or Covico wheel.

Other than a few restoration items like the 1932 head and cowl lights, Les has kept the Dresselhaus look, including the peaked grille shell. Even the slot mags were on it when he got it in 1983.

Middle Left: A 350 Chevy and auto transmission was the way to go in the late 1980s when Les redid it. However, the lacquer on the firewall is still original, and so is the finned coil cover.
Middle Right: That buttoned-and-rolled, green-and-white interior was a big part of this car's appeal, and it's all original other than a few modern updates. Bottom: Yep, it's even still got the white-covered spare on the back to match the top and running boards. All it needs are four chrome-belled pipes poking out under the back bumper.

The 'Dago Deuce Vicky

I was looking for lost hot rods in the San Diego area, so I contacted Andy Bekech, historian of the Prowlers, one of the oldest car clubs in the country. He asked, "How about my Vicky?" He started telling me about its rich history, then said, "It was on the cover of *Car Craft*, April 1959." I found a copy of that issue and said, "Wow! *That* Vicky?" The brilliant Ruby Maroon, chopped-top, Hemi-powered, white-walled 1932 on the cover of that small magazine was reason enough to include it in this book.

Then when he started telling me how it was originally Bob "Axle" Stewart's first car, that Bean Bandit Joaquin Arnette chopped it, it ran 127 mph at El Mirage in 1952, drag raced at Paradise Mesa, won car shows, and so on, I said, "Absolutely."

Top Left: This gutted, rusty 1932 Victoria might look edgy, but look closer—that's one cherry Deuce body for 1948. The next day Joaquin Arnett chopped it for $50. Bob Stewart was 13, and he was the son of Ed "Axle" Stewart, the guy who put "'dago" into dropped axles at his San Diego speed shop. *Top Right:* Car Craft April 1959 issue. *Middle Left:* With the top chopped 4 inches, axle dropped, headlights lowered, and grille shell filled, the wicked-looking Vicky made its debut at the Paradise Mesa strip around 1951. Note the Prowlers plaque. *Bottom:* All the Prowlers ran the lakes and Bonneville. With his own 3/8 x 3/8 flathead, on gas, Bob turned 127.4 best at B-Ville. By now (1953) the car was orange with a white top. This profile defines the term "Dago'd" (later known as a rake).

Top Left: Bob first painted the car a deep purple shortly before winning the Prowlers' first "Rod-Ability Run," which was covered in four pages in Hot Rod, February 1952. Joaquin Arnett's sectioned 1934 coupe won the Best Looking award.
Top Right: This is Stewart's Speed Shop, 1952. Bob drove the delivery truck (far left, with the axle bolted to the tailgate) to deliver dropped axles up and down California (plus ported and relieved flathead blocks) to earn money to fix up his Vicky. By this time it was repainted black. *Middle Left and Right:* Andy Bekich always loved that Vicky, and saved his paper route money to buy it in 1956 while a junior in high school. As money allowed, he first had Marty Moore paint it Ruby Mist Maroon. Then he installed a big, healthy, chromed DeSoto Hemi engine. Besides street and shows, he raced regularly at Paradise Mesa, seen here with whitewall slicks and new white interior visible. *Bottom Left:* Andy also learned to pinstripe in high school to earn extra bucks, laying the lines on his own car. By the early 1960s it had mags and bigger slicks. Good hot rods were supposed to evolve and constantly improve in that era. *Bottom Right:* Andy's big grin denotes an evolution with GMC blower, Hilborn injectors, and huge scoop made from a propeller nose cone mocked up for a show, not actual go. After this, however the Vicky got relegated to the garage as growing kids became a higher priority.

Top: When Andy finally got it back out 20 years later, the logical and typical thing to do was tear it down and rebuild it to contemporary standards. In 1980 to 1983 he stripped it to the bare frame and body, installed a 350 Chevy driveline with A/C and other amenities, and repainted the car in bright red paint with matching upholstery. Still the same car, but a different era. *Bottom:* Bob Stewart had meticulously restored his father's Deuce Hiboy to its early 1950s configuration, and in 2005, at a Prowlers' reunion, Andy got this photo of the two generations of original Stewart 1932s side by side. The Ed Stewart roadster is now part of the John Mumford collection. After another 25 years enjoying it in its 1980s version, Andy finally put the Vicky up for auction in 2009, and it's now part of Ken Lawson's early Ford collection in Longmont, Colorado.

Chapter Five: From the Yellow Pages

Little Yellow Roadster

The story of how this yellow Model A roadster was found is as amazing as the rest; it's just simpler. In April 2011, Verne Hammond and his Choppers club pal Deron Wright decided to spend the day at the huge, monthly, by-now-legendary Pomona Swap Meet. Did I mention huge? They started at one end, early in the morning, and walked all the rows of parts-for-sale stalls, not finding much. Sometimes you can find a gem—that's why you go—but most of the good stuff disappeared decades ago.

It was nearing 2 pm, the time when vendors usually pack up to leave, when they finally reached the other end of the enormous lot, and were about to give up and go home. But in the second-to-last row a fenderless, yellow 1929 roadster with a Deuce grille caught Verne's eye. It had some funky black upholstery, plywood floors, and sat on an A frame (not Deuce rails). It also had radial tires on wide wheels. The best part was an early Olds engine with finned aluminum valve covers, dual quads, and lots of chrome goodies in front of a chromed firewall.

A small For Sale sign in the windshield said "Built in 1958," and "Family Owned" with a price of $22,000. It looked as if it could have been built anytime between 1955 and 1975. It wasn't a classic-style hiboy. And neither Verne nor Deron recognized it in any way. Two older guys were sitting with the car, Mitch being the owner/seller, and they said Verne and Deron were the first, all day, to even stop and look at it. But Mitch didn't offer to lower the price, and he didn't mention anything about the car being in any magazines, let alone on the cover of *Hot Rod*. So Verne snapped a couple pictures of it with his cell phone, and they left. Their feet were tired and it was time to hit it.

By the way, if you're not familiar with Verne, his wicked-chopped, flathead-powered 1934 coupe (which has been seen in every magazine in the past decade), or the Choppers club, I refer you to *The Electroline Diaries* by Laurent Bagnard (CarTech Books, 2007). But these relatively young guys know their hot rod history, and have read most of the old books and mags.

So by the time Verne had gotten home to Burbank from Pomona, something in the back of his head said he'd seen that roadster somewhere before. He started by thumbing through the *Hot Rod* Yearbooks. And there, in No. 2, he found Ken Blackwell's *Street Jewel* (just a few pages past *Lepesh's Lalapalooza*, in fact). It was exactly the same car. The only differences were the wheels and tires, no cycle fenders, different upholstery, and two fours instead of six twos on the Olds mill. It didn't take Verne

Left and Above: *The headers, the wishbones, even the tiny King Bee foglights/headlights are the same as in the 1961 cover photo. You can see the six 2s on a shelf next to Verne's 1934 in the garage. The chopped 1932 three-window is another story for another time.*

Lost Hot Rods II

much longer to find the yellow A on the cover of the November 1961 issue of *Hot Rod*, with a similar Rickman two-page feature inside. Wow!

Verne quickly downloaded the photos from his cell to his computer, retrieved the ones of the roadster, then enlarged the For Sale sign. He could read the number and he called Mitch. Mitch said he had bought the roadster in 1973 "from the guy who bought it from Blackwell." He had repainted the yellow once, and made the other minor changes, but had stored it at a friend's house for years. He said he had as many as 175 cars at one time, but now he was "finally done." He had sold 15 rods since a recent divorce, and he'd let this one go for $20,000. He assured Verne it ran perfectly.

Verne didn't have that kind of money in his sock drawer, so he immediately put lots of his stash of collected cool stuff up for sale. He raised close to twenty grand, so a week later he called Mitch and made him a cash offer. Mitch thought about it a couple of minutes, said okay, so Verne and a friend drove about 30 miles to where the car was, test drove it, laid the cash on Mitch, and drove the roadster home.

That's basically it. Within a couple weeks Verne had the right wheels, tires, and hubcaps on it, polished everything up, and even found a boat-type steering wheel similar to the one in the early photos. He already has the 6-2's manifold and carbs to swap on, and is making new cycle fenders (though it really looks better without them). He'll redo the black upholstery like original, and maybe a top. But that's really all it needs. And thus ends a good, amazing, but simple story.

Top Left: *It's the same 1950 Olds bored to 338 inches, with a nasty-sounding Engle cam. I know nothing of builder Blackwell, but assume he machined the knurled caps on the chromed brake/clutch cylinders, like several similar small, machined parts on the car.* ***Top Right:*** *The upholstery looks better than it is. Verne plans to replace it and add a Moon gas pedal. The transmission is a GM 3-speed.* ***Bottom:*** *Note that the fenderwells are filled with smooth panels. Tiny taillights are made from 1941 Chevy park lights. They and the nerfs, pipes, and license mount are all original to 1961. Talk about lost and found.*

Chapter Five: From the Yellow Pages

The Stuckey Forty

One thing I can tell you for sure. Dave Stuckey built this custom 1940 Ford, not Rod Stuckey, as stated in the four-page feature in the October 1963 issue of *Hot Rod*, and again in a two-color photo mention in 1981's *Best of Hot Rod* book. Both were from Kansas and distant second cousins, but Rod strictly built dragsters in the 1960s and died young. Dave Stuckey is from Wichita, started building a channeled, customized 1932 sedan after school as an apprentice at Darryl Starbird's, then finished it as the famous *L'il Coffin* after he opened his own custom shop. He went on to build many customs, rods, and, yes, several drag machines.

This wildly customized 1940 Ford coupe was one of the first he did in his own shop, building it for Don Moore of Midwest City, Oklahoma, in 1962, and finishing it just before the final version of the *Coffin*. Short of chopping, channeling, or sectioning, Stuckey customized nearly every inch of this car, finishing it in what *Hot Rod* magazine called brilliant Sunkist Orange, but what was really a straight red toner sprayed over a bright yellow base.

Given those changing times, when traditional customs were evaporating, Don filled the interior with bucket seats, lots of black rolls, a Moon pedal, a 4-speed stick, and race gauges in a reworked dash. Outside he set it on a high rake with polished Gasser-style mags and big slicks in back. And the 283 Chevy had a polished 4-71 blower with a two-port Hilborn injector and scoop sticking through the hood.

With all that custom metalwork done in lead, it wasn't built for racing. And the blower and injector weren't street-practical. It was built to show. But other than the ample feature in *Hot Rod* (including a full color page), and another in *Popular Customs* (Winter 1963), this radical custom coupe was little seen for nigh on 50 years.

Stuckey said Moore dropped off a stock Forty and let him do pretty much what he wanted. "After two to three months of long hours, he picked it up and just disappeared. Upholstery? I don't know—somebody in Oklahoma." Dave said that around 1970 a customer wanted to buy the car and they looked everywhere but couldn't find it.

Ron Smith is an avid hot rodder who works for an oil drilling company in Odessa, Texas. He was in the middle of a 1932 coupe project when his son, Monty, who works at Performance Plus Automotive, called to mention that a customer had a 1929 Ford roadster pickup and a 1940 coupe—both older hot rods—for sale. He said the 1940 was featured in *Hot Rod* in December 1963. This was November 20, 2010.

Left: This is basically what Ron found in the garage in Odessa. The 283 now has a single 4-barrel and the gennie generator. The black paint looks better than it was (note blistering on hood), but not bad after being lost nearly 50 years.
Right: Someone swapped the 4-speed for a stick Hydro at some point, but otherwise this as-found interior photo looks identical to the way it was in 1963. Stuckey built the custom dash.

The customer's father, Sherman Emler, had owned a towing service, but had died five years earlier, leaving the two vehicles in a garage, where they sat, untouched. The son knew nothing more about them. Obviously Ron went to see him. Here's exactly what he said:

"Kenneth [the son] lived five minutes from my office. I went to his house and he opened the garage door. I like to have had a heart attack. The rear of the 1940 had a chrome Halibrand rear end, molded/flared fenders, 1958 Corvette taillights, nerf bars, molded drip rails. Wow! He showed me the 1963 magazine. The car had not changed except the color was black, the 4-71 blower was gone, the 4-speed was now a B&M Hydro with the Halibrand rear. The front end had dual headlights, Edsel grille, hood scoops, plus the interior, dash, and gauges were all perfect after 50 years. The tires and wheels were awful. I asked Kenneth where his dad got the 1940 and he didn't know.

"I bought both rods [the pickup had a tow hoist]. I took the 1940 to Johnny Alaniz who rewired it, replaced the Airheart front disk brakes, fuel lines, brake lines, etc. It hadn't run in 10-plus years. I installed Real Rodders Wheels with Michelin front tires and Hurst rear slicks. Then I took it to Sergio Cervantes at Texas Street Rods in Big Spring to repaint. He took it down to bare metal. Wow! All of the lead work was perfect. I contacted Dave Stuckey, who built this car just out of high school 50 years earlier. Dave told me not to paint it orange; paint it *red*. He gave me the numbers of the base yellow and the red toner. It turned out beautiful.

"I took it to Salina, Kansas, for the KKOA show [2011 Kustom Kemps of America]. On the way to Salina I went by Dave Stuckey's shop in Wichita. Met Dave, showed him the 1940 after 50 years, asked him to come to Salina (which he did). Dave signed and dated my dash 1962. Dave was glad to see the Forty. He saw his friends at Salina—Gene Winfield, George Barris, Bill Hines, Darryl Starbird. Stuckey is a *gentleman*. I love this car (even if it sits too high in the rear)."

I couldn't have said that better. Ron now has a polished 4-71 blower to reinstall on the original 283 after he gets it rebuilt and detailed, saying he wants to restore the car as close to its 1963 version as possible. Yes, and you could even lower the back a bit, I'm sure. But it's amazing to see this one-of-a-kind, time-warp Forty custom back out in the bright sun after its very mysterious, near-fifty-year hibernation.

Above: You'd have to see this color in bright sun to get the full effect. I don't know if Stuckey was the first to paint red over yellow to make it pop, but it's a good trick a few other rodders have used over the years. Note the rounded door corners and butted windshield. *Right:* When they stripped the paint, this is what they found: lots of good leadwork still in excellent condition. There was no rust anywhere, and the only plastic is on the hood where someone filled the blower scoop hole.

Chapter Five: From the Yellow Pages

You can barely see the big 1951 Chevy back window Stuckey mounted upside down in the 1940. One reason the back sits so high is the fully chromed quick-change someone added later, without cutting anything for clearance. But, mainly, this 1962-era show car tried to mix custom and Gasser elements.

Dave Stuckey actually had to tear himself away from a couple current projects in his cluttered Wichita shop to attend the KKOA Nationals in Salina, alongside one of his first custom builds.

The interior remains untouched, with many yards of black rolls in the headliner, package area, and trunk. Yes, those bucket seats do swivel.

The Titus/Southard/Cohen Roadster

I always thought of this 1932 as the Andy Southard, Jr., Bay Area Roadsters car. I knew Andy primarily as a freelance photographer from Salinas, California, whose photos were in all the early rod magazines. This car was a bright red hiboy, with a small-block Chevy engine, and some of Andy's excellent white pinstriping on it. But even then I'd get confused, because at that time Andy Southard had *two* red 1932 roadsters, one with fenders and one without. He sold the one with fenders to Andy Brizio (so it became a different, red Andy's 1932).

And this one eventually ended up with Andy Cohen. I had no idea, until recently, that this same car was also the well-known Lee Titus, black, full-fendered, fuel-injected Corvette-powered Deuce that appeared on the May 1959 cover of *Hot Rod*. That sounds like some powerful provenance right there, but wait until you hear who else has owned this currently lost and bedraggled Deuce.

Lee Titus owned a speed shop in Santa Monica, as stated on the white spare-tire cover on the back of this black lacquer roadster with the bright-red, Jack McNeil interior. With full fenders, bumpers, taillights, and spare, it was sort of a sleeper because under the full stock hood was a fuel-injected, roller-cammed 283 punched out to a then-huge 351 cubic inches.

Although the *Hot Rod* headline stated, "This One's for Keeps," it wasn't. The next well-known rodder to enter the picture was Neal East, who still had his blue 1932 coupe from the April 1958 *Hot Rod* cover, but saw this one offered in 1960 in the local "green sheet" ad paper for a price he couldn't pass up. It belonged to a young couple, had a stock 265 in it, still had Lee's tire cover on the back, but also had a vexing vibration in the driveline, which Neal figured was the cause of its sale. After many other attempted fixes, it turned out to be a misaligned torque tube.

Neal liked the gennie look, which he enhanced with wire wheels, blackwalls, and NOS items like a radiator cap and ornament. But in the six years he had it, the black lacquer was beginning to crack, and then Andy Southard called with a deal he couldn't refuse: he'd trade Neal his cinnamon-red, full-fendered 1929 roadster that had just been on the cover of *Rod & Custom* straight across for the 1932, as-is. Andy said he always wanted a Deuce, and Neal said, "Such a deal." Each drove halfway to Buellton, where they swapped pink slips and roadsters. That was in the summer of 1967.

It took Andy about 15 minutes to strip the fenders off his new Deuce when he got it home (all four of which ended up in Andy Cohen's garage, ironically). Next, knowing it needed new paint, finding a few "issues" with

Left: *A fuel-injected Corvette 283 bored anda stroked to 351 inches was the big surprise under the stock hood of Lee Titus' black 1932 in 1959.* **Above:** *Neal East bought the car with a stock 265 and a vibration out of a local ad sheet around 1963, and added wire wheels and other vintage accessories.*

Chapter Five: From the Yellow Pages

the original steel body, and wanting the grille shell filled again and smooth hood sides with small hot rod louvers, Andy took it to a well-known NorCal custom shop where it languished for three years.

About that time (1970 or so), Dick "Magoo" Megugorac set up shop in SoCal building traditional-style hiboys, so Andy made a deal for him to rebuild the Deuce in the Magoo style, which Andy photographed and Greg Sharp wrote about for a three-part series in *1001 Custom and Rod Ideas* (February, March, and April 1976). Eleven pages of coverage well document updates including new crossmembers, a 1956 Ford F-100 rear end on Corvair coil springs with a triangulated four-bar, a dropped Bell tube axle in front, and a basically stock 283 Chevy with aluminum Powerglide transmission. And there were hallmark Magoo items such as handmade front shock mounts also holding a V'd headlight bar and custom hairpin radius rods, all receiving the chrome treatment to enhance the bright red paint with white Southard striping. Finished in 1975, the car remained in this form until today, but the story continues.

Faced with a very expensive divorce the following year, Andy was forced to sell both roadsters. Andy Brizio got one, while this one went to—of all people—"Li'l" John Buttera. Obviously a bit stressed at the time, the only thing Southard remembers is Buttera paying the money, jumping in the roadster, and taking off for SoCal. Only then did he notice his Bay Area Roadsters plaque on the back, jumped in his own car, and gave chase. Andy said Buttera was already through the next town down Hwy 101 before he caught him to get his plaque back.

During the next ten years this car changed owners a few times—among friends—but never changed appearance. The next time I saw it was the day I met Bruce Meyer, around 1985. Bruce had invited a group of *Hot Rod* staffers to his house for lunch, and right in the front door of his large garage was this red hiboy. The garage was full of concours-winning classics; we were there to see the nearly complete Pierson Brothers coupe. But he proudly pointed to this roadster as his first hot rod (which he had bought from Jim Busby), and his current "go-to driver."

Not only did Bruce drive it all over, but he let his teenage sons use it, as well as anybody else, such as writer Ken Gross when he was visiting from the East. Bruce loved the fun, topless, trouble-free Deuce. But so did Bruce's good friend Andy Cohen, who (among others) borrowed it regularly. So finally, when Bruce got the Lobeck/Coonan Deuce, he agreed to sell Andy this one in May 1993. The only change Andy made was adding wide whitewalls.

If you're not familiar with the name Andy Cohen, he was partners with Jim DeFrank in a company called Beverly Hills Motoring Accessories, which many street rodders remember as the supplier of custom-fit car covers in the 1970s. During that same time, drag racers undoubtedly remember the awesome DeFrank & Cohen SS/AA Hemi 'Cudas and Darts that set many NHRA records from the late 1960s on, with Andy driving. Andy has long been involved in building and collecting early Ford hot rods and other special-interest vehicles of all kinds. In fact, the original fenders from Lee Titus' Deuce are currently on another Washington Blue and black 1932 roadster in Andy's collection.

Left: Andy Southard traded a show-winning 1929 roadster cover car for the Deuce, then had Magoo turn it into this red hiboy by 1975. Other than the Bay Area Roadster plaque, it's the same today. **Right:** After several more auspicious owners including Buttera, Jim Busby, and Bruce Meyer, Andy Cohen poses with his new red roadster in 1993, shortly after adding the wide whitewalls.

After driving the red hiboy plenty, he finally parked it in a less-than-weather-tight garage (actually an old stable) on his property on Pacific Coast Highway in Malibu, where it has developed an increasing degree of patina. That was its condition when I took the photos seen here.

However, Andy assured me that the only reason he let the car go is that he plans to fully and accurately restore it to the Lee Titus full-fendered version as seen on the 1959 *Hot Rod* cover. That's a noble plan for this amazingly pedigreed roadster. I hope it happens soon.

Top Left: Yes, this is the same Jack McNeil upholstery from 1959. Southard had it dyed black, but you can see some of the red wearing through on the driver's foot pad. Where all the early Stewart-Warner gauges and the round radio went, nobody seems to know. **Top Right:** The 283 is still exactly the same as it was in 1975, including blue paint, tin valve covers, plastic fan, and now-metal-sprayed Hedman Hedders that were chrome when Titus had it. **Bottom:** Cohen even has the original Titus fenders to reinstall if he wants to. He says the car is now indoors and dry, awaiting restoration.

Lupe Serrato's Sedan

When I took the new photos, Lupe Serrato of Upland, California, had owned this 1932 sedan a little more than 50 years. In all that time it's always been chopped, always a brilliant deep red, and always gorgeous. It's no wonder it got in magazines. In a two-pager in the November 1964 *Hot Rod*, called "The Old Family Sedan," the color was listed as "Oxblood Red." Earlier it got a small color shot as one of seven "Coupes & Sedans" on the cover of the August 1964 *Car Craft*, and "candy" was added to the paint's name, but it only got one black-and-white page inside. By May of 1965, it was bluntly titled "Chopped 1932 Sedan," with just seven lines of copy in *Popular Hot Rodding*, but the car was sporting a beautiful set of brand-new polished American five-spoke mag wheels by then.

This underscores what I've been stating all along: that finding an old hot rod that's still old is not only a rarity but an oddity, because the theme of rodding through most of its history has been to update and modernize old cars (or even new cars). Discovering an old rod or custom sequestered in a garage or barn for a few decades can be great fun today for the finder, yes. But it may not be much fun for whoever put it there. So this is a hot rod that's been owned by the same person for half a century, and he and his family have *enjoyed* it all that time. And, in the original hot rod tradition, they have updated and improved it over those years. Do we call this 1932 lost? Maybe not really, though it's been 45-plus years since it's been seen in a magazine. Would you say this car has provenance? I certainly do.

One reason it has always looked so good is because Lupe Serrato has been a custom painter most of his life. Then again, the reason he's a custom painter is because he's built cars like this. See how that works? In 1956 Lupe did two things. He got a job at Tate Cadillac in Pomona as a helper in the body and paint shop, and he got a 1940 Tudor sedan that he prepped and painted Titian Red, then took to TJ for full white T&R upholstery. He said by 1960, he sold the good-looking Forty for enough to buy a piece of property, with $250 left over to get a 1932 sedan that had already been chopped 3½ inches "by some elderly gentleman." The only problem was that the car was scattered in pieces all over Chino—the body here, frame there, and the fenders somewhere else. They never did find the grille shell.

But Lupe gathered it up, took the parts home to his garage, and built it into the beauty in the magazines. One of them noted that he was "detail conscious." He was, and still is. For the first build he mated a 1956 265 Chevy to a 1939 Ford transmission and 1940 rear end, topping the engine with a 1958 Corvette Rochester fuel-injection unit a friend gave him, matched with 'Vette valve covers and ram's-horn manifolds. He painted the engine yellow, the underside of the car semi-gloss black, and chromed the entire rear end (including spring, brakes, and wishbone), as well as the dropped and filled axle and front suspension.

Then he painted the body 1956 Buick Titian Red. But that didn't look as good as the candies and pearls that were coming into vogue, so he tried again, mixing his own Oxblood Red Candy by blending Brolite clear lacquer and maroon toner. You can see the result in the great color photo he took back then. The only thing he didn't do was the interior, stitched in black pleats with a single row of buttons, matched with a black top and running boards, which was the latest trend in 1964.

About that time Lupe and a partner opened their own custom paint and body shop, called Lupe and Johnny's, on Arrow Highway in Upland, with Lupe doing the paint and Johnny doing the custom metalwork. They were plenty busy shaving chrome, frenching lights, sinking antennas, and spraying beautiful colors. One of their biggest jobs, literally, was painting the Summers Brothers' record-setting *Goldenrod* streamliner.

The Deuce sedan got minor updates along the way, like the polished Americans. But when you're

Thank goodness for old Kodachrome! Great setting, excellent car, and a magnificent lacquer paint job mixed and sprayed by Lupe Serrato that he called Ox Blood Candy.

building and operating your own business, paying jobs take precedence. So the 1932 stayed pretty much the same for quite a while.

But by 1995, the kids who rode in the back seat of "the old family sedan" were grown up, and son Eddie inherited his dad's car-enthusiasm genes. So with Eddie urging him on and even buying new parts, they decided to tear the sedan down and give it a thorough upgrade to 1990's standards. This included a new SuperBell axle with disc brakes in the front, a complete Jag independent rear, a 350/350 powertrain, Glide seats inside with 1994 Lexus Light Oak leather upholstery, and many of the typical aftermarket products advertised in the street rod magazines of the day. Fortunately they were able to sell most of the original components (including the whole black interior) to help offset the cost.

But the big thing that set it apart from typical street rods of the day was the Serrato attention to detail—and gorgeous paint. Lupe and Eddie did 90 percent of the rebuild in Lupe's two-car home garage, including the all-new wiring done by Eddie. Lupe did, however, take it to the paint shop to spray it in a new Mitsubishi Red Poly over a black base, using DuPont Chromabase urethane products. These new paints look almost as good as the old candies and pearls, especially the way Lupe sprays them. Or I should say, "sprayed" because, in 2006, Lupe finally hung up the spray gun and sold the shop so he can spend his time at home building and flying his nicely detailed R/C model airplanes, and cruising in the old family sedan whenever he feels like it.

Top Left: This photo gives you a closer look at the gorgeous candy, plus some of the chrome underneath, including a dropped and filled 1932 axle, plus all attaching parts. *Top Right:* Before the car's completion, the entire 1940 rear end got dipped in chrome, too. This is the first Titian Red paint; good, but not as good as it got. *Bottom:* Same car, same body, same frame, even same license and horn—all updated to mid-1990s street rod standards. And Serrato family detail standards.

Top Left: The original 265 engine, plus the Corvette injector, were worth enough to pay for this more-reliable, tidy 350 and then some. This time Lupe painted the engine cream to match the interior. *Top Right:* Lupe selected interior materials to match those in his wife's new Lexus, replacing the old black pleats and buttons. *Middle:* How do you update a completely chromed 1940 banjo rear? A Jaguar IRS painted and polished to match the engine looks great and rides better. *Bottom:* You'll note the 1990s update didn't mean pastel, graphics, or smooth billet. Lupe kept the black top and 'boards, stock lights and bumpers, mag wheels, and didn't even need any pinstriping over his new deep, rich-red pearl metallic.

The Lepesh Pickup

When my son, Bill, called me from his shop in South San Francisco to tell me that a customer had brought him a 1941 Ford pickup that had recessed canted quad headlights, sculpted running boards, a rolled rear pan with custom taillights, and that it had been in shows in the Bay Area in the early 1960s, I was naturally very interested. The headlights reminded me of Dave Cunningham's candy-red Forty, but that was a sedan (see page 79). Bill said that when the customer, David Pozzi, got the truck it was Gold Metalflake, had a chromed early Olds engine with dual 4-barrels and crusty five-spoke mag wheels. The custom pickup had been in David's family a long time, and had been in his garage since the early 1980s. But he was only 21 when he got it, and was too young to know much of its history from back in the day. He just remembered this sparkly truck being parked in his uncle's backyard garage when they were kids, and how they'd lean their bikes against its gold tailgate.

Then Bill called to say, "It's in the *Hot Rod Yearbook* No. 2." I memorized that book when I was a teen, and when I turned to Lepesh's Lalapalooza, I recognized it immediately. Not only did it have the canted quads, but it was painted a deep Claret Red with bold white scallops around the lights, much like Cunningham's. Further, perhaps not coincidentally, the photos in the two-page 1962 feature were by the same Dave Cunningham.

With a little more research, I found a near-identical two-page feature on it in the October 1961 *Hot Rod*, plus it was one of three similar Forty pickups featured together in the October 1959 issue. In 1959 it had single DeLuxe headlights, 1949 Plymouth bumpers, stock running boards, bedrail pipes, the DeLuxe car dash, and Edsel wheelcovers with wide whitewalls. It also had a white interior with gold rolls.

Strangely, I also found another one-page feature in the June 1964 *Car Craft*, photographed earlier when it had white scallops around the 1940 headlights, chrome wheels with baby moons, and a 1958 Impala steering wheel. In all these features the 1950 Olds engine had plenty of chrome, but just one 2-barrel carb. Although it was never shown in its final Gold Metalflake version, this custom truck easily qualifies for this "Yellow Pages" chapter.

Here's the brief story. Nick Lepesh owned a used-car dealership, Lepesh Motors, in Sunnyvale, California. In all the magazine articles, no one is credited for the mechanicals, the bodywork, the paint, the upholstery, or even the pinstripes or scallops, so I have to assume that Nick did some of the work, probably in conjunction with mechanics, bodymen, or painters who worked for his dealership. I don't know, nor does anybody in David's family.

Nick was actually David's mother's first cousin. I assume Nick showed the truck until sometime in the mid 1960s, then parked it in the garage. He didn't drive it, but Dave said it ran. At one point Dave's dad tried to buy it, but Nick said no, he wanted to put stock fenders back on it and paint it black. Unfortunately, Nick died of a sudden stroke at the age of 61 in 1982. His wife didn't want the truck, but she wasn't going to give it away, even though a couple of nephews wanted it. Since one of them "already had too many old cars," she decided to sell it to Dave in 1983.

He installed a new gas tank and rebuilt the carbs and got the truck running, though he figured it needed a complete rebuild. Then (he blames it on his brother-in-law) first gear in the 1939 transmission went away, and Dave parked it in his own garage, saving it until he could afford to rebuild it properly. That took about 20 years.

These are the first photos taken of the nearly finished truck in exactly 50 years. Side mirrors and mild striping are planned. The Candy Brandywine paint is close to the original Claret Red.

Chapter Five: From the Yellow Pages

By 2006, Dave got the truck running again and put new tires on it, but then the brakes went out. And first gear was still gone. And who knew what was under that thick 'flake paint?

Roy Brizio's rod shop was right down the street from Dave's house. He decided a new Brizio chassis with IFS and a modern GM driveline would be more practical than trying to rebuild the old Olds and early Ford components. That part went smoothly. But when they had the original body sandblasted, it was in sad shape (as it was to begin with, according to the 1961 *Hot Rod* article). So Roy referred Dave to Bill's nearby shop for considerable sheetmetal rehab and replacement, which ultimately evolved into finish bodywork, luscious Candy Brandywine paint by Joe Compani, white upholstery in 1-inch rolls by Chris Plante, and all the details needed to complete the pickup.

Since it had been seen and shown in various configurations, Bill and Dave had to decide which to replicate. In its last form, the Plymouth bumpers were replaced by handmade nerf bars, and the Dodge taillights had been replaced with 1963 Impala lights and a frenched license plate set into a rolled pan. Bill made new front nerfs, and had to remake the rear pan, tailgate, and sculptured running boards, but the four fenders and most of the bed are original, after much repair. Some items, such as the spotlights and sidepipes, were eliminated, but Bill had to make the chrome reversed rims from 1950 Ford centers and 5- and 6-inch Buick outers to match the 1960s originals.

When these photos were taken, a few details were still left to do, such as a chrome radiator cover and some subtle pinstriping, as seen when it was displayed for the first time in nearly 50 years at the 2012 Grand National Roadster Show. I hope Dave is enjoying this beautiful pickup, back on the street once again.

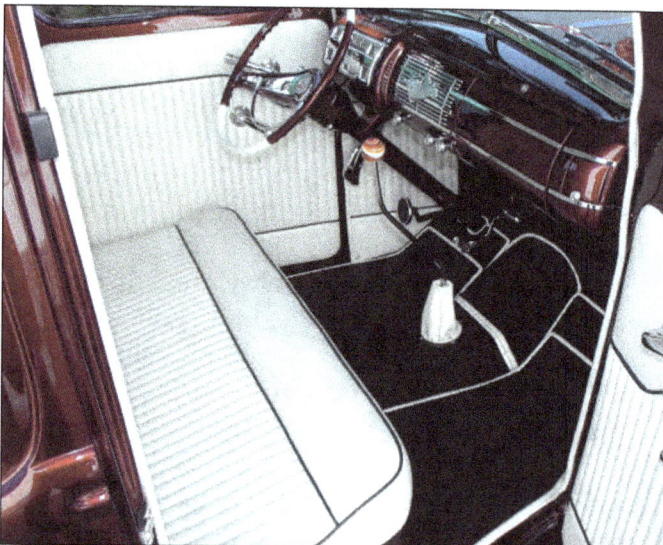

Top Left: This is how the truck was last seen in 1961, with white scallops, spotlights, bed pipes, and Plymouth bumpers. Note the white pleated upholstery inside, and how closely the new wheels match these. *Top Right:* Although both had to be replaced, the 1940 DeLuxe car dash and 1958 Impala wheel were in the truck by 1959. Lots of 1-inch white pleats, including a band in the headliner, are early 1960s style. Note the Merc door handles. *Bottom:* Though faded, this is a rare color shot from 1961, showing the 1958 Dodge taillights in the fenders and the rear "grille." These were changed to the current rear design when the truck was redone in gold 'flake in 1962–1963. The new version will have milder striping and no scallops.

Top Left: The new engine nestled neatly in the Brizio chassis is a basic GM 350. The chrome emblem on the firewall is from Lepesh Motors, Sunnyvale, California. Detailing is impeccable. *Top Right:* The original 1950 Olds engine and Ford transmission that came out of the truck, along with a few of its many show trophies from the 1950s and 1960s. *Bottom:* Original fenders and bed were saved, with much work. Magazines say the gas door is from a 1953 Pontiac. The rolled pan with 1963 Impala lights and frenched plate was the final version.

Buried Treasure

T his chapter is titled "Buried Treasure" because it's about cars that have been tucked away in garages, basements, or even barns for years and decades.

Chapter Six

Chapter Six: Buried Treasure

Murphy Tiffany's Deuce

Everybody remembers the August 1961 issue of *Rod & Custom* magazine, the first big one, with Neal East's gorgeous gold Deuce roadster with the white upholstery and chrome wheels, set on the beach in sunny California with kids in bathing suits with surfboards. The Woodard-East-Moeller-etc. roadster epitomized the current hot rod trends of 1961, has been restored twice, and was voted one of the Top 75 Deuces of all time.

But what about that other roadster, whose tail-end is partially seen on that cover? It belonged to fellow L.A. Roadsters member Murphy Tiffany, whose stated objective was "making it reminiscent of the 1940 era." So it had black paint and upholstery, orange Kelsey wire wheels, blackwalls, cowl lights and handles, and a healthy three-carb 59A flathead. But, man, the kids weren't into that number then, you dig Daddy-O?

I first heard about this buried treasure when I moved to Orange County, California, in the early 1970s and joined a car club. Everybody seemed to know about this original, complete 1932 roadster stored in the back of some guy's garage, untouched, that he wouldn't sell or even let anyone see. It was supposedly in the Huntington Beach area. I had visions of an old garage full of junk, dust, and cobwebs with a full-fendered roadster buried in the back under blankets, boxes, and lampshades. After 20-some years people stopped talking about it. In fact, I can't remember exactly how I found it, but it certainly wasn't what I expected.

Another early L.A. Roadsters member, Lee Kasabian, bought the roadster from Tiffany shortly after the magazine coverage and installed a Corvette dual-quad 283 in front of the 1939 transmission. At the same time, young Bernie Kretzschmar and his two older brothers were heavy into building hot rods at their father's shop yard in Hawthorne, near where Kasabian kept his roadster. Also located in this hot-rod-hangout industrial area was Dick Bergren, who had a 1932 three-window in the middle of a top chop.

Kretzschmar had an impressive fleet, including a 1940 coupe, a 1932 Fordor sedan with a dual-quad 283, and a 1934 five-window with a built flathead. In 1963, Kretzschmar and Bergren decided they wanted to join the L.A. Roadsters, so Bernie sold all three of his rods to buy the roadster from Kasabian for $1,500 (big money in 1963), and Bergren traded his brown, chopped three-window to Doyle Gammel straight across for a T-bucket roadster (that story has been told elsewhere).

The only things Bernie did to his new roadster were install a set of chrome wheels and have Tony Nancy build a white top and side curtains for it. Otherwise Bernie drove it everywhere, showing it at the Winternationals in 1963–1964, going on roadster runs, and towing his

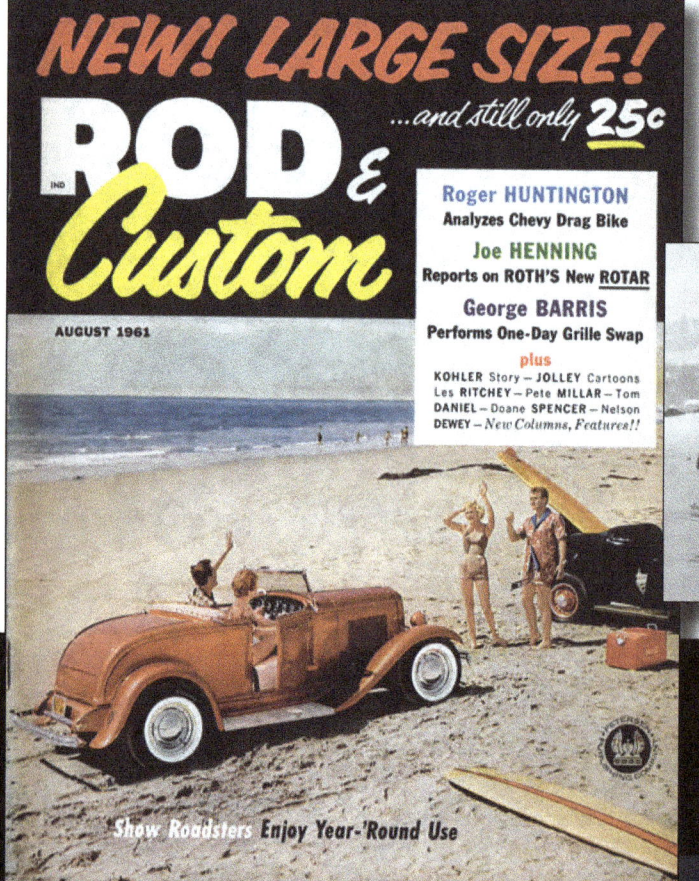

Left: The black Deuce got second billing on the first full-size Rod & Custom cover. Worse, the magazine hired young models to pose with the cars. *Above:* In 1961 hot rodders definitely were not into resto-rods or retro-rods, so Tiffany's beautiful black Deuce roadster wasn't nearly as interesting as the gold one with all the chrome, white tuck-n-roll, and Corvette engine.

Lost Hot Rods II

crackerbox boat to the lake. He even drove it to work when he got a job with Carroll Shelby beginning in 1964. Bernie began building Cobras and Shelby Mustangs at the "factory" next to LAX on Imperial Boulevard, but soon moved up to "race mechanic," building chassis for Trans-Am race cars and other special projects.

By the time Shelby's enterprise was winding down, Bernie had racked up 120,000 miles on the roadster, and the 1939 transmission gave out. In the early 1970s Kretzschmar joined the Costa Mesa fire department, moved to Huntington Beach, got married, started a family, and parked the 1932 in his mom's garage. It wasn't dirty or dusty.

As his family grew, Bernie sold one house and bought a bigger one, back when this could be quite profitable, especially in a SoCal beach area. He did it again. Then he bought some rental property and built some apartments. By 1991 he built an extra garage at one of his complexes, for his own projects, and moved the still-complete and original roadster there. He wasn't ready to restore it yet, though.

Top: Today this same Deuce, in nearly the same condition, is treasure to any hot rodder. Yes, it's buried in the back of a garage, but not under dust and cobwebs. Right: This was the best shot I could get of the car. That's the same dual-quad 1958 'Vette 283 that was in the car when Bernie got it in 1963. It's also the same black lacquer and dent-free, rust-free sheet metal.

Chapter Six: Buried Treasure

First he had a couple Shelby Mustang projects in mind. In 1997 he put together a 1965 R-model clone built specifically for VARA vintage road racing, which he has been doing at tracks across the country. Next he built a 428-powered 1968 Shelby GT 500 convertible for his wife, Diana, to drive on the street. And when I visited their latest house in Costa Mesa, in the garage sat a beautiful, black, just-finished GT350H fastback.

A few avid collectors keep calling about the pristine 1932 in the back of the garage, but Bernie still says a flat no to selling it. It's been waiting very patiently all this time, and as soon as Bernie is ready to quit racing his Shelby Mustang, the roadster will get its turn. There isn't that much to do, and Bernie has amply demonstrated he knows how to do it.

Top Left: Tony Nancy sewed the top in the early 1960s. Bernie added chrome rims and newer tires. The hood, grille shell, and radiator are inside the rumble seat, along with a new 1939 transmission, waiting to be installed. **Top Right:** Other than a Covico wheel and missing transmission and floor, everything here is the same as it was in 1961, including Jack McNeil's black upholstery. **Bottom:** Here's what's keeping the Deuce in the corner. Bernie built the 1965 "R clone" fastback for himself to race, and the 428 GT500 for his wife to drive. The 1932 comes next.

The Unknown Roadster

This channeled 1930 Model A first came to my attention through hot rod artist Darrell Mayabb, when he photographed it shortly after longtime Denver rod-builder Gary Vahling acquired it and cleaned it up a bit. These photos ran in the small *Hop Up* magazine No. 10, asking if anyone knew anything about it, but no one did. At that time the car had no engine and little interior, but it did have a 1941 Lincoln O.D. transmission. It also had a 1955 dime glued in the center of the T steering wheel, which might be a clue to when the car was built. Vahling got the car from Bob Conner, who had it stored for many years, but knew nothing of its history.

Vahling and Mayabb both have plenty of hot rod connections, but the only person they could find who knew anything about this car was rodder Ed Koski of Fort Collins, Colorado. In 1963 Ed lived in Greely, a few blocks from the State University. He had an Olds-powered 1929 roadster at the time, and one day this light-blue, channeled 1930 A roadster drove up to his house. Ed grabbed a camera and took several snapshots. On the back of one he wrote the name "Bob Flager." Ed remembers the guy was an engineering student at the university, possibly from North Dakota (though the roadster had 1963 Colorado plates). That's the only time Ed met him, and he never saw the car around town afterward. What really adds to the mystery is that the paint and chrome on the car is already quite weathered in these photos.

Ed and Flager didn't discuss who built the car or where it came from, but its heavy channel and even the pastel-blue color indicated an Eastern style. The car was quite well constructed; handmade parts such as the rolled pans, three-piece louvered hood, 1950s nerf bars, 1940 dash, and especially the V-windshield (made from a 1938–1939 frame and 1927 T stanchions) set this roadster apart. It was show quality, if not magazine feature material. It's unique and identifiable. But nobody seems to know anything about it.

Darrell had given me photos of the car, and I planned to see it while I was in Denver. What I didn't know was that Gary, in the meantime, had sold it to his younger brother, Frank, who had already installed a 1953 Merc engine, new wiring and brakes, Plexiglas for the windshield (including "deflectors" above the frame, like the original), and even new white tuck-and-roll upholstery (including in the trunk), making it fully drivable. He'll probably add some more hop-up goodies to the engine in time, but he figures he'll leave the car's long-cultivated patina the way it is, at least for now.

While I was at the shop where Gary works, and Frank brought the roadster for me to photograph in its current state, who should drive up but Bob Conner, delivering a car on his rollback hauler. So I took the opportunity to ask him exactly when and where he got the roadster. I didn't get an exact answer (Gary says that's the way he is), but it certainly did add to the story.

Other than some cleaning and new wheels, tires, and hubcaps, this is how the roadster looked when Gary Vahling finally got it about five years ago. The hood top and sides were handmade from steel, but the lower rolled panels were made from the 1930 hood tops. Crafty.

Bob not only transports cars, but he buys, sells, or rents them, so he's always on the lookout for anything interesting. He said he was pheasant hunting, by himself, around 1970, near Hudson (northeast of Kersey, which is seven miles east of Greely). In the distance he saw a roadster sitting under a lean-to attached to a barn. So he hiked over, found the farmer who lived there, and asked about the roadster. All the farmer said was that it "came with the place," and he couldn't sell it because he didn't know whose it was. It sat on four flat tires and didn't move.

Bob figured the guy didn't own the property so he kept track of the car for the next 17 or 18 years. But then Bob saw that the property had been sold to a developer in the late 1980s. He contacted them and offered to clear the property, including buying the tractors, other farm machinery, and—oh yes—that old jalopy. He said it still had the flathead in it with three carbs, Harrell heads, headers, and so on, but it was frozen, so he sold it.

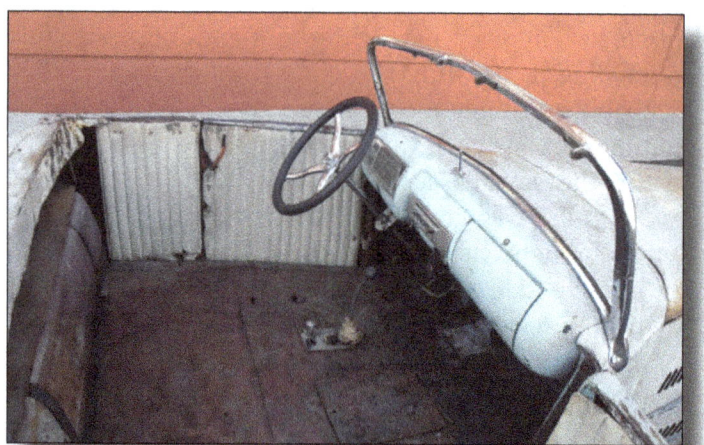

Top: Given what we know of this car's history, let alone what we don't know, it's incredible that parts like lights, nerfs, hood, fenders, dash, and windshield are all still there. Middle Left: Even the radio was still in the 1940 dash, which was molded to the 1930 cowl to fit the custom windshield frame. A handmade shifter operates the Lincoln transmission, with a separate lever for the overdrive. Seats were gone, but the floor is intact. Middle Right: Here's how it looked the day Bob Flager drove over to Ed Koski's house in Greely in 1963. The hood sides are off, and the cycle fenders appear to be in gray primer. Bottom Left: Bob removed the hood to show off the much-chromed 1938 Ford flathead. Note the red firewall, white-rolled seat, and clear deflectors above the windshield. It appears never to have had a top. Bottom Right: The rolled pan was made from the rear portion of an A sedan roof. But note how weathered the blue paint and chrome is, even by 1963. Is that the Toad on the Vespa?

Gary heard through a friend that Bob had this neat old roadster, so he went over to see it. It was outside, under tarps, still on four flat tires, but now with the engine gone. Gary made a good offer, but Bob said no. This continued for at least two years before Gary finally got the car. Despite the major parts I don't know about, this is still a pretty amazing story. What's even more amazing, given what I now do know of its history, is that it is so well preserved. There's no rust beyond what you see on the surface. And the roadster still looks pretty much the way it did when it visited Ed Koski's house that day in 1963 and he snapped some pictures of it.

Top: And here's how it looks today. Frank Vahling had to add new upholstery, an engine, and new wiring and brakes, but not much more. *Bottom Left:* Frank had the Lincoln transmission rebuilt and the Merc mill is stock inside for now. The red firewall is from 1963; the blue overspray might indicate the car was all red at one time. Who knows? *Bottom Right:* Jerry Weatherman installed new white upholstery to match that in the 1963 photos.

Chapter Six: Buried Treasure

1933 in the Basement

This one is literally buried—under a strip mall somewhere in the suburbs of Denver. I can tell you how it got there, when, and even why. But I can't tell you exactly where it is because this is another one Joe Haska led me to on our one-day wild goose chase of lost hot rods in the greater Denver area. All I can tell you is that we found a single-story, 1960s-era stucco strip mall, situated perpendicular to a main road, with maybe eight storefront shops in it. We drove around to the street behind, and there was a small lower parking lot at the back of the long building, with a pair of doors (just wide enough to get a car through), leading into what appeared to be a basement under all the stores.

Joe found out there were cars in there because he knew someone who did some maintenance on the building, knew Joe was into old cars, and told him there were five or six of them stashed in the basement. After a little detective work, Joe discovered the building belonged to Bud Zimmerman, and talked him into showing him his car stash. The one we were most interested in was a restored and slightly rodded 1933 Ford roadster. Joe had seen it, and even photographed it, a few years ago, and had kept in touch with Bud ever since.

Of course Bud didn't want to sell it, or any of the other cars, which included a stock 1923 turtle-deck T, a 1970s-era injected Chevy sprint car, a Mark IV Lincoln, and a couple other 1920s-era cars. One was a huge touring that was well-preserved, quite rare, and supposedly worth a lot of money. Bud (who appears to be in his 80s) demonstrated how the engine still turned over by hand-cranking it for us. But it was the 1933 roadster we wanted to see. Of course it was in the last room of the long, dark, cluttered basement. Lighting was minimal, and it didn't smell all that great in there either. But the 1933 was worth seeing.

There wasn't much light or room to get pictures, but Bud's all-original 1933 Ford roadster has been sitting right here since 1976. Woodlite headlights (made in the 1930s) dominate the front.

Lost Hot Rods II

Bud said it had been a "field car" on a farm in Kansas that he got in the early 1970s, and rebuilt himself. After repairing the body, he painted it metallic blue, redid most of the chrome, added Thunderbird chrome wire wheels, and installed new seats and upholstery from LeBaron-Bonney. He didn't say what size or year the engine is, but it's a 59A with Edelbrock heads, an Edmunds intake manifold, and two Holley carbs with original Edmunds air cleaners. It appeared to be in running condition, although the firewall-mounted battery was missing.

Of course the most unique feature of the car is the pair of Woodlites Bud installed. He was pretty proud of his finished product—definitely more restored than rodded—so he entered it in a big Ford V-8 Club show in Estes Park in 1976. To use Bud's words, the 1933 got a "poor reception" from the restorers and, even though his was the only car entered in his class, he got no trophy. He said his only recompense was "blowing the door's off the President's 1940 coupe" on the way home. But he was so chagrined by the whole thing that he parked it in the basement then, and that's where it has sat for going on 40 years now. I'm sure Joe keeps tabs on it. But I doubt it's going anywhere.

Top Left: Bud was into midgets and sprinters back in the day, so this Edmunds- and Edelbrock-equipped flathead has some pop, but he wasn't more specific than that. Top Right: It's got a 1939 transmission and LeBaron-Bonney seats, but everything else looks pretty original. Bottom: It has a dropped axle in front and 1940-style juice brakes, to which Bud adapted T-Bird wire wheels, including the spare.

Chapter Six: Buried Treasure

Deuce in the Loft

I'm not sure how to handle this one, but I think the best way is to leave all names and the exact location unspecified. That way I hopefully won't hurt anyone's feelings. This is a lost hot rod I'd been hearing about for a few years. In fact, a couple of the Finders mentioned in this and the first book had told me about it, but it was a fairly well-guarded secret.

The story was that a guy in a small desert-foothill community somewhere between Los Angeles and San Diego had a gorgeous, much-chromed, metallic green, ex-drag-race 1932 five-window coupe sequestered in his garage, in perfect condition. Jacked up in the front, with slicks in the back, but with full street accessories (fenders, lights, bumpers, etc.), it supposedly looked just like Harry Luzader's 1932, only a darker green. And, like Luzader's, it was raced through the 1960s and was then parked in the garage, making one or two brief appearances locally since then, but not seen for about 30 years.

This obviously sounded very intriguing. I kept waiting for one of my informants to take me out there to see and photograph it, but it was pretty far away and this didn't happen. I finally got the owner's name and phone number. I started calling and leaving messages, but he didn't know me and I got no calls back. I then learned from one of my informants that he had seriously broken his leg in a falling accident, and was slowly healing. He had a cast with wheels on it, and had a hard time getting around. So I put it aside; I had other cars to find.

Then, months later, I got a call from the guy. It took me a few minutes to remember who he was. He told me he'd been busy working on his house; that's how he fell, off his own scaffolding. In fact, he was building an extra garage to house the Deuce and a Model A Sport Coupe his father had restored. The Deuce was on a lift, with the A under it, and since he was still in his cast, he wouldn't be able to get the 1932 down. But I was welcome to come out and see it. After what I'd heard about the car, how could I refuse?

The problem was that it was about a 200-mile round trip and we were having a summer heat wave. But I had to go somewhere in that direction, and figured I'd at least go see this hidden Deuce I'd heard about for so long. I

The owner had just finished building the garage on the right, with the covered Model A on the bottom and the Deuce on a lift above it. Note there is no driveway. The scaffolding in the middle is what he fell from, raising one of those beams.

Lost Hot Rods II

think it was 107 degrees when I got there. The guy was quite friendly and accommodating, even though he had a hard time maneuvering in his roller-cast. He showed me into a new, narrow, two-story garage he had just built on the front of his house, where both cars were stored.

When I saw the dark green Deuce up on the lift, I was pretty disappointed, to put it bluntly. I was looking at the underside of the car, and there was no chrome, let alone shiny paint, in sight. I couldn't see that much of the body of the car, though what I saw looked straight and nice. But there were some very wavy fiberglass fenders on the back, with wide 1960s tires hanging out, and clear plastic flaps screwed on to cover them. The guy said it had a 265 in it, with a single 4-barrel, and I believe a 3-speed stick with something like a Pontiac rear end. It ran mid 14s in C/Gas in the 1960s, which he said was respectable and fun. Although it was streetable, he just drag raced it at local tracks. I didn't see the interior, but it appeared to be basic black. He briefly mentioned something about his father getting angry when he started cutting braces out of the inside of the body to make it lighter. That didn't sound good.

Top: This is about as much as I could see of the long-stored 1932. The body looks straight and the green enamel paint is shiny. But just like Harry Luzader's? Not exactly. Bottom: I admit it probably looks a lot better from above than from down here. But the 'glass rear fenders were lumpy and those flaps don't do much for the Pos-A-Traction tires protruding from them. They're on real mag American wheels though.

Chapter Six: Buried Treasure

ran. Getting the Model A out and getting the 1932 down that day was out of the question. Besides, this new garage didn't have a driveway in front of it. So I took what pictures I could of the Deuce on the rack. I figured I'd go back later, when the owner was out of the cast, and we'd get it out for better photos. But, to tell the truth, I don't think that Deuce is coming out again. It hasn't been out in 30-some years. He hasn't done anything to it since the 1960s. He built that garage to *keep* it in. I think it's a Zen thing. So what you see is it.

I uncovered the 1928 Model A underneath it, and it looked very nice. His father had done the restoration on it, but was now too old to drive it, or something, but it ran.

I of course mentioned this to my informant, wondering at the discrepancy between his description and what I found. He had last seen the coupe at some sort of racers' reunion party. It was a very long time ago. He was young; it was dark, it was late, and he admitted he had been drinking a bit that night.

Top: The only chrome I see down here is the oil filter on the 1956 265. **Bottom:** The 1928 is nice, but it's bone stock other than accessory wheels.

Lost Hot Rods II

The Craigslist Coupe

You might have noticed that several lost rods in this book could fit in one chapter just as well as another. The main reason I'm putting this well-preserved, 1950s-built 1934 three-window in the "Buried Treasure" chapter is that it doesn't fit anywhere else. It was never in a magazine, wasn't built for racing (though it did plenty), and wasn't famous or a well-known show winner. If young Nick Osborne hadn't snagged it on Craigslist.org, I could have included it with the "Keepers," because this hot rod was built and owned by the Girod family of Burbank, California, for half a century.

Nick and his dad, Kirk, run a family metal company that once supplied mesh liners for Hellings air cleaners. Both are much into cars and automobilia, and Nick already had one nice, patina'd, fenderless, flathead-powered 1934 three-window retro rod in his garage; his dad had salvaged it as a shell with a tree growing through it. Because of that, one of of Nick's friends, who was browsing for Oldsmobile parts on the Internet, phoned to say he had just seen a 1934 coupe advertised locally with an "Olds Rocket engine." There was one photo, but no price. It looked good, so they called right away, figuring to go halves, buy it, and flip it. It turns out it was so good Nick's dad said, "Let's get it and keep it." Which they did, but it wasn't easy or cheap.

The person who put the ad on Craigslist.org was Robert Girod's widow. He had passed away a year before, and their children had no interest in the car. By the time Nick and his friend got to the house to see it, Mrs. Girod had already gotten hundreds of calls from all over the world, but she said they had "first dibs." They offered $20,000, but she said it wasn't enough. I have no idea what Nick actually paid, but he was soon going home to get a truck and trailer; he didn't even know if it ran. It turns out it did run, and quite well. Nick and Kirk have no buyers' regrets.

Mrs. Girod didn't know the car's whole story, but she knew a lot. She had photos, registration tags going back to the mid 1950s, and even "a stack of tickets" her husband Robert got speeding and racing on River Road. Plus Nick contacted Robert's brother, Richard, who still lives in Burbank and who filled in some details.

Here's what Nick learned. Robert and Richard bought the coupe as a stocker around 1949–1951. They started building it as a hot rod with a flathead, but blew the engine. So they sold the car to a friend "with money," who had the stout, three-carb Olds engine built (they don't know where). However, a couple years later this person fell and hit his head on the car, and died. So Robert bought the car back. Richard said he used to drive it quite a bit, and remembered "blowing many transes." He dates the great photo of the three brothers with the car at 1958, so it was sometime not long afterward that Robert and Richard painted the black lacquer that's still on the car, probably in the same driveway where several photos were taken and where it was when Nick bought it.

I wish more of those photos could be shown here. But even they leave some questions unanswered. For instance, a few taken in the mid 1960s show an interior with bucket seats upholstered in nice, black rolls. Where did they go and why does it have the minimal upholstery it does now? Also, in all these photos the rear splash apron is missing—why? It's still not there. Yet the entire early Ford rear end under the car today—axle housings, springs, shackles, backing plates, and wishbone—are all chrome plated, as are the window frames and several engine parts. Did Robert have an in with a chrome shop? I don't know.

When Nick got the car in 2008 (with some help from Dad), it had been sitting for some time. So they took it to the Kennedy Brothers in Pomona (who did the work on Nick's other 1934), not only to get the engine running properly, but to do some front-end work and redo the brakes (moving the master cylinder from the firewall to under the floor). Nick said there was a white top insert in the roof, which blew off during the trailer-ride to his house, and which he is replacing. Other than that, he says, the car is done. I might suggest one more thing: finally putting a splash apron on the back. Why not?

I've got to start with this cool photo. Those are the Girod brothers, Michael, Robert, and Richard (on the Triumph), circa 1958. Their 1934 coupe has the Olds engine, a gonk in the left front fender, and no paint or chrome yet.

Top Left: Robert and wife Monica lived in the same house in Burbank for years and both worked in the nearby movie studios. Robert stands proudly with his 1934 in the driveway, now painted black lacquer with plenty of chrome, sometime in the 1960s. Note the whitewall slicks on the back. *Top Right:* A color shot of the Olds mill from the 1960s. Note the chrome master cylinder on the diamond-plate-reinforced firewall. It was exactly the same when Nick got the car. *Bottom:* Nick added the whitewalls to match the 1960s photos. But other than a little clean and polish, this is how he got it.

Top Left: It took a little carb-cleaning to get the 324 Olds running, and it's stout. Dig the Spalding Flamethrower ignition. Nick doesn't know what's inside, but it sounds like it might even have a roller cam. *Top Right:* There was nicer upholstery in the 1960s; who knows what happened to it. The Kennedys rebuilt some floorboards, moved the pedals there, and added gauges to the middle of the dash. *Bottom:* Nick is obviously quite pleased with his Craigslist.org score of a cherry, gennie 1950s hot rod. The top insert blew off on the way home. He'll replace that. How about a rear pan?

Chapter Six: Buried Treasure

Race Cars

The only thing worth less than a 15-year-old Cadillac is an out-of-date race car. And race cars of all types become obsolete faster than any other type of vehicle.

If you want to remain competitive, you've got to rebuild or update your car each season. Older cars get handed down to racers in lower classes, where they usually get beat-up, butchered, patched together, or ultimately wrecked beyond repair. So how in the world have so many early dragsters, Altereds, Gassers, Funny Cars, sprinters, midgets—you name it—turned up in the past 10 or 20 years, since "Nostalgia Racing" of various types has become so popular?

Long-wheelbase dragsters, in particular, aren't very easy to keep. But they keep coming out of the woodwork. Searchers find them in basements or hanging in the rafters. I've found and restored a few myself. But I can't explain how so many still exist, and continue to be found. The following sampling includes some amazing, esoteric examples.

Chapter Seven

Mrs. Swallow's Midget

I think this is my favorite story of the whole book. It certainly qualifies as lost, and I consider any open-wheel cars that race on circle tracks—preferably dirt ones—as hot rods. That includes midgets and sprinters.

You might not know the name Billy Felts if you didn't follow dirt track racing on the West Coast, but he was a standout both in midgets and sprint cars in the renowned California Racing Association (CRA) and others that ran in California and the West. Billy started driving midgets—Offy Midgets—around 1971, and then moved up to full-size sprint cars by 1975, continuing racing both, as funds permitted, through 1990. Although he can't claim any major championships, as often as not you'd find him in the trophy dash on any given night, winning his share.

But one thing he was always known for, besides his driving, were his meticulously built, painted, and chromed cars. There was good reason for this. He was meticulous, but he also owned, and still owns, a chrome shop. It's called MJB Plating in the small town of Rialto, just west of San Bernardino. That's where this story develops.

Mrs. Hazel Swallow, age 81, also lives in Rialto. Her husband, Calvin, a certified welder and mechanic, died in 1992. One of the half-started projects he left behind was an old midget race car he bought in 1980. It was in a small shed on the back corner of the half-acre lot where she lived. About all she knew about it was a hand-written tally sheet of parts he had bought to refurbish it, mostly from Don Edmunds Auto Research. At the top he had written "Curtis Craft Offy Race Car." He didn't spell it right, but it was the real thing.

Hazel decided she wanted to donate the race car to some museum as a tribute to her late husband. There were several in the area, and she called or wrote all of them, but none was interested in this unrestored race car with no known history or famous name. In a program for a local car event, she happened to see a small ad for MJB Plating in her hometown, and it mentioned "Motorcycles, Boats, and Race Cars." Given that, she called. Billy answered and Hazel explained she had an old race car that she wanted to put in a museum, but she wasn't having luck; could he help? Billy asked "What kind of race car?" When she read off the sheet, "Kurtis Kraft Offy," Billy's ears tingled. "Oh really? I used to race those." It turned out Mrs. Swallow lived three blocks from Billy's shop. He asked if he could stop by that evening, when he closed, to see it.

Top: Here's what Billy found inside the shed when he arrived with his truck and trailer. You never know what's hiding in suburban garages. *Bottom:* The small shed at the back of Mrs. Swallow's lot.

Top: Here are the pieces Billy brought back. Calvin bought the car in 1980 and had Edmunds add the cage. He likely repainted it, since his daughters' names are on the cowl. I have no idea what the "M" is for, or any of the car's history. I borrowed the repro Kurtis nose and grille from metal-master Dennis Webb (Anahiem, California), who had just made it for a similar restoration by Arlen Kurtis. Hopefully he will make the new body for this one. *Bottom:* The 1970s 'glass body and 1980s cage are Edmunds, but the chassis is early 1950s Kurtis Kraft. Note the Bell wheel and early gauges.

When Billy got there, and she opened the small shed, it didn't look like much. It had a 1970s fiberglass body (Edmunds) with no recognizable names on it, a 1980s cage, four threadbare slicks on Centerline wheels, and a Cosworth Vega engine sitting nearby. But the closer Billy looked the more he saw: a leaf-spring tube axle in front with spot discs on Halibrand knock-off hubs, parallel torsion bars in back holding a Casale quick-change, Norton steering, and a Halibrand in-and-out box. Then, in a back corner he saw it—a disassembled, but complete 110 Offy DOHC midget engine, Hilborn injectors, mag, and all. Billy was obviously excited about what he saw, as he named all these components for Mrs. Swallow. And yes, despite the more recent Edmunds cage, it was an early- to mid-1950s Kurtis chassis.

About this time Hazel's friend, we'll call him Dick, arrived in some Volkswagen-powered MG-like kit car. He's a car guy, and starts telling Billy, "Hey buddy, this is some good stuff. Don't think you're going to get it cheap just 'cuz Hazel doesn't know what it is." Billy was already telling Hazel, "This is out of my league. I couldn't afford to buy this. I'll try to help you find…." When Hazel promptly turned and said, "Zip it, Dick!" Then she slowly turned back to Billy and said, "Okay, I've decided what I'm going to do. You obviously know and appreciate what's here. I'm going to give it to you." Billy was dumbstruck. But not Dick; he started yelling, "You can't do that!" Hazel simply raised her finger to shut him up, and said, "I'm 81 years old. I can do whatever I want." Billy could hardly believe what he was hearing, but it was true.

Of course there was a slight catch. She had three daughters, and their approval was needed to give away their father's old race car. They were all in Texas, but she was sure there wouldn't be a problem and agreed to call him in a couple of days.

Sure enough, two or three days later Hazel called Billy, said she had a typed agreement from her daughters (Joy, Melody, and Star) and to come get the midget, which, of course, he did. The agreement Hazel wrote said, in part, "We do this realizing we have found a person with great passion for midget race cars as their dad [did]. We will appreciate it if some sort of memorial in the form of a small plaque or whatever is found appropriate. Keep yourself safe Bill, and we hope you have years of enjoyment with it. That is what Dad would have wanted!"

I swear this is all true. You can see the pictures. Of course it will be completely and meticulously restored, like any of Billy's own midgets, hopefully with a properly reproduced aluminum Kurtis Kraft body.

Pretty good story, huh?

Top: The quick-change rear is a rare 1950s Casale midget open tube.
Bottom: A Cosworth Vega engine came with the car, but the real gem is this 110-ci midget Offy, serial No. 122, that appears to be complete less pistons, and very rebuildable.

The Mach IV Mustang

Everybody who knows anything about drag racing knows about Tommy Ivo's *Showboat* dragster, built in 1961 with four fuel-injected Buick engines. They probably also know Tom McCourry bought it in 1966 and had Tom Hanna build an aluminum Buick Riviera "wagon" body for it, called the *Wagon-Master*. But far fewer know about Gary Weckesser's Ford-powered four-engine 1969 Mustang Funny Car called the *Mach IV*, and even they would probably be surprised to learn Gary still has it. He is rebuilding the engines right now to run it at tracks across the country, at least through the Mustang's 50th anniversary in 2014.

Gary grew up in Wisconsin and started his racing career with 1940 Ford and Willys Gasser coupes. But by 1963 he'd moved to Van Nuys, California, because it was the hotbed of drag racing and dragster building. One question I forgot to ask Gary was exactly *why* he wanted to build a four-engine Ford dragster, but I figure that's sort of immaterial. He was apparently influenced by McCourry's *Wagon-Master* because when he went to Frank Huszar's Race Car Specialties (RCS) to begin the project in early 1969, his initial plan was to fit some form of Ford station wagon body. Huszar built the frame, and Weckesser became good friends with RCS machinist Roy Steen, who helped him design and build the unique driveline for the four 351 Windsor engines.

Ivo's car had the two right engines coupled to drive the rear axle, and the two left ones reversed to drive the front. Weckesser's coupled all four in a custom-machined three-gear transfer case feeding a (first-ever) four-disc Schiefer clutch with a single drive shaft through the middle, powering both the front and rear axles.

In the middle of this project (which only took eight months to complete), Gary moved north to Watsonville, California, and connected with Kent Fuller (builder of Ivo's car), who was then in nearby Scotts Valley. Fuller not only convinced Gary that a new 1969 Mustang F/C body would look better and be more aerodynamic, but he reworked the back half of the RCS chassis for the lower profile and cut and reformed a Fiberglass Trends body to fit. Pat Breslin of Custom Speed & Marine in Watsonville built the then-new 351W engines, with injectors custom-made by Enderle and magnetos by Joe Hunt. It was then painted by Bill Carter, first in candy blue over pearl white, then in blue 'flake the next year after it ate a guardrail and had to be rebuilt. It was sponsored by Galpin Ford during this time.

And, yes, it certainly did run. During initial testing at Fremont Dragstrip it clocked a 203-mph pass—on pump gas. But the NHRA had outlawed four-engine cars from competition by then, so the real purpose was to put on a smoke-filled show. That it did, and quite well. So Gary not only toured the car all over the United States and Canada for booked-in exhibition runs (like many wheel standers were doing), but he also paired up with McCourry for side-by-side smoke-fests, both cars running in the 175- to 180-mph range. Weckesser said they raced each other hundreds of times.

Holy smokes!

The immediate question was, "How did you see?" Gary answered, "I couldn't, for the first 1/8 mile." The other thing you have to understand is that you can't really steer a car spinning all four wheels. It's like driving on ice. So Gary said he got the car to go straight by testing and jacking weight into one side or the other, plus playing with front and back gear ratios, "Then I'd have to drive by feel or instinct to half track." Soon he figured out how to angle the center pipes on the engines to blow smoke away from the windshield,

which helped some. He said he and McCourry never hit each other, but they both swapped lanes—twice—on one run, which sent the guy in the timing shack at the top end running away, yelling, "You guys are crazy!"

After a second crash in 1972 in Canada, where he rolled it five times in the lights at 180 mph, Gary was smart enough to rebuild the car again and take it on the show circuit for the next three years, "Where they pay you whether you smoke the tires or not, and you can't break anything." However, by 1978 he had moved back to Wisconsin to raise his daughters and pursue his long-haul trucking business, and the car wasn't seen for more than a decade. Then, by 1989, he got it out, gave it a new paint job, got it running, and brought it to the first Hot Rod Reunion at Bakersfield to put it on display, which he has done at similar events since. Now, having just retired from trucking, he plans to make more smoky runs with this amazing car. Catch one if you can. Keep the rubber down and the shiny side up, Gary!

Top: In its first Carter paint job of smoke-swirled candy blue over pearl white, the Mach IV starts to smoke all four slicks on an exhibition pass at Suffolk Raceway in Virginia. Middle: The second Carter paint job, in 1971, was blue 'flake. Note the center pipes now angled to clear smoke from the windshield. Bottom: The tube chassis was originally by Frank Huszar of RCS. It and the 'glass body were reworked by Kent Fuller in 1969. This was its third paint job.

Top: The engines are mated back-to-back (with two running in reverse rotation); then a custom gear case connects them on this end to a single four-disc clutch, with a driveshaft running to the front and back axles. *Bottom:* Yow! Which is scarier, a vision-impaired four-engine Mustang at speed, or the proximity of those people and cars, with no guardrail? This was the Holtville track, an old air base in the SoCal desert near Mexico.

Chapter Seven: Race Cars

The *Magwinder*

Two things here. First is a minor theme in this book I might call "cross-referencing." That is, more or less by happenstance, a few cars have been connected to the same person, or else different people have owned the same car. An example of both includes Greg Sharp's 1941 Ford pickup in Chapter Three, his Dave Marasco–built 1929 roadster pickup in Chapter Ten, and Dave Marasco's current 1929 RPU in Chapter Eleven. This car is a second vehicle closely connected to Jack Chrisman.

The second, larger theme that has been prevalent is mystery. There's a fair amount of mystery to explore in this one.

The first two *Sidewinder* dragsters, fielded by Mailliard-Reed-Jones and usually driven by Jack Chrisman, were quite well known because they were very successful. Many didn't know there were two, because they looked quite similar, with a blown Chrysler Hemi mounted sideways behind the driver, chain drive on the left side, and a full aluminum body with a vertical tail behind the engine.

This one, the brainchild of team owner Chuck Jones and builder Kent Fuller, was called the *Magwinder* because its extremely low, lay-down tube chassis and most of its Wayne Ewing-shaped body was made of magnesium. When it debuted in a red-white-blue scalloped paint scheme by George Cerny in the August 1961 issue of *Hot Rod*, with a small color photo in the lower corner of the cover, it was very advanced for its time. The article stressed safety features, as if the NHRA was afraid of the car. Some photos showed a mocked-up Chrysler and bare 6-71 blower, and the copy stated it ran a 750-hp 454-inch blown Chrysler Hemi, but also said, "Pontiac engine now used. Best run to date, 171 in 9.22." This was on gas,

Top: Chuck Jones said the car was finished like this by 1959. The "S" on the nose and the Tony Nancy seat was a Sidewinder snake medallion. The engine is supposedly a tilted blown Chrysler, but there are no visible clues. **Bottom:** This photo, taken at Lions in early 1960, shows how futuristic the *Magwinder* looked compared to the best dragsters of the time. That's Jack Chrisman, second from the telephone pole, standing between it and the much the more successful *Twin Bears* car he also drove.

Lost Hot Rods II

Top: There was no engine, and a tube axle replaced the original Volkswagen front suspension, when I took this photo in 1983 in the driveway of the house in Orange. That's Chuck and daughter Stephanie. *Bottom:* I don't know who added the wing or mirrors, or much of its in-between history, but the car was in surprisingly good, complete condition.

Chapter Seven: Race Cars

during the fuel ban, but it doesn't say what engine turned that time. I've seen photos of the car running, but I've never seen any photo of either engine, in running condition, in the car.

The fact is that this futuristic, scary looking, weird-design new dragster wasn't successful. Despite its extremely light weight, it didn't win races. Why? After its appearance in *Hot Rod*, it wasn't seen again. The story I heard at the time was that it wouldn't run straight, because the big horsepower twisted the live tube rear axle like a torsion bar, making the car turn. This was likely a myth.

The true story, as told by son Steve Chrisman in the book, *The Chrisman Legacy*, is that Jack was seriously hurt returning from a run when the car's push-bar broke, and the push truck hit the rear slicks, vaulting it over the back of the car. The bumper hit Jack in the back of the head, slamming him into the steering wheel, which broke his jaw and knocked out some teeth. He wasn't "scalped" as some stories at the time said (more myths). But it put Jack out of commission for at least six months.

When I talked to Chuck Jones recently, he said this happened in late 1960 (before the *Hot Rod* article), and that it effectively ended the team, even though the car wasn't hurt. Chuck was based in Orange County, California, and so was Pontiac Super Stock racer Hayden Proffitt at the time. Chuck said he tried Proffitt as driver, but he'd never been in a dragster before, let alone one like this, and didn't take to it readily. However, Jones (who eventually competed in Formula 1) wanted to go road racing, so he left the car with Hayden, who put a Pontiac in it.

Things get a bit hazy at this point. Chuck said Proffitt had the car about a year and Jack Engle ran it with an Olds. Then Jones got the car back in 1962, but gave it to some guy from Orange who put a blown small-block Chevy in it. This person supposedly had the current, source-unknown, pearl-yellow (with candy-green scallops) paint job done. I heard (from Andy's brother Julian, among others) that the car ended up hanging on the wall in the late Andy Alvarez' paint/restoration shop in Costa Mesa for years. But Jones claims he got the car back again in 1973 or 1974, and that it hung on *his* shop wall until 1978. I just learned that Jones owned the building Alvarez was in, so they're both right. After that, Jones stored it in a friend's garage in Santa Ana.

What I know for sure is that, when I was trying to locate lost early dragsters for an article in 1983, I had heard that the *Magwinder* was stored somewhere, in good condition. I found Chuck Jones, who told me to meet him at an old house in downtown Orange, right across the street from Chapman College (the house is now gone, replaced by new Chapman buildings). When I got there, he took me around back to what looked like a weathered, one-car garage. Inside was the complete *Magwinder*, less engine.

This was nearly 30 years ago but I remember a dirt floor. Maybe there was a garage door that was locked. But for some reason Chuck and I had to pick up the dragster, turn it on its side, and carry it out a regular door. It wasn't easy, but I was surprised it was light enough to do that. I know this part of the story is correct, because I have the photos to prove it.

When we were done photographing the car we had to carry it back into the garage. Sometime later Chuck donated it to the Garlits Museum in Florida, where it remains today, looking just as it did in 1983, or 1973, or maybe sometime in the mid 1960s. That's as much as I know.

And it looks exactly the same in the Garlits museum today.

The Chevy 88

This one involves not only some mystery, but even a little noir. But I can't say too much about it, if you know what I mean.

The car itself was no mystery at all to me. When Bill Bartlett from Rohnert Park, California, (north of San Francisco) came by my booth at the West Koast Customs meet at Santa Maria a couple years ago, and started describing an old drag car his family had acquired in 1987, it sounded familiar. He said it was a 1939 Chevy coupe, featured in *Hot Rod* in 1958 when it had a GMC six in it, and again in *Car Craft* in 1960 with a chopped top and a Chevy V-8. When he said it had no fenders, I knew exactly what it was. I said, "Did it have a big '88' painted on the doors?" He said, "Yeah! That's it. How did you know?"

Surprisingly, I saw those features long before I had an inline-six-powered old Chevy of my own. Maybe it had something to do with my ongoing involvement with GMCs. But that car just got my attention. A 1939 Chevy coupe, with its pointy grille and hood, looked like a streamlined race car with the fenders removed. A decklid full of louvers and Moon wheelcovers added to the look. And the chopped top perfects it. Why aren't there more race cars like this? I'm pretty sure it's the only fenderless 1939 Chevy coupe I've ever seen. The big surprise for me was seeing it again, after all these years, in nearly original condition.

When the car appeared in the March 1958 *Hot Rod* it was built and owned by Darrel Redfern of Fairoaks, California (near Sacramento). It had the body channeled over the stock frame, all fenders removed (with stock inner fender panels in the front), and a big 320-inch GMC with five carbs set back under the middle of the cowl. Running a 1938 Packard transmission and skinny whitewall slicks, it had won B/Altered class at nine out of ten races with best times of 114.90/12.94. I assume it was white (doesn't say) with a big "88" on the doors (in most photos). It didn't occur to me until now that 88s are usually Rocket Oldsmobiles. Maybe Redfern was implying he could blow off those rapid V-8s, which he could.

By September 1960 the car got a small photo in the top corner of the *Car Craft* cover. The feature inside was photographed by George Barris, and the Chevy had its lid lowered 5 inches by Sam Barris. New owner, Jim Hicks, was credited with white enamel and green scallops, retaining the 88s on the doors. The GMC was replaced by a six-carb 265 Chevy V-8, which actually ran a tad slower.

What I also never noticed until now is that the front wheel wells were filled with flat, smooth panels, while stock rear fenders were significantly narrowed and molded to the body, with a flared lip, greatly cleaning up and streamlining the back of the car. I assume Sam Barris also did this work, and I now realize he had moved back to Sacramento by then, where this car was located, and probably did the work out of his garage. That's cool.

Above: By 1960 the car had a chopped top by Sam Barris, a six-carb Chevy V-8, and white paint with green scallops. A year or two later, at Oakland, it appears to be orange with white scallops, and has won a whole bunch of trophies. **Left:** Here's how the 1939 looked in 1958, even before the 88s were added. The much-louvered aluminum deck panel is now the floor in the trunk area.

Chapter Seven: Race Cars

Top: Other than newer slicks, this is just how the Bartletts got the car in 1987. Note the small scoop in roof, which may have been added for Bonneville in 1963. *Bottom:* I assume Sam molded narrowed fenders to the rear. I don't know why the deck lid was changed, but the push bar makes it stationary.

Where the car was, what it did, and who owned it between 1960 and 1987 is the mystery. As you can see, the car is now orange with white scallops in nearly the same pattern. It also has a 1963 Bonneville "Participant" decal in the windshield. I just checked a 1963 Bonneville program and, sure enough, a team of Hicks-Shannon-Peterson from Marysville, California, (north of Sacto) had entered a 1939 Chevy as No. 881 with a 283 Chevy in B/Comp. Coupe, and with a supercharged 354 Chrysler as No. 880 in A/CC. However, there's no mention of the car in *Hot Rod's* 1963 coverage, and I have no other indication the car actually ran, or had a blown Chrysler in it. Bartlett has a photo of the car at the Oakland Roadster Show, apparently in the orange paint and with the Chevy V-8, but without the decal in the windshield, so I have to assume this was before 1963. But that's all I know—or can surmise.

The noir part of the story involves "some lady in Truckee" (on I-80 in the Donner Pass) who had a car on a trailer in her garage (I don't know how long, or where she got it), who maybe owed some money to somebody for some illicit substances. The car changed hands a couple of times, still on the same trailer, and Bill Bartlett heard it might be available. That was 1987. The Nostalgia Drags were going strong in Fremont, and it looked like a perfect car to participate. Bill, his dad Bill, Sr., and brother Brian all chipped in to buy it. It still had a six-carb small-block Chevy in it, which they briefly got running. Bill said it was really loud and the carbs were really leaky. But they found out the Packard transmission was busted. They started to rebuild it to run with a 4-speed, injectors, and 9-inch rear. But when the rules changed, requiring a full cage and other new equipment, they decided to leave the car as-is.

It's been a while, but it's still "as-is" today.

Left: The interior has changed little since 1958. The 1939 Chevy box was neatly converted to center steering. Top cuts, visible inside, are also neatly done. **Right:** The engine, headers, and mag are original; injectors are mocked up. The Bartletts were planning to run the car at the Nostalgia Drags until current NHRA regulations were imposed. So it stays preserved for now.

Chapter Seven: Race Cars

Missing Mercs

Custom cars are all about style and fashion. So most of the classic customs of the 1940s and 1950s got rebuilt and "modernized" as often as teens' hairstyles and hemlines changed with the current fads.

If the owner of a custom car couldn't afford to keep modifying its body, or at least having it repainted in the latest trendy style—both of which were expensive—his chances of selling it were slim, and it would either become a daily driver, or pushed out in the backyard to fade and rot, if not crushed for scrap.

For a time during the 1960s and 1970s, custom cars fell totally out of fashion and disappeared altogether. Until people began finding them stashed in garages, barns, or backlots—probably faded and moldy, if not rusty or rotted, but ultimately savable.

Like old race cars, a surprising number have been found. Unfortunately restoring one usually takes considerably more work. Of course chopped Mercs are the Holy Grail of early customs. Here's just a sampling of what I tracked down.

Chapter Eight

Chapter Eight: Missing Mercs

Steve Gonzales' 1950

My, how time flies. When I photographed Steve Gonzales' beautiful persimmon-lacquered 1950 Mercury for the cover of the August 1977 "Special Chopped Merc Issue" of *Street Rodder* magazine, he was a 16-year-old junior at Cantwell High in Montebello, California. When I reconnected with him and his Merc recently he told me he'd just turned 51 and the oldest of his five kids is 15. Whew. I had kept track of Steve as he joined the Dukes of SoCal, installed hydraulics in the car, and became very active in the lowrider scene. But it was the usual story of family, children, church, and work that led Steve to finally park the Merc in the garage 21 years ago.

What prompted him to get it back out was the hugely successful "Customs Then and Now" exhibit at the 2011 Grand National Roadster Show in Pomona, for which he got the very well-used Merc cleaned up and sprayed with a fresh persimmon basecoat by Tommy Brizuela of Ventura. I was pleasantly surprised to see it there. Now Steve is getting ready to pull and rebuild the engine as the next step in restoring this lost custom.

Here's the story. Steve's father, Blas, learned the bodywork trade back when it was done with lead and paddles. After seeing the *Hirohata* Merc at the L.A. Motorama, he decided he needed a custom like that, and built his own 1951 Merc very similar to Steve's, except it was 1956 Chevy Sierra Gold and didn't have the chopped top. It was the family car. Steve remembers riding in the back as a little boy, and seeing its picture in family albums. By the age of 12, Steve decided he wanted a car like that. Surprisingly, his dad spotted one sitting behind Jay Ohrberg's Mr. Roadster shop in North Hollywood, and bought it when Steve was 14. The roof had been cut and tacked by none other than Joe Bailon (they discovered later), but it needed a lot of work, which Blas and Steve began immediately.

First they added 1951 rear quarters with Lincoln taillights, and extended the front hood lip to look like the *Hirohata*. Blas also recut the roof to make it a hardtop with better flow at the back. All this was done with lead, paddles, and vixen files. The car had a tired 283, so they swapped in a 1971 350 and Muncie 4-speed. Steve was driving the car in primer with his learner's permit.

Greg Sharp said he was following this chopped Merc's progress because he's a custom nut, and he was still an LAPD "motor cop" at the time and Blas headed the LAPD "body shop." I was planning the chopped Merc issue of *Street Rodder*, but even in 1974 there were hardly any chopped Mercs to be found to photograph for the cover. Greg suggested this one, but I wasn't sure it could be finished in time. I didn't find out until now that Blas and Steve got all-fresh chrome

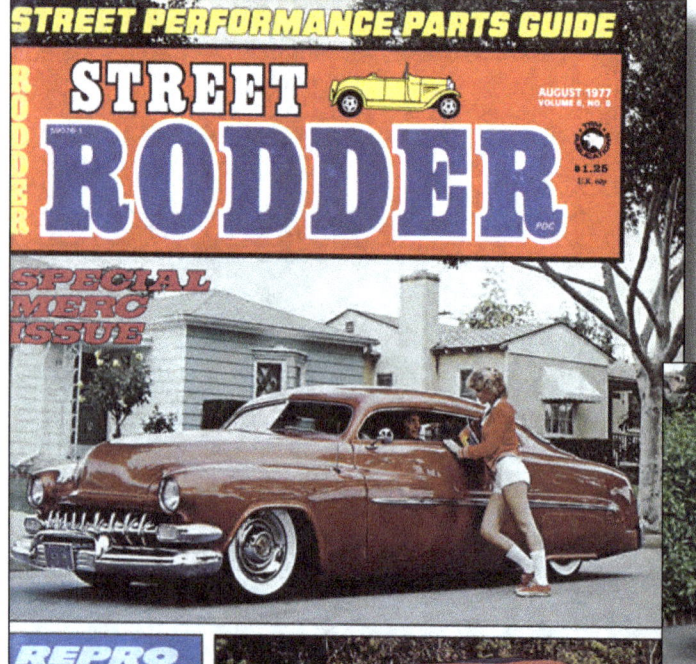

Left: I took this photo in front of the Gonzales home in Montebello, with Steve and his high-school girlfriend Sandy. **Above:** The headlights, hood lip, fender flares, and hardtop roofline were influenced by the *Hirohata* Merc, all done in lead by Steve's dad in the family garage. The side trim is 1955 Chevy.

Lost Hot Rods II

Top: It's a 1950 Merc with 1951 rear quarters, to which Blas added Lincoln taillights, like the Hirohata. **Bottom:** Steve finally got the Merc out of the garage and gave it a fresh persimmon basecoat for the big custom display at the 2011 GNRS show. Yes, this is Steve's first car—the one he drove to high school. There've been some miles, but both are in pretty good shape.

for the car done two days before I photographed it, and sprayed the acrylic lacquer and rubbed it out the day in between! It looked plenty good, as you can see in the early photos.

I also had no idea how much Steve drove this car. After joining the prestigious Dukes club in 1979, he got a job at *Lowrider* magazine as a show promoter and photographer. Over the next ten years Steve drove this Merc to Phoenix, Tucson, Albuquerque, San Antonio, Houston, El Paso, Denver, Las Vegas, and up and down the West Coast setting up, promoting, and photographing shows for the magazine. He has no idea how many miles are now on it. But there are plenty, especially for a car that was displayed and won trophies at several of these shows as well. It deserves the long rest it got. And it certainly deserves the full rebuild Steve is just beginning.

Top: Inside the trunk is a now-classic set of hydraulics all plumbed in hard line by Raul's in 1981. Bottom Left: Although worn by much use, the rust velour was stitched by Joe "Yoya" Ruiz of J&R in 1977 over a 1977 Cordoba front seat, wraparound 1965 T-Bird rear, and 1970 Riviera door panels. Bottom Right: This 350 Chevy has been ridden hard. The engine compartment was once buffed in black lacquer with plenty of chrome, and will be again soon.

Merc in Repose

How do I describe my longtime, good friend Ron Rothstein? I can't. Not in this space. In that same 1977 Special Merc Issue of *Street Rodder* that had Steve Gonzalez' car on the cover, we ran a three-page story on a club called the Mercs of SoCal, showing 20 of the members' 1949–1951 Mercurys lined up side by side. Only three were chopped, all of which were unpainted, and Ron's 1951 was one of them. That was 35 years ago, and Ron's 1951 is still unpainted. In fact, it looks nearly the same now as it did then, just with more patina. There's lots of patina at Ron's place.

I can't remember if it was before or after 1977 that Ron started sending me long, hand-written letters at *Street Rodder*. He obviously loved the custom cars, he was intelligent, he picked up on nuances many others missed, and he had what I like to call sardonic wit. We became pen pals. It wasn't until many years later that I finally met him in person, and visited his house in a section of L.A. appropriately called Palms. By then he had driven the Mercury many thousands of miles, and parked it on blocks on a covered patio behind his garage.

Top: Shortly after 1977 Ron sprayed the Merc in pastel primer, as seen here in the evening in front of his house. Decades later, Ron is grayer and the Merc has more patina, but not much else has changed. *Bottom:* Ron cut a back door in the two-car garage behind his house so he could store more cars behind it, such as his chopped Merc. He restored the small-block Ford-powered Healey, which looks good and runs well.

Chapter Eight: Missing Mercs   143

Top: I think Ron calls this Mercury preservation. It's a green thing. **Bottom:** Here's how I found it. Under the wraps is one nice, mildly chopped 1951 Merc, patiently awaiting a paint job or other rehabilitation.

His attention was then focused on three other vehicles; namely a yellow Austin Healy roadster with a 289 Ford engine he inherited from his dad, a well-patina'd 1952 Ford F-1 pickup with a twin-carb six that was his daily driver, and a somewhat rusty 1956 Chevy Bel Air hardtop that was his back-up driver. Also in the garage/yard were: his first-car, a Chevy-powered 1931 A sedan that he drove to Ohio and back as a teen; a complete 1949 Merc convertible (now mostly disassembled) he bought for $100; a 1939 Chevy four-door he's making into a lowrider bomb; and a 1951 Merc chassis with a hopped-up flathead that runs and drives.

Is Ron a hoarder? I don't think so. He works as a freelance mechanic, and often customers' cars come before his own. Plus he's slow and methodical. And he can't pass up a good deal on a good old car. He's never paid more than $500 for one, including this Merc.

He got it in 1973 when he was 20. It was parked at Sepulveda and Pico, and the guy wanted $500. Ron and a friend each put in $250, intending to flip it. But no one bought it for $850, so Ron bought his partner's half and kept the car. He called Barris to ask how much he would charge to chop it; George said $3,000. So Ron found Korky's Kustoms in Van Nuys in the phone book (Dick Korkes), who did it for $850. He found a set of Cadillac wire wheels for $20 each at Economy Auto Wrecking. With cut coils in front and blocks in back, that's how it looked in *Street Rodder* in 1977.

Many years, many miles, and three engines later, Ron somehow convinced metal master and Merc connoisseur Paul Bragg to redo the chop. So Ron took it to Bragg's huge home shop in Paso Robles, where he helped a little, but mostly watched as Paul cut and shaped the sheet metal, hammer-welded it together, and finished it in lead.

With the new roof in primer, Ron drove the Merc some more, picked up a good Cadillac OHV engine to put in it someday, collected other parts, and even got the front seat nicely upholstered. But then it got parked in 1997, and there it sits today, waiting its turn.

Obviously there's way more to tell—and show—about this car, Ron, and each of the vehicles in his yard. But I'll leave you with something Ron said just the other day: "I think if a car is lowered right, has a good wheel-and-tire combination, and runs reliably, that's all it really needs."

As many of you know, I personally like paint and chrome. But I also basically agree with what Ron says. As for this Merc, it's about time to get it back to the "runs reliably" part. Yes?

Top: The current Merc mill has finned heads and twin carbs on a three-pot intake, backed by a 3-speed overdrive transmission (as in all Ron's cars). It's ready to run. *Bottom Left:* The seat's upholstered, the dash is original, and the floors are good; it's pretty cherry. *Bottom Right:* This is the new chop by Paul Bragg. Ron figures the car needs no further customizing. The blue plate reads "Into It." Note the 1956 Chevy in the driveway.

Chapter Eight: Missing Mercs 145

Charlie Lopez' Merc

Do you remember there was a chopped Merc issue of *Street Rodder* before the one in 1977? It was the November 1974 issue, and that was a very long time ago. I'm not completely sure why we did it. I think it was mainly because Jerry Weesner had submitted drawings showing how to chop a 1950 Merc top, along with illustrations of four classic chopped Mercs (did you know Jerry was an illustrator?). I had been on the staff about a year, and was all for promoting custom cars. But there just weren't any customs around. *Rod & Custom* had died its second death six months earlier, but there hadn't been any customs in it for years.

I can't remember how I met Charlie Lopez, either. He was well known in the lowrider community of Orange County for doing custom bodywork and paint out of his garage in Midway City. I was just as much a fan of lowriders as I was of customs, and there were plenty of lowriders around then. I happened to know Charlie was building a chopped 1950 Merc, and had taken photos of its construction. The fact he had just finished it probably had something to do with the Merc issue. In fact, it was the only finished chopped Merc I could find anywhere in California to photograph at that time. The only other one in the issue was the *Graffiti* Merc, which I photographed on display at Universal Studios. That was it!

The connection between lowriders and custom cars is that most lowriders are custom cars, but not many custom cars are lowriders. You either get that or you don't. I seem to be one of the few people who truly likes both. But I didn't get any complaints about this car being on the cover of *Street Rodder* magazine. Apparently readers were as hungry as I was to see a chopped Merc again.

Charlie's Merc was named the *Nostalgia Sleeper*, but it was definitely a lowrider, complete with full hydraulic suspension. It was also strictly a show car, so Charlie kept rebuilding it every year, making it wilder to win more show trophies. Within a few seasons, he had cut out the roof for a full-length sunroof-type tinted Plexiglas panel, and he had changed the doors to hydraulically lifted gull wings. So it kept winning trophies and became pretty famous in the car show/lowrider world. It was featured in red-metalflake paint in *Lowrider* magazine in 1978. But by the 1980s I had lost track of Charlie, and the Merc disappeared, as do so many show cars after a few seasons.

Apparently Rogelio Cevallos who briefly published *Classic & Custom* magazine in San Jose got the car in the early 1980s and had it for some time. I've seen photos of it at the first West Coast Kustoms meet at Lake Nacimiento (pre–Paso Robles) in 1982. But the next time I saw the car was at one of the KKOA Spectaculars in Iowa (I think) many years later. I was surprised to see it in the Midwest. It might have still had the red 'flake paint, but whatever it was had weathered significantly and was peeling. I didn't meet or see the owner; I just saw it sitting there on the grass, looking pretty forlorn. Nobody was paying it much attention.

How it got to Lexington, Kentucky, is another mystery that even Barry Sexton, the guy who owned it, didn't know. I'm not sure how long Barry had it, but he didn't seem to know any of this Merc's history. The car looks as if it's had a few owners and a few paint jobs in the last couple decades. The significant amount of chroming Charlie had done on the car (including the entire frame) was all green. Yet what's surprising is how original and intact the car is today, given what it's been through.

In 1974 Street Rodder *magazine was two years old and an A&W root beer was 15 cents. And Charlie Lopez' lowrider was the only chopped Merc to be found.*

Conrad Garcia of Downey, California, happened to see an ad for it on the HAMB a couple years ago and immediately recognized it. A builder and collector of lowriders and rare classic Chevys today, he said Charlie's Merc made a strong impression on him when he was young. He considers it a significant and historic car. So he jumped at the chance to buy it, and drove to Kentucky with his truck and trailer to bring it home. Other than cleaning, he hasn't done much so far. But he says everything on it works, including the hydraulic suspension and doors, and most of the 1980s interior is surprisingly good. He plans a full restoration to the red metalflake version, which it deserves. So I can catalog this one as lost and found, and hopefully saved.

Top: Charlie chopped the roof himself and did all other work in his home garage including the silver 'flake paint. Murals were big in the 1970s—on everything. *Bottom:* The same stripes are still on the firewall. Charlie worked in a chrome shop too, so nearly everything on the car eventually got plated, including the whole frame.

Chapter Eight: Missing Mercs

Top: The Merc now sits in Conrad's shop with some rare Chevys and a couple other customs. It has a few bruises, but it's in surprisingly good shape after all these years and who knows what adventures. *Middle:* Even the full-length Plexiglas sunroof Charlie added in 1976 is in good shape. No telling how many paint jobs it's had. *Bottom:* This still-quite-red velour dates to 1978. Charlie chromed the whole dash when he first built the car.

Jimmy Doyle's Bailon 1952

The only thing Joe Bailon loved as much as spraying Candy Apple Red paint with gold scallops, was building chrome tube grilles. Some curved out, some curved in. This one does a bit of both. I can't say this semi-custom 1952 Mercury convertible he built for Jim Doyle of San Jose in 1959 is one of my favorite Bailon builds, but it did exactly what it was supposed to do. It created plenty of attention, got on several magazine covers, and won plenty of show trophies.

I should call these 1950s show cars "Meteors" because they burned so brightly and beautifully for such a short time and then—poof—they were gone. This one was featured in six magazines in 1959 alone, but by 1962 both it and Jimmy Doyle fell from sight. I know none of either's history until sometime in the mid to late 1970s when the car, sans top, interior, and paint, showed up parked on a levee in the Sacramento Delta with a For Sale sign attached. There was no house nearby. That's all I know.

Bruce Guy bought it because he was a Ford restorer/collector with about 200 cars, and he knew this was the rarest Ford Motor Company convertible model ever produced. He planned to restore it to stock.

But before that happened, he traded it to Trevor Thomas, who lived in the gold country near Placerville and had about 300 cars stored in turkey sheds (do they count as barns?). At some point in the 1980s Joe Bailon learned he had the car, and made a deal to restore or trade for it. It got sandblasted and primered, but that's as far as it got. It went back in Trevor's turkey shed in 1985. It had no engine, transmission, top, or seats, and all external trim and other parts were stuffed inside. Trevor's intention was to restore it to stock too, but he finally realized that wasn't going to happen.

Butch Gardner of nearby Shingle Springs is a well-known NorCal car show guy who built several cars including a chopped 1957 Merc and a chopped-and-sectioned 1955 F-100. Like Trevor and Bruce, he was another Ford guy, but he liked customs. One day in 1996 Trevor called Butch and said, "I've got a car you need." When he said what it was, Butch's initial reaction was, "Yes, it's a significant Bailon custom, but it's kinda ugly." However, he warmed to the idea, especially when Trevor said, "I don't want money. I want that gennie 1954 Ford two-door Mainliner you have." Butch agreed to trade straight across. He was pleasantly surprised when Trevor delivered not only the Doyle Merc, but also a four-door parts car plus a low-mile 351-C Ford engine and C6 transmission.

He started the restoration the day after Thanksgiving 1996 with the goal of making the 1998 Oakland Roadster Show, doing everything in the spacious, well-equipped garage/shop on his property. When he re-stripped the body, he was surprised to find all work from the doors forward done in lead, with all the rear done with plastic filler. Butch ended up making nine patch panels to fix rust he found under the plastic after chiseling it off. He also rebuilt the suspension using parts from the donor car, and installed the newer Ford engine and transmission (it had a Chevy previously). Then Paul Sheehy did the final bodywork, prep, and paint in 1996 Ford Mustang Laser Red, which looks very close to Bailon's original Candy Apple.

With new upholstery in white Naugahyde and red frieze to match the door panels that were still in the car, plus a new white top (by West Coast Customs in

Doyle's Merc got three photos on this cover, just one of six magazines in which it appeared in 1959 alone.

Chapter Eight: Missing Mercs   149

The background is almost as good as the custom car in this 1959 motel setting. Those are 1958 Chevy quad lights. Everything else on this front end was handmade by Joe in his inimitable style.

Above: Radiused rear wheel wells were typical of skirtless 1950s Bailon customs. The rear is formed of 1953 Studebaker front pans, with twin 1956 Packard taillights in the handmade fins. Candy-apple-red lacquer with gold scallops was Bailon's signature. *Right:* The car was in sad shape when found on a Sacramento levee in the 1970s. The sagging door panel was the only interior remnant left.

Placerville), Butch did display the car at the 1998 GNRS (held in San Francisco that rainy year), which is where I first saw it. Butch said he also showed it at Sacramento and Portland that year, drove it about 1,000 miles that summer, then had it in a special custom car exhibit at the Petersen Museum from 2001 to 2002.

That's the last I saw of it, because when he got it home he drained all the fluids and parked it in his spare garage, having other cars and projects to drive or work on. It took some sleuthing on my part to find this Meteor once again, plus some work to photograph it, because it didn't run and I couldn't push it up the steep driveway outside the garage.

But it is now fully drivable, and beautifully and accurately restored, right down to the 1958 Imperial wheelcovers with bullet centers. This is an original, well-known Bailon custom, not a clone. Whether you think it's ugly or beautiful, it's the only real 1950s-era Bailon car I can think of that exists in restored condition, other than the *Mystery* Ford now in the Oakland Museum. Butch figures he's done his part by saving this historic custom; he'd like to see it go to some museum as a tribute to Joe. Or you could buy it and restore it back to the rarest convertible the Ford Motor Company made.

Top Left: Butch's restoration is beautiful and accurate. New Mustang paint comes as close to candy red as you can get. *Top Right:* The restored interior even has red frieze to match the original. The car also has a new white top. *Bottom:* Given the "before" photo, you can appreciate how much work went into this restoration.

A Bit Different

By now you've probably figured out that I consider hot rodding a way of doing things, a mindset, even a culture—not merely a type of vehicle. It involves not accepting things the way they are, but wanting to customize things, personalize things, and make things better. It means not buying off the rack, and it usually means doing it yourself. Because it's a culture, and we're part of that culture, most of us have fairly stringent parameters for what's considered a rod or custom and what isn't. On one hand, I agree. On the other, I say you can hot rod just about anything.

Right in the pages of *Hot Rod* magazine we've seen everything: hot rodded sports cars, Indy cars, dune buggies, pickup trucks, boats, motorcycles, bicycles, go-karts—you name it. To really stretch it, I'd say you could even hot rod your house, your wardrobe, maybe your golf clubs or lawnmower. There's a fine line that determines what is hot rodding and what isn't, and it usually takes a true hot rodder to tell when it's crossed.

I wasn't sure what to call this chapter. "Oddballs" was on my outline for a long time. At least I kept this to vehicles, and ones with four wheels at that. A couple are unquestionably hot rods—have even been featured in rod magazines. But all are a bit different. "Diversity" is the current hip buzzword. Consider this the diversity chapter.

Chapter Nine

Chapter Nine: A Bit Different

The Barris *Bearcat*

My first example is the farthest stretch. Its owner considers it a hot rod. It's an old car. It's completely hand-crafted. It's modernized, using some traditional hot rod techniques. And it was built by Kustom Kar legend George Barris.

It's called the *Bearcat*. It was patterned closely after an original 1914 Stutz Bearcat, only 30 to 40 of which exist today, valued at up to a million dollars each. But this is one of two that were commissioned to be built by Barris for a short-lived TV series called *Bearcats!* that aired on CBS in the fall of 1971. The hour-long show starred Rod Taylor and Dennis Cole, who roamed the World War I–era West in a new 1914 Stutz Bearcat, seeking wrongs to right for clients such as banks, railroads, or governments in exchange for a blank check.

John Boyle, who now lives in the Spokane, Washington, area after a career in the Air Force, likens the show to "a cross between *Have Gun Will Travel* and *The A-Team*." He watched all 13 episodes that ran, which turned him on to brass-era autos and this one in particular (thinking it was a real Stutz, of course). Later he learned from an article in *TV Guide* that two near-identical movie cars had been built by Barris (plus one less-accurate, more-gaudy version he kept for personal promotion).

Due to his career and constant relocation, it wasn't until 1997 that Boyle contacted Barris to see if he knew anything of the TV *Bearcats*. George had no idea where any of the three were. John had also become involved in a Stutz Club. Through it he located a Stutz expert/restorer who said he had been contacted by one of the Barris *Bearcat* owners, looking to sell the car. But he lost the number. You know how it goes. A couple weeks later he called back with the number of an elderly Philadelphia attorney who was selling his car collection. John

Top: Did you ever see this on TV? That's Rod Taylor driving this Barris-built Bearcat *in the show of the same name that lasted 13 weeks on CBS in 1971. Bottom: This car, now lovingly restored by John Boyle, was one of two built from scratch in the Barris shops. John found it in a 30-car collection in Philadelphia, where it had been for ten years. A local restaurateur owned it for at least a decade before that.*

According to his research, John says an Italian craftsman named Andre De Stefanis, who previously worked for Gene Winfield, hand-built the all-steel body on a custom chassis as his first job in the Barris shop. Supposedly they had a real Stutz to copy, and this is a close duplicate, with a 120-inch wheelbase. However, the engine is a 223-ci pre-1964 Ford six. The rear end came from a 1965 Mustang. It had a Corvair steering box. The front axle looks like a narrowed 1950s Chevy pickup. And it had some actual hot rod parts such as Stewart-Warner gauges and a Moon aluminum fuel tank and gas pedal. John kept the Moon tank and small pedal, but replaced the non-working Stewart-Warner–gauges with new, more period-looking VDOs. The extensive

called the number, "Got photos of the Stutz, sent them to Barris for verification, got a reasonable quote on the car, and sent a check. I finally had the very car I saw on TV 30 years before. Now I had to work on it."

It turns out this was the first car built for the show, with a Ford pickup 4-speed transmission (the other one had an automatic). It was in good condition, but needed a few parts replaced plus a complete restoration (the paint was peeling). John admits he had no experience working on cars beyond high school auto shop, but his friend, Charlie, was game to help him. You can see the excellent results.

restoration required finding a wheelwright (in Oklahoma) to duplicate the cracked wooden wheels, and someone (in California) to rebuild the custom brass radiator, among several other things.

Whether you consider this custom-built car a hot rod or not, it was originally constructed to a much higher level of accuracy and detail than the typical prop car, to be sure. And John has rebuilt it to a higher level yet by "sweating the details," as he put it. Best of all, like any good hot rod, he can now take it out on weekends and drive it around so he, and everybody who sees it, can fully appreciate all the sweat he put into it.

Top: The wood dash had to be replaced, but all sheet metal is original. John added brass-rim VDO gauges. Check the small Moon gas pedal, Hurst-type shift knob, and angle-iron cowl-light brackets. John made the new, more accurate brake and clutch pedals. *Bottom Left:* The surprise under the hood is an early 1960s Ford inline six. Not only did it fit the car, but it was a strong, rugged engine that sounded right. *Bottom Right:* Under the back is a Mustang 8-inch rear, complete with drum brakes adapted to fit real wood-spoke wheels, which had to be remade.

Creighton's Mystery Bug

First, you have to understand that Volkswagens have been hot rodded and customized every way you can imagine—bugs, microbuses, dune buggies, dragsters, etc. I've seen them built as customs, lowriders, beach cruisers, hippie wagons, and classics. My favorite style, called the "Cal Look," takes its cues from hot rodding with big-n-little tires on chrome or mag wheels, radical front-end lowering, de-chroming, louvers, nerf bars, and dual-carb engines with custom exhaust. Unfortunately, such rodded VW Bugs have never been well accepted by the street rod contingent. I truly don't understand why. So, worldwide, they have their own magazines, associations, and events. If there were an all-time Top 100 of rodded/customized Volkswagens, the one shown here should be at least in the Top 5. Most VW fanatics know this car. They just don't know much about it—when or where it was built, who built it, or what became of it.

Second, although I've been intrigued with this chopped and channeled 1955 Bug ever since I first saw its single photo in *Rod & Custom* in 1967, I'm not the one who tracked it down, located the owner/builder, and actually found the car. That kudo goes to Burly Burlile, a longtime VW fan from Mendon, Utah. He found Creighton Muller at his large Lakewood Auto Body establishment in the Tacoma, Washington, area, and went there to see and photograph the car recently. Creighton is the one who found it about 12 years ago.

For most, this story begins with a single, small, black-and-white photo of this chopped, black, lowered VW sedan in the "Roddin' at Random" section of the March 1967 *Rod & Custom*. The caption stated only that the picture was taken at some show, by someone, long ago. No further clues. Two months later a reader from San Francisco sent in four photos taken at the same show, stating it was built by Creighton Customs in San Diego years ago, and that it was chopped 6 inches, channeled 4 inches, and sectioned 3 inches. It had 1956 Olds headlights, 1948 Pontiac taillights, 1955 Dodge side trim, Jaguar seats, a dash full of Stewart-Warner gauges, and push-button doors, hood, and deck. Most of this was basically accurate. You could also see the handmade nerf bars and louvers in the bonnet, liberally drilled custom wheels, right-hand drive, and lots of black tuck-and-roll inside. But that was it. This amazing Bug was never seen or mentioned again.

Here's a brief synopsis of what I have learned about this car, so far. Hopefully Burly's full story will get printed in *Hot VWs* magazine. It deserves it.

Creighton Muller got into rods and customs in San Diego by 1949 or 1950, hung around Stylers Custom Shop to see what they did, and taught himself to hammer and weld. By 1952 he was gaining a reputation for chopping tops, working out of his parents' garage. In fact he became known as the kid who would chop anything for a couple hundred bucks, but he preferred

Left: *Although taken ten years earlier, this completely unidentified small photo in the "Roddin'" section of the March 1967* Rod & Custom, *was the first anyone saw of this amazing chopped and sectioned 1955 Volkswagen. Many have been chopped since, but none as proportionally as this.* **Right:** *Two months later, a reader sent in four more photos of the mystery Volkswagen, including this tuck-and-rolled interior with lots of Stewart-Warner gauges, drilled pedals, and right-hand drive. Still no date or I.D. other than "Creighton Customs," and no mention of the likely first-ever hydraulic suspension.*

Lost Hot Rods II

to be known as "Custom by Creighton." What he really wanted to build for himself was a chopped and channeled 1934 Ford three-window coupe, but all he could find were rust-buckets.

Then he saw one of the new Volkswagens first imported in 1955, which didn't look all that different from early Ford coupes, but had all brand-new sheet metal for $1,800. So he bought one. And immediately started cutting it up. First he channeled the body (and floor) 3½ inches over the chassis (or pan) to get it low. Then he noticed this European car had bosses for steering on the right side, and said he decided to move it over there "just for fun." Then he made his own wheels using the VW centers with 13-inch rims in front (15 in back) to get it lower, but the 1½-inch road clearance wasn't practical.

The aircraft industry was big in San Diego, with lots of surplus stores. Creighton hooked up a pair of hydraulic wing-flap struts in place of the shocks in his front suspension, with a 24V aircraft pump. He said on six volts it was slow, but worked well enough to keep from getting tickets. He drove the car that way to Bonneville in 1956 (this being, I believe, the first-known hydraulic suspension).

In early 1957 he chopped the top 3 inches (the car apparently wasn't sectioned), and finished other custom work. With custom-made manifolds to mount two Solex carbs on the engine and an Isky cam and bigger Jahns pistons, he finally painted the car black lacquer and had the interior done by Kizer's over Jaguar seats. In this form he entered the car in shows in San Diego and San Bernardino, but it received little attention, both because it was a foreign car, and it was black.

Then, Creighton says, he got drafted into the army for the first time in early 1958. Ultimately spending nine years in the service, he sold the Volkswagen to Bruce Crower (who wanted to run it at Bonneville) in 1959. But Bruce was getting a divorce, and sold the Volkswagen to Bob Garcia, his clutch guy, who spent a lot of time traveling the country helping dragster guys tune their Crower clutches. Bob removed the engine to use in something else, and took the car apart, removing the seats and stashing the fenders, doors, and other parts inside. It sat like that, outside, at some relatives' body shop in San Diego (National City) for at least 30 years.

Meanwhile, Creighton's army travels took him to Tacoma, Washington, where he opened his first body shop in 1962. Obviously a talented and motivated guy, the shop grew to the point that he eventually opened two more. Today, at age 77, Creighton divides his time between his three large collision repair shops in the Tacoma area and his three homes in Hawaii. He has a modest collection of cars including a chopped 1950 Merc custom, a couple T rods, and a Gull-Wing Mercedes, to name a few.

However, he always wondered about that first chopped Volkswagen from 1955, and asked friends he knew in San Diego to be on the lookout for it. One of his buddies from Chula Vista made a concerted effort, and finally found Bob Garcia, who not only still had the car sitting outside a shop, but even had the pink slip. Creighton bought it back in 2000, and spent a year rebuilding it, giving it a few updates such as a newer IRS transaxle and 2,180-cc engine with dual Weber carbs. Having been told by a couple of magazines in the past that black cars don't get on covers, this time he decided to paint it bright candy red with candy-blue flames.

Ironically, however, this didn't work either, since at least one VW magazine told Creighton, "We're not into hot rod Bugs now. We want the kind with all the aftermarket accessories on them." Creighton's not into roof racks and mud flaps, so he says the car has basically sat at his shop for the past ten years. He'd be interested in selling it for a decent price. Personally, I'd love to see this historic, classic, custom Volkswagen get the recognition it deserves.

While Creighton was growing his body-shop business in Washington, his Bug was sitting outside a much smaller body shop in National City. This is how it looked when he got it back 30 years later.

Chapter Nine: A Bit Different

Top: Creighton's business is rebuilding wrecks, so it only took a year to redo his 1955 Bug, making a few modernizations such as a newer driveline, which required slightly widened rear fenders—still with the same 1948 Pontiac taillights.
Bottom: The nerf bars weren't back on yet, but it has the same louvered bonnet, upside-down 1955 Olds headlights, Dodge side trim, and drilled wheels. Creighton wasn't going to paint it black this time though.

Lil' John's Corvette

Once again, this is a car that could go in more than one chapter of this book. It qualifies for the "Yellow Pages" since it was featured in the July 1983 issue of *Hot Rod*. It could also go in the "Race Cars" chapter since it spent most of its life on drag strips. It ran very close to 200 mph at El Mirage, and competed at Bonneville in 1981, 1985, and 1987 (and still has the inspection stickers in the window to prove it). So why is it here in the "Oddball" chapter?

When John Harvey of Los Lunas, New Mexico, first saw this 1958 Corvette in the 1970s, it was racing at Famoso dragstrip near Bakersfield with a fuel-injected Boss 429 Ford hemi engine(!). The car was gutted—no dash, no interior except a bucket seat and roll bar, a tube axle in front, cut-out rear wheel wells, and coil springs with ladder bars in back. It was a race car, not a candidate for restoration. When John bought it in 1978, even the Ford engine was gone, so he dropped in a big-block, bracket-race-style Chevy engine and continued to drag race it.

However, the car was white and John is a custom painter. So it soon got prepped for one of Lil' John's candy jobs in Brandywine, Tangerine, and Pagan Gold. At the same time he scored a Hilborn-injected, 488-inch, late-Chrysler Hemi that had been machined by Keith Black, and had all the good stuff like a Moldex crank and an Isky roller cam. John installed it with a beefed Torqueflite and polished tin paneling in the now-good-looking (and running) race car. I photographed it for *Hot Rod* in June 1981; they ran it two years later. Why does it have a woman in a bikini standing next to it? Umm . . . it was something *Hot Rod* was doing then. What can I say?

After a stint painting cars for Reggie Jackson in SoCal, John moved himself, his paint shop, and his various cars to New Mexico, south of Albuquerque. Since it was pretty far to a dry lake or any drag strip, John decided to completely rebuild the old warhorse Corvette into a stout, very candy-red street machine. John didn't want to completely erase the car's race heritage, so he retained the roll bars, the tube front axle, and most of the suspension. But he added a dash, upholstery, cooling system, street fuel tank, exhaust system, and so on. After restoration of the abused 'glass body, he sprayed it a brilliant candy red with white coves. For an engine, he went back to a nicely detailed big-block Chevy, this time topped with a 6-71 blower and twin 4-barrels.

John had just finished it in 2005 when I went to Los Lunas to photograph him painting a different red Corvette for my book *How to Paint your Car on a Budget* (CarTech Books). In fact that's John and the Marlboro Maroon 1967 Stingray on the cover.

While I was there, John said, "Why not photograph the 1958 and see if we can get it in *Hot Rod* again?" Sounded good to me, so I did. But when I sent the photos to *Hot Rod*, they said, "Oh no. It's got big tires sticking out of the back and a blower sticking out of the hood and it sits funny. We don't do that anymore. It needs to look like a race car. A road race car. You know, Pro Touring. Try the Corvette magazines." So I sent the photos to two or three of the Corvette magazines, stressing the car's rich racing heritage and how it had been "saved" and returned to the street. They were aghast. They said this poor 1958 Corvette had been mutilated, ruined.

So that's why it's lost. It can't find a home. You're the first to see it in print, in its new street form, here in the "Oddball" chapter of this book. I don't know about you, but I think it's a hot rod, with or without a woman in a bikini.

Despite being gutted for racing, with a tube axle in front and no interior, the 1958 'Vette didn't look too bad when John got it. This is with a big-block Chevy he first installed for brackets.

Chapter Nine: A Bit Different

Top Left: For the next racing version in 1981, John sprayed the car with three shades of candy. The slicks on Cragars were for the drags, where it turned 9.85 at 146 mph. For lakes runs, it had tall Indy tires and a chute. **Top Right:** The Hillborn-injected Hemi was strictly a racer with a 1/2-inch stroker, Isky roller, and all the good parts. It ran 196 on a 200-mph record at Bonneville. **Bottom:** Nope, this is no Pro Tourer. We used to call this a hot rod.

Top Left: The new Rat motor is plenty stout, but it doesn't have to prove anything on the track. That's been done. This one's for street, and purely for fun. *Top Right:* John had to add things like a passenger seat, a dashboard, a steering column, and a bit of upholstery to make this old race car streetable. *Bottom:* John's specialty is custom bodywork and paint, which is evident in the brilliant candy red on this very smooth 1958 Corvette.

Marlan's 'Vette

This is the car that's never been seen. That should qualify it as lost. And since it's a significantly modified L-89 1969 Corvette (originally a Tri-Power, big-block, 4-speed car) owned by the longest-tenured staff-member of *Hot Rod* magazine, I say it qualifies as a hot rod.

If you've read *Hot Rod* magazine anytime in the past 35 years, you should know the name Marlan Davis. He's been the technical editor there as long as I can remember. It's a position for which he is eminently qualified and does an exemplary job. He can spout GM part numbers, aftermarket cam specs, and all the gear ratios used in Muncie 4-speeds from memory. Besides his in-depth tech stories, for decades he's been the guy who finds answers to readers' off-the-wall questions in his "Pit Stop" column in the back of the magazine, and he very rarely makes a mistake. To call Marlan a gearhead is a gross understatement to which he'd probably take exception.

Marlan was already a fixture on the *Hot Rod* masthead when I arrived there in 1983. He started working at Petersen Publishing as some sort of gopher in 1976 because he happened to live in the same neighborhood as Dick Day, by then a company V.P.

But Marlan had gotten "the Corvette" even before that. He was still a teenage box boy at Hughes Market in the Valley when he saved up enough nickels and dimes to buy this coveted big-block, 4-speed, T-Top 'Vette for $4,000 in 1974. And like any teenager with this kind of car, it didn't take him long to blow the first engine. He says it ate a timing chain.

He went through two more. But by 1979, being on the *Hot Rod* staff by then and being tutored by C. J. Baker (his predecessor as tech editor and a GM big-block expert), Marlan bought a 12.5:1 L-88 427 crate motor to put in it. But first he wanted to rebuild the brand-new engine to his own specs. The Corvette has never run since.

It's not because Marlan couldn't build the engine. With C. J.'s guidance, he had it bored .060 over, lowered compression to 10.4:1, and installed a Crane roller cam and rockers. He had Ken Sperling at Air Flow Research port a set of L-88 aluminum heads for it, got Doug Thorley to build custom headers, and topped it with a modified Holley 850 double pumper on an Edelbrock C-454 high-rise intake. To everybody's surprise but Marlan's, it pulled 578 hp at 6,800 rpm on 92-octane pump gas on the dyno. That's the engine in the car now.

I think it was in the car when I met Marlan. But then he was swapping out the Muncie for a Doug Nash 5-speed. Then he was getting the rear end blueprinted by Tom's Differentials. Then he was adding genuine GM fender flares so he could install road race tires on Jongbloed three-piece wheels, after installing a complete, adjustable Guldstrand suspension. I heard a lot about this Corvette, but I never saw it.

Left: *This is most of Marlan's Corvette. He has all the pieces, somewhere. If it had a radiator, it could probably start and run.* **Right:** *Given the kind of power numbers the magazine touts from test engines these days, 578 hp from a 430-incher sounds almost tame. But when Marlan built this one, himself, in the early 1980s, it was impressive. It's dyno'd and ready to go, one of these days.*

I'm not really sure what stage of assembly or disassembly it was in when I met him. But the latest thing then was aircraft plumbing. Marlan became obsessed with braided-steel hose, hard line, and AN anodized-aluminum fittings in perfectly memorized dash sizes. It was his goal to replace every fluid line on the 'Vette—from radiator hoses to the vacuum lines that opened the headlights—to certified aircraft AN lines and fittings. To Marlan, using a rubber hose or screw clamp on a performance automobile was something worse than a mortal sin.

Another thing that set back the car's construction about that time was the Sylmar earthquake in the Valley. Since Marlan lived in an apartment without a proper garage, he kept the 'Vette at his dad's house, which wasn't far from the epicenter. I think he'd just had the car painted red, and I know it was on jack stands when the quake hit. Not only did it throw the Corvette on the ground, but it knocked his dad's house off its foundation. So the car sat while the house got rebuilt. Then, the car got repainted red by Rob Spoon. Of course, to paint it, Marlan disassembled it further.

Marlan's Corvette has become the ultimate "garage car." Of course I've kept in touch with Marlan over the years since I left *Hot Rod*. I often inquired about the Corvette, and got vague answers. But not too long ago Marlan moved to a house way out in the high desert north of L.A., and I knew he built a big, multi-car garage to go with it. I knew he'd moved the Corvette there, and that it was, at least, intact. So I figured this book was a good excuse to finally go see the lost rod I'd heard about for 30 years. It is there, painted, and on wheels. It's ready to run. It has AN lines and fittings everywhere. But there's still a little bit of work to be done. Well . . . quite a lot of work.

Top Left: How many AN fittings can you count in this photo? The car even has braided-steel aircraft radiator hoses. Marlan prefers anodizing and cad plating to chrome. Check the safety-wired manifold bolts. The suspension is by Guldstrand. *Top Right:* I'm not sure if this is a wiper motor or vacuum pump—maybe both. Note that aircraft hoses still need to be attached to several AN bulkhead fittings. *Bottom:* Those fender flares came with a GM part number, believe it or not. It has a way to go, but at least it's now in reassembly mode, I think.

Chapter Nine: A Bit Different

Low-Buck C-Cab

When I first started working at *Street Rodder* magazine in the early 1970s, I could look out my office window and see, way across a large vacant field, a little old house fronting on Orangethorpe Avenue, with an even older red barn behind it. I didn't know who lived there, but I could see a red 1956 Ford ramp truck going in and out of the dirt drive leading back to the barn, often carrying things like a beat-up 1957 Chevy race car or dilapidated hot rods. When I saw it towing in a derelict, black 1929 roadster on Deuce rails with a V-windshield, I had to go over and investigate.

I looked like a young long-haired hippie, and the guy in the barn was a redneck trucker with a buzz cut. He looked at me warily, but when I told him who I was and where I worked, he became downright friendly. He said his name was Dave Williams, and that he'd just turned the barn into a rod-building shop. The 1929 roadster was one of the original Knight Riders from Fullerton with a Duke Hallock windshield that he was going to rebuild for a customer. I was obviously quite interested.

Then he pointed to a pencil drawing on a sheet of loose-leaf paper tacked to the wall. On it was drawn the profile of a 1920s-era C-Cab stake bed truck. He said, "I'm going to build that next." Little did I know then that Dave would become one of my best friends, and that, yes, he built that truck. Using little more than an ancient arc welder and several hand-made metalworking tools, I watched him build the entire thing, by himself, from the ground up, in less than a year.

His retired dad came over and helped him sand the tongue-and-groove ash wood he used to build the cab and bed, but that was it. About the only parts on the truck he didn't make himself were the brass headlights and the non-functional T radiator on the front, plus the drive-line (though he modified a lot of parts on that). He even sprayed the Ferrari Red paint right in the barn, before he had someone add old-time gold-leaf striping and lettering.

At that point he was calling his new business Custom Metal Fabrication, with the C-Cab as a calling card. Two years later he realized that selling inexpensive metalworking tools mail-order, like the ones he made for himself, could be more practical, and Low Buck Tools was born.

Remember, this was the early 1970s. T-Buckets were prevalent, Resto-Rods were in, and C-Cab trucks were considered extra cool. Dave's was not only completely hand-built, but with plenty of paint, chrome, varnish, and gold leaf, it was significantly nicer than most. I didn't have to argue much with the powers at *Street Rodder* to let me photograph it for the June 1975 cover. Two months later Gray Baskerville photographed it for *Hot Rod*.

Left: Other than the brass headlights and radiator, Dave Williams hand-built everything you see on this fictitious C-Cab truck. **Right:** Having been a big-rig owner/operator previously, he incorporated a few early Kenworth parts such as the air cleaner. Dave punched his own louvers on an old Betz press.

Lost Hot Rods II

But after getting the magazine exposure, and one or two show trophies, Dave started using this truck as a truck. He hauled parts on it. He got rid of the 1956 Ford, built a car trailer, and used it to tow projects in and out of the shop, as well as his wife's Chevelle stock car to the track. That's the way Dave is with all his projects. He loves the building part the best; he finishes them beautifully and then he drives the wheels off them. "Rebuild" is not part of his vocabulary. He'd rather start the next fun project.

So he drove this C-Cab about 150,000 miles over ten years or so. Then he parked it in the corner of a big garage on his property. I think one of the U-joints in the 'Vette rear went out. Nothing major, but not something Dave wanted to fix. I forget what the new project was. But the C-Cab sat there for several more years as the tires went flat. Then somebody called out of the blue, wanting to know if Dave still had that old truck. He always loved it, and could he buy it? Dave said, "Sure," and charged him way less than he should have. That was maybe ten years ago now. The guy took the truck home, put it in his own large storage garage, took a bunch of parts off it, and then let it sit until the tires went flat again.

Then somebody else called wanting to know if the old truck was still around. Dave said he knew where it was, and that the guy would probably sell. So when Dave took him over to see it, I tagged along to take some pictures. At least the guy pumped the tires up. But he didn't even blow any of the dust off. The prospective buyer said, "No thanks," so there it sits.

Top: Dave parked the truck about 25 years ago, figuring it had served its purpose. Fortunately it's been inside all that time, and is in surprisingly good shape. The new owner removed the parts you see in the foreground; that's all he's done. *Bottom Left:* The engine is a late 1960s GM 292 six, with a TH-400 transmission. Dave fabbed the 180-degree tube headers and the unusual "updraft" intake that worked quite well. *Bottom Right:* You can see Dave's workmanship in the brackets and linkages to mount the Corvette IRS. It also has Corvette four-wheel disc brakes. Not bad for a mid-1970s shop truck.

Collectors

In the first book, I made a point of not including cars, regardless of how lost or important they were, if they were sequestered in someone's private car collection where people couldn't see and appreciate them. There are probably more of these collections than you can imagine, and that's where far too many rods and customs go when they get lost. This time, however, I asked a couple of enthusiastic car collectors if they'd be willing to let people visit their collections, and they said, "Sure!" In a couple other cases, it wasn't feasible to arrange for public viewing, but the cars in question are taken out and driven often enough that your chances of seeing them at some rod run, show, or public museum are pretty good.

Chapter Ten

Chapter Ten: Collectors

Dick Martin's Deuce

This is one of the most amazingly preserved original 1950s hot rods you will probably ever see. I'm not talking about a car that was a beater in the 1950s, and is still a beater. I mean it's a show-quality, black lacquer, white tuck-and-rolled, fully chromed, early Olds-powered, chopped 1932 Ford five-window coupe that looks almost exactly the same now as it did when first finished in 1955.

Why is it in this book? Well, this perfect Deuce wasn't so much lost, as it was never found. It wasn't on the cover of a magazine, it won no big show trophies, and it was never even *in* any magazine (as far as I know) until I first saw it in 1975. That's when it showed up at the first street-rod drag meet at Irwindale Raceway, driven by young Arley Myers and his wife. It was sort of out of context because it didn't come to race, and I'm not sure how many others there really noticed it, but it knocked me over.

Arley had spent some time polishing it, but this car was perfect, from its dropped headlight bar and filled grille shell to its Pontiac taillights and fully chromed rear axle. The black lacquer paint and the white upholstery looked brand new. Even the undersides of the fenders were polished black, if I remember correctly, and the whitewall tires were 18 years old. It was a total time warp. In fact, that's what I titled it when I featured it in the March 1976 issue of *Street Rodder*. According to the story, Arley's unnamed uncle bought the car 18 years earlier, apparently chromed the rear-end components, but otherwise stored it in his garage, unused and unshown.

Arley's uncle bought the car from Dick Martin in 1958, and that's how I knew who built it. Martin was from Inglewood, California, and I knew Neal East had a similar Deuce coupe in that area about that time. Neil said he knew the car; it was one of the nicest around, and he had seen it locally, but didn't really know the owner.

Well, I was quite surprised to learn just recently that Dick Martin is not only still around, but retired on a 10-acre horse ranch where he keeps his current 1932 five-window, 1956 F-100, and 1939 Cabriolet, among others.

I assume the tires are new, but everything else you see in this photo, other than the rearview mirror, is original to 1955. Dick Martin sprayed the black lacquer in 1954. He got the idea for the strips on the running boards from his wife's MG.

lacquer himself in 1954, and then had Jack's Top Shop add the white upholstery.

Dick even had photos of the car, in primer, and then beautifully finished in 1955. But, to be honest, it looks exactly the same today. Dick said he entered it in the 1958 L.A. Motorama show, but sold it immediately afterward (for $1,800) because his father told him he had to quit hot rodding if he wanted to join (and inherit) the family's lucrative construction business. He's glad he did.

After Arley Myers got the car out of its 18-year slumber, I saw it at lots of SoCal rod runs for a couple years, then—poof—it was gone again. Apparently some 1932 collector saw it and had to have it. Then it went to another collector, and another. After a few more years it popped up at SoCal rod gatherings, such as the Outriders picnics, driven by the affable Jack Underwood of Costa Mesa, who had traded a 1932 roadster for it.

He told how he built this 1932 from a stocker he bought in the early 1950s for $25. He swapped the body for a chopped three-window he already had (with a chromed dropped front axle) because he liked the five-window better. He said Harry Jones of L.A. (who did the Pierson coupe) chopped the top 2½ inches, and Harvey Goldberg (who worked at Howard's) helped him build the 303 Olds bored out to 338 inches. He said he painted the black

Jack's not one for cleaning and polishing hot rods, but he kept this one in pretty good condition—considering he drove it whenever he felt like it—during the 14 years that he had it. But Jack said he finally tired of maintaining it, since he didn't build it himself, and he

Top: The chrome on the "W" headers, made by Al Barnes at Howard's, is faded, but otherwise the bored Olds, running a Howard's cam, is the same. Dick said he used adapters to mount four 2s on the dual-four intake because he knew how to tune 97s, but not the "new" 4-barrels. *Bottom Left:* Jack's Top Shop did a whole lot of rod and custom interiors in the 1950s, including this one in 1955. From 1950 Ford door handles, to 1940 column shift, to mid-1950s Stewart-Warner gauges, this is all original. *Bottom Right:* The chrome may be showing its age, but there's plenty of it, including the Houdaille shock, fender brace, and bumper bracket.

Chapter Ten: Collectors

that's what it needs). And he shows his cars frequently around the country, so others can enjoy them. This coupe was in the NHRA Museum in Pomona when I photographed it, and it should still be there when you read this. Further, he unhesitatingly agreed to let anyone visit his collection, housed in a large old red brick building in downtown Madison, if you make an appointment ahead of time (email him at RVMClassics@gmail.com and leave a phone number where he can reach you).

needed space in his garage, so he sold it to racer/collector Jim Busby about ten years ago. It again made the rounds of West Coast collectors, stopping at Don Orosco's for a bit, before current owner and caretaker Richard Munz, of Madison, Wisconsin, finally acquired it.

This is good news for a number of reasons. Richard really loves and appreciates hot rods with history. Once he adds one to his significant collection, it usually stays there (being preserved, or getting restored if

The 30-some car collection is mostly rods, including such icons as the Tommy Foster, Neal East, and Chuck Price 1932 roadsters, the Bill Breece and Hart/McCandless 1932 coupes, to more recent cars such as two by Don Thelen and two by Roy Brizio. His latest project is a full restoration of the Chuck Porter 1950 Ford F-1 pickup (seen in the first *Lost Hot Rods*). Plus his collection was a scheduled stopping point on the road tour to the 2012 Goodguys Indy event. If you go to Madison to see his neat stuff, tell Richard thanks for sharing.

Top: Dick said someone after him chromed the rear end, including the torque tube and wishbone. A little polishing and this underside would be in show condition again. **Bottom:** The running boards are handmade from sheet metal. Note the chrome fender welt. It's all as it was in 1955.

Dave Dias' Pickup

Early in my infatuation with hot rods, one style I really loved was the 1928–1929 Model A roadster pickup. There seemed to be a spate of them clustered around the San Francisco Bay Area that turned up in magazines around that time (1960, give or take, and magazines were the only way I'd see them then). Most were black, all were full-fendered, and they all had shortened beds. Two of my all-time favorites are right here in this chapter. I built models of them. I'd probably have built a real one, except there's no way I could fit in its small cab.

But what was it about the Bay Area and Model A roadster pickups? It wasn't until recently that this question occurred to me, and I figured out a plausible answer. The greater San Francisco/Sacramento area, which has always been a hotbed of hot rodding, is at the northern end of the San Joaquin Valley of Central California, which is still one of the most fertile and active agricultural areas in the United States. There were lots more farms than cities there.

And if you have a farm, you have at least one farm truck. And since this was the warm—usually hot—central valley of California, a lot of those farmers bought roadster pickups; way more than farmers in other parts of the country. Los Angeles was just as warm, but more citified, so people there bought roadster cars instead of pickups, for the most part. And why Model A roadster pickups? Because Ford quit making them pretty much by 1932. A few of these roadster pickup rods used 1927 T bodies mounted on an A chassis with A fenders and beds, but nobody wanted to build a hot rod on a T frame by the 1950s.

Dave Dias of Concord, California, went a little further than most in reshaping his 1928. First he Z-cut and kicked up the rear of the 1928 frame 5½ inches to get the rear to sit low. Then he moved the body back about 6 inches to make room for the big 1949 Cadillac V-8 he punched out to 342 ci. Being a sheet-metal worker, he then made a longer three-piece, louvered hood. And behind the body he shortened the pickup bed to a mere

You really need to see this pickup in profile to appreciate how Dias rearranged it. He also usually ran it with the top off. Plus it always had "wide-5" 1939 wheels, without hubcaps (like track roadsters) when he owned it. But here it is outside at Pleasanton, shortly after Joe Rogers finished the restoration.

Chapter Ten: Collectors 171

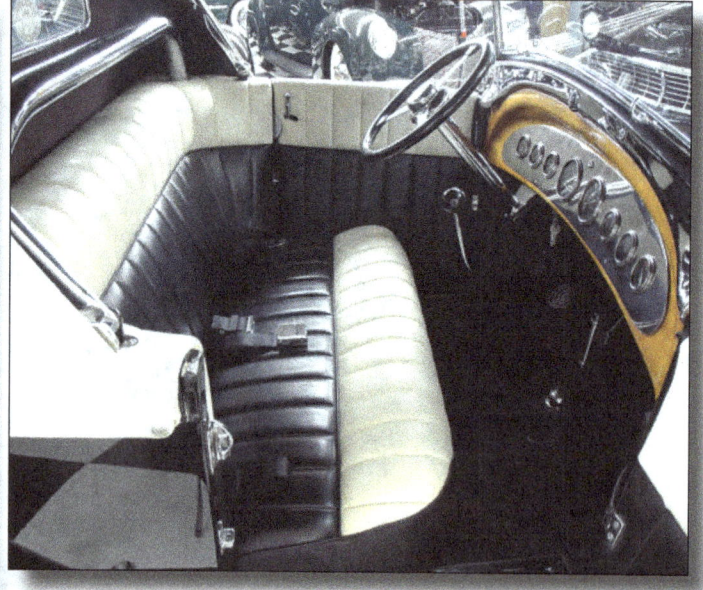

Top: It happened to be pouring rain the day I took these photos, so I had to do it inside where John Mumford keeps part of his growing collection. Other than the wheels, everything you see here is restored as it was in 1962. **Bottom Left:** Dias moved the gas tank under the bed and added a chrome firewall. Moving the body back allowed plenty of room for the Cadillac V-8, including a stock fan. Even the carbs are chromed. **Bottom Right:** Dias also carved the wood dash and added eight Stewart-Warner gauges. The short roll bar is original. Sid Chavers duplicated the upholstery. Note the three-spoke Bell wheel.

3 feet. Finally, he added sleeker 1931 fenders, bobbing the rears several inches to match the bed, and adding a sheet-metal apron between them. With the A windshield chopped a healthy 4 inches and a short, chromed roll bar just peeking above the back of the cab, this all combined to give this black roadster pickup a look somewhere between a 1940s sports car and a dirt track racer. Dias' choice of wide-5 1939 Ford wheels, as well as white upholstery rolled over the cab's edges, added to the track roadster image.

But then lots of chrome, plenty of white upholstery, nicely finished wood in the bed and on the dash, and details like roll-out tool trays mounted under the raised bed wood, dispelled any thoughts of actual racing on dirt. Yet, to be honest, I don't know much more about Dave Dias and his excellent roadster pickup than what I read in those magazines (April 1962 *Hot Rod*, specifically).

Apparently it never left the area and never got changed, because the first time I saw it in person was at the 1993 Oakland Roadster Show. Rodder Joe Rogers of Brentwood (just east of Concord) had acquired it, and had Roy Brizio completely restore it. It was repainted, replated, and reupholstered exactly as it was to start. The Cadillac engine was rebuilt but kept the same. Other than a few steering components, the only visible change to the truck was a set of red-painted steel 15-inch wheels with early Ford caps and rings on 1940 brake drums in place of the black 1939 wide-5s.

So why is it in this chapter? After showing it and driving it to a few local events, Rogers didn't use it much, and finally called Roy asking, "Know anyone who might want to buy the pickup?" This was about ten years ago, when John Mumford was not only beginning his exquisite rod and custom collection (*Ala Kart*, the Sam Barris Merc, etc.) but was moving it into the other half and upper floor of the large building Brizio's Rod Shop occupies in South San Francisco. John immediately bought this significant roadster pickup and added it to his collection, where I photographed it recently. Unfortunately, John's collection is not open to the public. Fortunately, however, this one is among his drivers, and he keeps it near the door and uses it fairly often. If you visit Brizio's during Roy's annual open house on Mother's Day weekend, you just might see it.

The red and white striping is Tommy the Greek style. You can see a hint of the chromed rear end. Dias bobbed the 1931 rear fenders to match the much-shortened bed.

The Marasco/Sharp Pickup

Dave Marasco is a consummate machinist by trade, and a woodworker by choice. He has a large, well-outfitted shop for each behind his house in Carmel Valley, California. These are good talents to have if you're going to build a hot rod pickup.

Dave lived in nearby Salinas when he began cultivating these talents and became excited about hot rods. The first one he built was a 1929 Model A coupe, sometime before 1962. Salinas was also home to photographer/pinstriper Andy Southard, who had just joined a prestigious new club called the Bay Area Roadsters (BAR), and Dave wanted to be a member, too. Dick Mendonca, another BAR member who happened to be a photographer and who drove another of these black, full-fendered, short-bed 1929 roadster pickups, happened to have an extra parts-car pickup that was basically his leftovers.

Dave bought the body and bed to swap onto his completed chassis in place of the coupe body. To say that he had to do some work on this cast-off sheet metal before he painted it black lacquer is an understatement—but something Dave does very well. Like so many similar roadster pickups, including Ray Silva's that shared the April 1963 *Rod & Custom* cover with Dave's, he shortened the bed (12 inches) and moved the body back (4 inches) to get the right look.

I forgot to mention the louvers in the splash aprons, another thing I love about these pickups. Using the 1932 grille and tri-power 265-ci V-8 already in the 1929, Dave routed new wood for the bed (as he did for Silva's), then built a signature wood luggage rack for it.

Before photographing Marasco's and Silva's trucks, Southard pulled a whole lot of red and white pinstripes on Dave's. At that time his pickup rode on chrome wheels that Dave said he drilled with holes "for detail." Shortly afterward he had Joe Wilhelm fabricate a horizontal-bar grille to fit the 1932 shell, like Silva's.

In Chapter Three I introduced Greg Sharp and his yellow 1941 Ford pickup (not that he needs any introduction to most rod fans). Greg had recently joined the LAPD and had vague longings of joining the vaunted L.A. Roadsters club when he visited a Roadster Roundup in Visalia in 1969. There he learned that Marasco's beautiful roadster pickup was for sale. It took Greg about two seconds to decide a better roadster would be hard to find, and with it he could join the club. So that's what he did.

It was hard to improve on the pickup, but Greg made some minor, tasteful changes. The first was a set of Buick Skylark wire wheels. Next he had Eddie Martinez redo the upholstery in the same Oxblood tone, but with nice rolls to go with the pleats. In this form Greg fulfilled another hot rod dream: entering and wining first in class at the Oakland Roadster Show in 1971. Afterward, he took the 1929 to Jack Hagemann's shop to have a three-piece hood built, complete with louvers and lunch-box latches. After a coat of black lacquer, he had Andy add more pinstripes.

Greg drove the pickup so much, on L.A. Roadsters outings as well as other runs, that he had the grille, fenders, and tailgate repainted (and restriped by Andy) after eight years to repair road rash. That was more than 30 years ago, and things remain the same. In 1999, Greg was proud to have his now-historic roadster pickup included in the 50th Anniversary Oakland Roadster Show. Then, having retired from the LAPD after 28 years, Greg embarked on a new more-than-full-time job as Curator of the NHRA Museum in Pomona. Since the 1929 was spending too much time sitting on the floor

If that magazine looks worn, it's because I bought it in 1963 and read it a thousand times. There are six pages of Marasco's and Silva's similar trucks and photos by Andy Southard.

Lost Hot Rods II

Top: I asked Greg to give me a picture of the pickup when he owned it, and this is the one he chose. He added the Buick wires and hood; these trucks do look best with the top off. *Bottom:* This is how the 1929 looks today in 3 Dog Garage—unrestored. Most of it dates to 1962. Some paint was redone in 1970. All striping is by Andy Southard.

there (and since he was finally rebuilding the 1941), Greg succumbed to an offer from Ross Myers to acquire the pickup to add to the exquisite 3 Dog Garage collection in Boyertown, Pennsylvania, in 2003. Greg had owned it for 34 years.

The 3 Dog collection is set up as a museum, displaying 50-some vehicles, primarily rods, customs, and Trans-Am vintage racecars. The Myers' Trepanier-built 1936 Ford coupe won the Detroit Autorama Ridler Award in 2007. Other classic rods and customs in the collection include Fred Steele's and Tony LaMasa's famous 1932 roadsters, two Dick Courtney Hallock-windshield 1929s, the Larry Shinoda/Don Montgomery 1932 three-window racer, the black Jerry Yatch Carson-top 1940 Merc custom shown at Pebble Beach, and the similar bronze 1936/1940 shown in the first book when owned by Doug Hall. The best part is that 3 Dog Garage welcomes visitors, by appointment. To schedule a time, email 3DG@comcast.net. This one is well worth the visit.

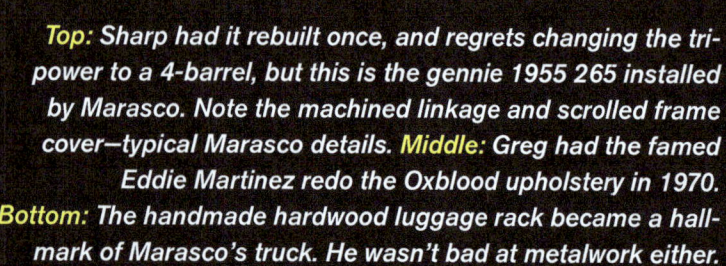

Top: Sharp had it rebuilt once, and regrets changing the tri-power to a 4-barrel, but this is the gennie 1955 265 installed by Marasco. Note the machined linkage and scrolled frame cover—typical Marasco details. Middle: Greg had the famed Eddie Martinez redo the Oxblood upholstery in 1970. Bottom: The handmade hardwood luggage rack became a hallmark of Marasco's truck. He wasn't bad at metalwork either.

176   Lost Hot Rods II

Sidney Allen's First Deuce

I first met Sidney Allen when he was the only person to answer my ad in the back of *Hot Rod* magazine to sell my *Low Buck Special* Altered for $7,500 in 1985. He bought it, and he still has it, along with about 25 other significantly better hot rods he has gathered into a couple of large garages in Longview, Texas.

I'm not sure I'd call Sidney a collector, as such. He's been a hot rod enthusiast since he was a teen, and he has had the wherewithal in years since then to acquire a few cars that particularly appealed to him, as well as to have a few constructed by builders he admires. Two of those are Dick Megugorac and Art Chrisman. One of Sidney's better-known vehicles is a bright yellow, blown Chrysler Hemi-powered 1956 F-100 pickup, built by Art Chrisman, that graced the cover of *The Rodder's Journal* No. 9 in 1998. Of course he still has that. Later he bought the equally yellow, SOHC Ford-powered 1932 coupe Art built for Mike Martin, then the slick, gorgeous, black 1956 Nomad seen in *The Rodder's Journal* No. 31.

Of all the Magoo-built machines, you probably know the yellow 1928 phaeton he built for Mickey Knight that was one of Steve Coonan's early photo features seen on the cover of *Street Rodder* (September 1978). More recently Sidney got the chopped 1950 Merc Dick built for himself. And one I love is the black 1932 Vicky Sidney had Magoo build several years ago, then recently had Art stuff with a 6-71-blown, four-port Hilborn-injected Chrysler Hemi. Those are just a few examples.

But the car featured here is the "Keeper" red 1932 three-window that Sidney has had since he was in high school in Roswell, New Mexico (Class of 1962). He traded a sleeper 348 Tri-Power 1958 Chevy Biscayne straight across, and it came with a 265 Chevy, 1940 brakes, dropped axle, and red paint. Sidney's dad sold John Deere tractors, and working summers in the shop, Sidney built a 365-inch 1956 Cadillac engine for it with three twos, a hot cam, and other good parts, that he installed in 1961, along with a B&M Hydro he had shipped from

There are a whole lot of serious hot rod collectors around the world today, but very few who can say they still have the same Deuce coupe they drove and drag raced in high school. Sidney Allen can. Magoo rebuilt it a second time in 1985, doing what he called a "cut and tuck" on the front fenders to shorten the frame horns and remove the spreader bar.

California. Besides street duty, it was good enough to win B/Gas at the 1961 NHRA Regionals in Roswell, beating 1960 national points champ Buddy Garner, and there's a picture in the July 1961 *Hot Rod* to prove it.

When Sidney left for college, the Deuce got parked at the back of the John Deere lot, after he sold the engine and transmission. Next came marriage and family. Then his dad moved the dealership to Longview in 1969; and when Sidney joined the business, the Deuce almost got lost in the shuffle. His younger brother fortunately hauled it out, but it got stuck in the back of the lot, fenders stuffed inside the cab, again.

Sidney wasn't ignoring it; he was saving up to rebuild it. When he saw Magoo's 1929 hiboy on the cover of *Hot Rod* in 1974 (between vans and 'Vettes), he got motivated, gave Dick a call, and even flew to his house in Canoga Park, California, where he was building rods out of his garage, with wife, Lois, stitching upholstery.

He liked what he saw, and by 1977 he shipped the Deuce to Magoo, telling him to keep all the original body and the dropped axle. Besides new red paint, the other stipulation was for a Halibrand V-8 quick-change rear end. Otherwise Dick did his usual 1970s-but-traditional build, using a four-bar at the front, angled ladder bars in back, but buggy springs at both ends. In went an LT-1 350 Chevy and Turbo 350 transmission. Dick did the outside in Porsche red, and Lois did the inside in Buckskin 'Hyde. In this form it was featured in the July 1977 *Rod Action*, riding on typical Magoo chrome rims with red centers and early Ford caps.

This was Sidney's re-entry to rodding, and the red coupe got enough use that by 1984 he thought it needed rebuilding again, so he sent it back to Magoo's shop. This time they decided on some 1980s-era changes, most notably billet taillights, a gas tank cover with an inset license, and removal of bumpers and spreader bars. Less obvious are the slightly trimmed front fenders and splash apron, and inset grille. Surprisingly, they opted to retain hinges, handles, running boards, and even the top insert. Then Dick re-sprayed it in Magoo Red and Lois redid the upholstery.

Top: This is how the Deuce looked after a drive in the snow, probably home from school, one winter day in Roswell, New Mexico, in 1960. *Middle:* The billet taillights are evidence of the 1980s rebuild. Magoo shortened the rear horns as well, building a cover for the fuel tank, and supposedly bobbing the rear fenders just a touch. Note the Halibrand quick-change barely visible underneath. *Bottom:* The Dominion aluminum cylinder heads for small-block Chevys, with four valves per cylinder and shaft-mounted rocker arms, were a good design and worked well. But this engine, built by Reher-Morrison, might have the only working set in existence today.

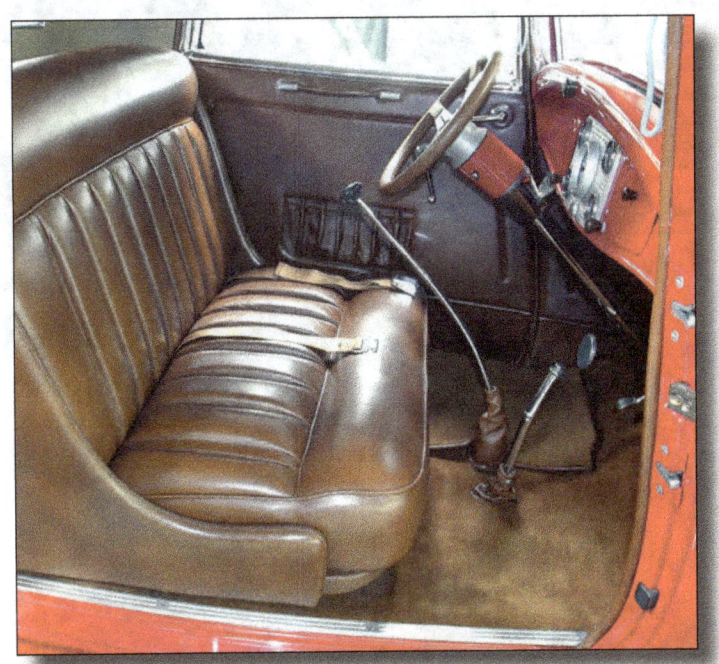

Nothing much has changed from that 1985 rebuild, except Sidney saw an article in the December 1997 *Hot Rod* for some new 4-valve heads for small-block Chevys from a company called Dominion Performance in Torrance, California. Sidney ordered a set, and now thinks he might be the only person who did. Not only that, but he enlisted the well-known Reher-Morrison shop in Arlington, Texas, to build a whole new engine around them. He said this Deuce's drag racing days are long over, but it runs plenty strong, and the heads work very well.

Plenty good for tooling around East Texas, or the occasional farther rod run, which is all Sidney has planned for his very longtime 1932 coupe. Unfortunately his garages aren't set up for visitors, and Sidney is plenty busy running what he calls his retirement business, a local scrap metal and recycling plant. But he does exercise his hot rods regularly, and you're very likely to see one at any given event or show, come the weekend.

Top: In 1977 Magoo made the floorshift from the top of a 1939 Ford transmission. Lois redid the stock interior in the same buckskin style again in 1985. *Bottom:* Talk about lost hot rods—I had to show a picture of my old *Low Buck Special* nostalgia racer. You'd probably rather see more of the famous Tony Nancy 22 Jr. injected Buick roadster next to it, right? Well, this is where they both are.

Chapter Ten: Collectors

Recently Departed

This chapter is about hot rods that were here, and then were gone. There are a million of them. Of the cars that won the Ridler or AMBR Award, how many can you name from the past five years? And where are they? How about the last ten years? How many cars that were on the covers of *Hot Rod*, *Car Craft*, *Street Rodder*, or *Rod & Custom* in that time span have you seen lately? Where do they go? Or cars built by Troy Trepanier, Rob Ida, Scott Sullivan, Pete Chapouris, Boyd Coddington, or John Buttera, for that matter.

You can probably name a few, but plenty more are lost. I could easily write a whole book just on such well-known or briefly famous cars that have come and gone in the past five, ten, or even twenty years. Think about it. I'll just present a few here. And I'll readily admit that what seems recent to me might seem ancient to you. It's all relative.

Chapter Eleven

Marasco's New Pickup

Since you saw the beautiful black Model A roadster pickup that Dave Marasco built 50 years ago in Chapter Ten, you might remember the modern version he built in the early 1990s, which deservedly got its share of magazine attention, as well as winning the first-ever Goodguys Street Rod of the Year award in 1991. Jeez, that was more than 20 years ago!

How come we haven't seen it since?

Unlike so many award-winning rods that get bought for big bucks by collectors and then squirreled away never to be driven or seen, Dave has no intention of selling this incredible roadster pickup. As an expert machinist, he built it over a five-year period; much like a sculptor creates a work of art. When I last photographed it for the February 1991 issue of Rod & Custom magazine, it took four full pages and 17 photos to show all the incredible hand-fabricated and machined details on, in, and under this vehicle. He started with some Brookville repro body panels, some gennie fenders, and a 350 Chevy engine and transmission, and made just about everything else himself. Obviously I can't show all that here, but you get the idea.

However, unlike a work of art that gets put on a pedestal and dusted once in a while (like some rods and customs do), Dave also built this one to drive. He's put 26,000 miles on it so far. That's not a whole lot in 20 years, but that's not being stored in the garage under a cover, either. You'll note that this roadster has no provision for a top. It's a fair-weather rod built for fun cruising around town. And that's what Dave has been doing with it.

When I arrived recently to photograph it again, he simply opened the same garage door and backed it out. He didn't take time to clean and polish it, because it wasn't dirty. It fired right up and ran fine. And by the time I was nearly done taking pictures, I could tell he was getting a little antsy, "Are you about done? Tonight's our little cruise night over at the Baja Cantina, and I want to get there before it gets too crowded." That's where you'll

This truck is black, there's not a ripple or crease to be seen anywhere in it, and it looks good from any angle. About the only things not made or massaged by Dave in this photo are the Eric Vaughn wheels and the tires.

find Dave's new roadster pickup most any Thursday night. Other times you're likely to see him cruising Monterey or Carmel, maybe with one or two of the grandkids on the way to get ice cream.

Dave said he sold the first 1929 in 1969 to expand his home-based machine shop, where he's done freelance contract machining to support himself and his family all his life. He used that machinery to build this pickup, and he plans to enjoy the fruits of his own labor as long as he has a license and fun places to cruise.

Top: Dave assembled the bed from Brookville pieces, cut to the shape he wanted. Note the rolled pan with a cut-out for the license ("Ford Fever"). The taillight stands are handmade. *Middle:* Besides a bunch of hot rod goodies inside the four-bolt-main 350, Dave machined the valve covers and air cleaner from billet aluminum, helped build the brass radiator, and even made his own dipstick—besides all the other stuff you see. *Bottom Left:* Bill Manger stitched the seats, but Dave milled the dash insert, then made the cab rail, bed floor, and of course a luggage rack out of various rare woods. Plus he made the pedals, column, hinges—everything. *Bottom Right:* That's a Winters center section, but Dave made his own stainless axles, disc brakes, gas tank, and complete exhaust including hangers and the mufflers. It's a keeper.

Chapter Eleven: Recently Departed

Guy Ruchonnet's 1934

As the story went in *Hot Rod* magazine in January 1988, then-15-year old Guy Ruchonnet found this much-chopped 1934 three-window body in somebody's backyard in the dark of night, and the owner needed bail money. Guy doesn't say how much he paid, but it wasn't much—nor was what he got. That was in 1976 in Livermore, California, just east of Pleasanton, where Guy was a high school student taking classes in Auto Shop and Metal Shop. Guy started doing some metalwork on the iffy body, which not only was rusty but was chopped crooked, and quickly realized he needed more talent before he proceeded. He took a summer job in a local body shop, and then went to work there fulltime.

It took him ten years to build the car, but he learned a lot more than bodywork and paint during that time. He welded his own frame from 2 x 3-inch tubing and fabricated his own front axle and coil-over/four-link front suspension. He also paneled the interior in bead-rolled and polished aluminum, including a six-point cage.

Guy says the 392 Hemi came out of a blown alcohol dragster, running parts like a Schneider roller cam, 10.5:1 Arias pistons, C&A aluminum rods, four-bolt main caps, ported and polished heads, a 6-71 blower on a fabbed intake, a Don Zig mag, and Hilborn four-port fuel injection. The beefed 9-inch rear runs 5.13:1 gears on a spool.

Yes, it has lights and a license, and such street amenities as front disc brakes, a radiator and remote belt-drive water pump, a good-size fuel cell, and a pair of big batteries in the trunk to get it started. But even Guy admits that—especially running on alcohol—this is not the sort of hot rod you drive to cruise night regularly or use to take the kids downtown to get ice cream. If it had a newer body, such a car would have been labeled Pro Street back then, and snidely referred to by some as a "fairground queen."

But this bright orange beast did exactly what it was supposed to do; it got attention and was featured in *Hot Rod* magazine. It showcased the sort of fabrication and

How'd you like to see this in your rearview mirror? The car does make a statement, doesn't it?

finish Guy could produce in his own shop, which he had just established.

On the other hand, besides driving into and around fairgrounds at rod events, Guy really wanted to make this a dual-purpose car that could drive some on city streets and run respectably down a drag strip. He tried both, several times. The problem was that the former alcohol race engine didn't want to do it. Head gaskets were the problem, combined with the high-compression pistons. The heads were O-ringed, but if Guy used copper shim gaskets to seal the cylinders properly, they sprouted leaks at all the water passages because of the radiator, water pump, and full cooling system. This could potentially "hydraulic" and break the engine. But composition gaskets (either steel or copper faced) that sealed the water passages, immediately blew out due to the high compression. "It'd blow the head gaskets on the burn-out," recalls Guy.

He took the car to Fremont and to Sears Point, making a total of about 25 passes down the quarter-mile, but never got times better than 11.20 at 125 mph. He actually did this after he pulled the blower in frustration, mounted a pair of large 4-barrels on top of the blower manifold, and ran it on gasoline. He also tried running the carbs on top of the blower with gasoline, which made the car more tractable on the street, and he did drive it from Livermore to the Goodguys event in Pleasanton (about a 20-mile trip) a few times. But this was a lot of work, and Guy's new shop was starting to fill with customers, and then his first son was born in 1991.

So that's about when Guy decided it was time to park the car in the corner of the shop, and wait until he could give it the proper attention to rebuild the engine with a new piston/rod combination that allowed it to run the way it should.

And that is exactly where the *I'd Winn* coupe has been ever since. When I called to verify that's where it was, Guy said he'd robbed a few parts off the engine, the transmission was out, and the mag wheels sorely needed polishing. I told him just to bolt the injector back on and make it look functional, and forget about the rest. The fact that it's there, he still owns it, and now I know where it is, is what's important. That it still looks damn good, not to mention wicked and nasty, is just that much better. Plus he mentioned that he has a new combination figured out for the engine, and he's just about ready to rebuild it and give it another try. We can all be watching for that.

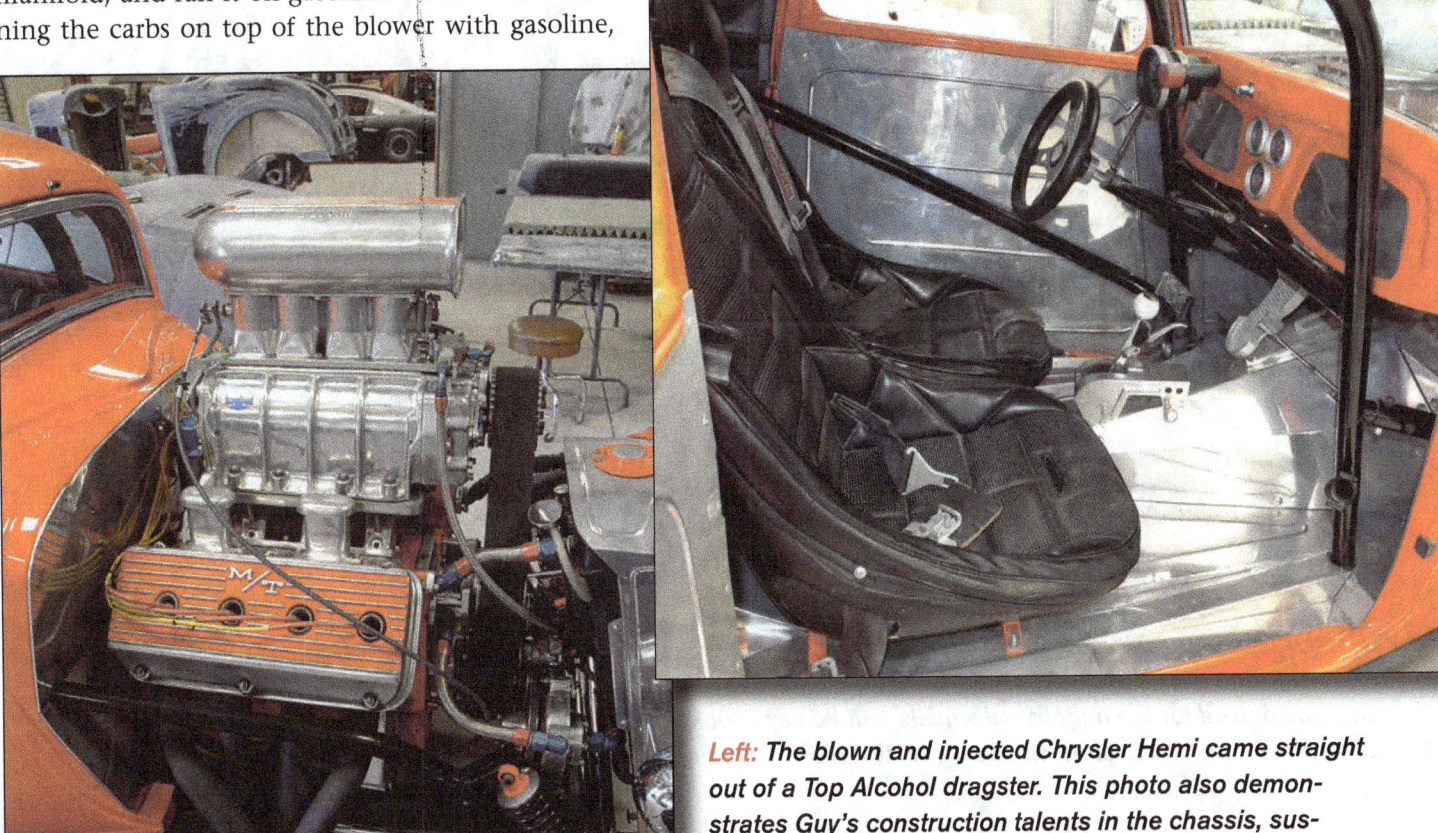

Left: The blown and injected Chrysler Hemi came straight out of a Top Alcohol dragster. This photo also demonstrates Guy's construction talents in the chassis, suspension, and sheet-metal departments. **Right:** It has a passenger seat, but this isn't your typical commuter car. Guy had to build everything in here, too. The transmission is a beefed Powerglide.

Guy apologized for the unpolished wheels, but I'd say it looks pretty good for having sat in the shop corner for the past 20 years. All he had to start with was a rusty, crooked-cut body. Guy made everything else.

The *Flashback 1957* Chevy

Let's end this book with another mystery and a small victory. The victory is that I finally found the *Hot Rod* magazine giveaway car from 1984, the *Flashback 1957*. It's not that the car was exactly lost. I knew more or less where it was and who owned it since 1988. It's just that, for some reason, he'd never let me see it.

In the 1980s, *Hot Rod* magazine put on a big event called the Super Nationals, which helped draw entries by giving away lots of huge raffle prizes, including complete engines and even complete cars. By 1984 the Super Nationals got so big they moved it to the Indiana State Fairgrounds, and the grand raffle prizes were a new Ford pickup with a car trailer, and a bright orange, fully rebuilt, mildly customized 1957 Chevy Bel Air post.

I was a senior editor on the staff then, and I was more or less put in charge of the build-up of this car, which started as a $450 clunker. This was also a strange period when, due to supposed liability concerns, *Hot Rod* staffers couldn't openly own hot rods, and project cars couldn't be mechanically modified. So the primary rule governing the build-up of this giveaway car was that it had to be built with stock, factory components. Fine, but rules were made to get around.

I'm from a generation that blended hot rod and custom car sensibilities to create cool street cruisers. The rules didn't say anything against custom bodywork, but we were *Hot Rod* magazine, so it had to be performance-oriented. So I hired artist Steve Swaja to illustrate some potential ideas in the February 1984 issue when the project was announced. These included nosing, decking, molding off the "gun sights" on the hood, maybe molding in the upper grille bar, and making a custom grille of some sort. Besides adding hot rod louvers in the middle of the hood, one of my favorite ideas was to punch real louvers in the front fenders, where the fake ones were. I chose the orange color, and of course the car sat on a rake. It also got the first set of Eric Vaughn's Halibrand-style Real Wheels.

To fit this early 1960s theme, the power choice was simple: a Duntov-cammed, dual-quad 270-hp 283 Corvette engine, followed by a 'Vette 4-speed and 4.11 Posi rear. Finding the right carbs and manifold was difficult even then, but they are correct. After the engine was rebuilt with factory-correct TRW parts inside, it was liberally painted, polished, and chromed, as was the whole chassis, as seen on the June 1984 cover. Chuck Lombardo's California Street Rods did all the work on the car, including bodywork, louvers, paint, engine, and final assembly. For the interior, Ciadella made stock-style seat covers to match the paint, and we added a 1958 Impala wheel and Sun tach on the column to go with the Hurst shifter.

As shown in the October 1984 issue, Deuce hiboy owner Steve "Kidneybean" Crocker had the lucky raffle ticket to win the car at Indy. I was off photographing a car somewhere else, and didn't see the actual transaction, but I heard from several sources that the car was sold and bought three times before it ever left the fairgrounds; I don't know for sure. That's part of the mystery. But I never saw it again until recently.

In 1988 Petersen decided to bring back *Rod & Custom* magazine, and I volunteered for the job. So I went to the Kustom Kemps of America (KKOA) big meet in Holland, Michigan, that year to photograph cars. One was a lavender-primered, slammed 1951 Chevy fastback.

This 1984 cover left no doubt that this 1957 Chevy was a highly detailed, body-off-frame build-up—considerably better than your typical giveaway raffle prize.

Top: The finished car was what you might call an early 1960s-style mildly customized hot rod. It might look better a tad lower in the front, but that was against the rules. It looked pretty good as it was. *Bottom:* After 25 years, here's how I finally found it, in Austin, Texas. I'm not sure who painted the black primer, or when, but apparently the car sat outside and weathered at some point.

The owner was Jimmie Vaughan, then of the Fabulous Thunderbirds, and the guy with him (who looked like a pro football player) who went by "Tonky." We ended up going to dinner that night, and Tonky mentioned he had (among other cars) an orange 1957 Chevy built and given away by *Hot Rod* magazine. I was quite surprised, and told him how I'd been involved in its construction. Of course the car was in Austin, Texas, where they were from. He didn't say how he got it.

I became friends with Jimmie (photographing his Chevy again for *Rod & Custom* after it was painted) and saw Tonky several more times. I asked about the 1957, but he was always vague, saying it wasn't in good shape, or some other reason for my not seeing it. I'd heard from custom painter Gary Howard that Tonky brought him the car in the mid 1990s to fix a small dent and touch up the orange paint, but then he left it there a couple years. Apparently a divorce and contested property had something to do with it.

The next thing I heard was that Tonky had the car primered black and drove it to one of the first Roundup rod runs in Austin. That was the only time people saw him drive it. But knowing that, I called and asked if I could photograph it for the first volume of this book. He didn't exactly say no, but he wouldn't say yes. It wasn't long after that, in 2009, that Tonky suddenly passed away. The *Flashback 1957*, in primer, as well as his 1957 Corvette, T-Bird, and 1932 roadster all went to his son, who simply goes by "T." Perhaps as a tribute to his dad, but also through some intercession by Lee Pratt, T said I could finally photograph the 1957 on a recent visit to Austin. He was out of town at the time, so I couldn't drive or move it. But he told me where it was, and let me take pictures. I could hardly believe it when I finally saw it, but here it is.

Top Left: After all these years, it's truly amazing the car is as original and complete as it is. Other than the exterior primer coat, virtually everything is still the same, from the knock-off wheel caps, to the single-bar grille, to the little louvers in the front fenders. **Top Right:** The seat covers seemed to be sun damaged more than anything else. But the Impala wheel, Sun tach, Hurst shifter, and chrome window frames—it's all still there. **Bottom Left:** The chrome and paint has weathered under the car, but I have a hunch it would clean up pretty well with some polishing and detailing. **Bottom Right:** Things would probably clean and polish up just fine in here, too. We didn't put fuel injection on it because that was too pricey at the time; now those numbers-correct Corvette dual quads are perhaps more rare and expensive. We didn't have the keys to take it for a ride. But at least I found it.

Afterword

And so continues the hunt for lost hot rods. The stories are all a bit similar, and yet distinctly different. There are plenty more to find, and more stories to tell.

This, obviosuly, has not been a shopping spree. You don't need a bankroll to participate and enjoy this hunt. in fact, as I have said, it's more like a fishing trip—catch-and-release fishing. Searching for, and actually finding, on of these long-lost or hidden hot rods is the fun in itself.

How do you do it? There are many ways as there are stories in this book. Whether it's peeking behind neighborhood garage doors and backyard fences, networking with car club members, or trolling with your own rod to see who has "one just like it," plenty of possibilities are portrayed here. Try it and see what you find. Who knows? You might even snag a "Keeper." That's perfectly okay, too. Good luck!

Additional books that may interest you...

LOST HOT RODS *by Pat Ganahl* Author Pat Ganahl attempts to answer the questions about whatever happened to some of the great, legendary cars. Nearly all of these vintage rods and customs were found in urban or suburban garages—possibly right in your neighborhood—where they were parked years ago, maybe to save, perhaps torn apart for a rebuild, or in many cases they are projects that were started years ago and just never finished. The condition of such finds ranges from musty piles of parts, to dusty and cobwebbed originals, to pristine, still-show-quality beauties. Vintage and modern photography combine to make this book a must-have for hot rod enthusiasts and archeologists. Hardbound, 8.5 x 11 inches, 192 pages, 200 color & 100 b/w photos. **Item # CT487**

RAT RODS: Rodding's Imperfect Stepchildren *by Scotty Gosson* Rat rods are high on style but low on budget, and that's why so many love them. This book is a celebration of this trend, and almost as importantly, the lifestyle that accompanies it. Never has rodding been so cosmetically indifferent, so socially oriented, so affordable, and most importantly, so much fun! Author Scotty Gosson watched the rat rod trend start, grow, and blossom into what it is today. He shares the story with sharp wit, honesty, and a smile on every page. Cars from all over America and around the world are featured, and no two are the same. Softbound, 8.5 x 11 inches, 160 pages, 450 color photos. **Item # CT486**

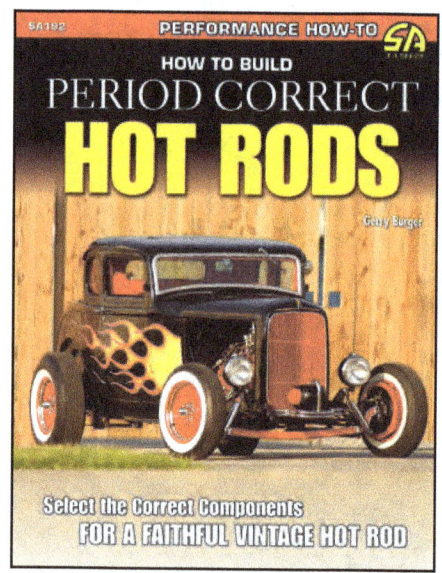

HOW TO BUILD PERIOD CORRECT HOT RODS *by Gerry Burger* To build a faithful traditional hot rod, you must pay close attention to details—select the parts of the right era and make sure those parts work in harmony with one another. After all, the goal is to build a pure, stripped-down, go-fast car that captures your personality and stirs the soul. Author Gerry Burger takes you through each component group, chassis, engine, induction, body, drivetrain, and others. All the options are covered in detail for a particular time period, so your hot rod is faithful to its era and style. You are shown how to build a vintage hot rod from the 50s, 60s, and 70s, and of a particular style, such as East Coast, West Coast, and dry lakes. Softbound, 8.5 x 11 inches, 144 pages, 350 color photos. **Item # SA192**

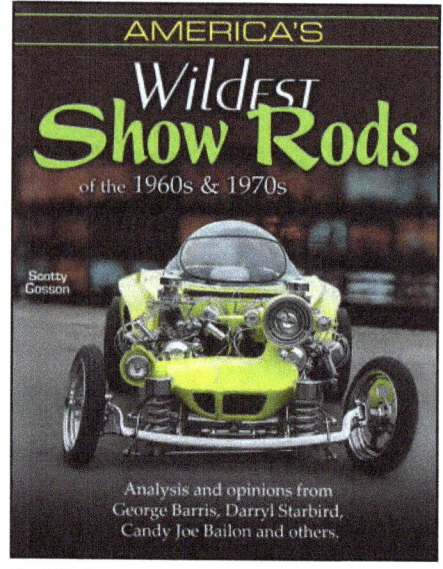

AMERICA'S WILDEST SHOW RODS OF THE 1960s & 1970s *by Scotty Gosson* In the 1960s and 1970s, a new breed of car was developed—the show rod. What began as visions of futuristic cars eventually morphed into cartoon-like representations of cars. This book features iconic cars from builders such as George Barris, Ed "Big Daddy" Roth, Gene Winfield, Dean Jeffries, "Candy" Joe Bailon, Bob Reisner, Darryl Starbird, and Tom Daniel—all important characters in promoting, designing, and building these insane pieces of rolling artwork. This unique book is a round-table discussion featuring all of these great customizers discussing the era, their builds, and each others' rods. Softbound, 8.5 x 11 inches, 160 pages, 300 color photos. **Item # CT510**

Check out our website:

CarTechBooks.com

✓ Find our newest books before anyone else

✓ Get weekly tech tips from our experts

✓ Get your ride or project featured on our homepage!

Exclusive Promotions and Giveaways on Facebook Like us to WIN! Facebook.com/CarTechBooks

www.cartechbooks.com or 1-800-551-4754

www.ingramcontent.com/pod-product-compliance
Lightning Source LLC
Chambersburg PA
CBHW081445070526
44586CB00019B/2233